The Seven Archetypes of Fear

Varda Hasselmann
Frank Schmolke

The Seven Archetypes of Fear

Analysis and Treatment

translated from German by Roswitha R. Bergmann

About the Book

The authors portray our archetypal fears as an intrinsic part of the human condition. They present it in a completely new, clearly structured format. The basic fears of any human being are an indispensable part of his soul structure. They are fixated during infancy according to clearly definable rules. Out of seven archetypal fears, the soul selects two to deal with in each single incarnation. Over the course of many lives and in always new variations, they contribute to the spiritual growth and meaningfulness of human existence. Conversely, a surplus of fear can be reduced by insight and understanding or with therapeutic assistance. Theoretical discussions and practical notes of advice complete this novel philosophy of the soul.

About the Authors

Dr. Varda B. Hasselmann was born in Germany in 1946 and grew up in Italy. She followed a career as a lecturer of medieval languages and literature at the University of Göttingen. To her own amazement, in 1983 she discovered her unusual mediumistic talent, which she combines with her competence in humanistic sciences. Her husband Frank Schmolke, born in 1944, studied English and German literature. He is the intellectual mentor and motor of their lifelong cooperation. They published numerous works on the wisdom of the human soul. Their organization SEPTANA® offers an extensive seminar program on the subject. Their book *Archetypes of the Soul®* is available in English from amazon.com.

Varda is also the author of two well-known novels and a collection of short stories.

Contents

Appendix 331

Introduction

Fear is a fascinating phenomenon. It is inseparable from being alive. It is necessary for growth. Fear is a most useful tool provided by existence when skillfully employed.

This is the perspective we would like to convey to our readers. People, although being sensitive to the fears of others, often avoid looking at their own fears for very comprehensible reasons. Yet we consider it extremely rewarding to do just that – with curiosity and interest but without judgment. It is consoling to assume that each one of us shares their archetypal fears with millions and millions of other people. They form part of the human condition.

With this volume on the seven archetypal fears of human beings we intend to provide new ways of perception. Archetypal fears, according to our Source's soul teaching, are a requisite part of any soul structure. They are chosen out of necessity before incarnation and fixated in earthly reality during infancy. The individual fear structure henceforth crucially determines the path of experience and the development of every single character. Nobody, as long as they live, can do without their archetypal fears. But our soul chooses which combination of two out of seven it wants to explore in a single life. To deal with all seven of them simultaneously would be overwhelming.

So we are focusing our reader's gaze firmly on the Seven Archetypes of Fear, to make basic human anxieties and their stereotyped modus operandi more transparent. Once we have learned to observe the tactics that fears operate in ourselves and others, we create an inner distance. Only then can we understand, tolerate and laugh. Cognitive distance is an important premise to respond and act in a new, different way and with more freedom of decision towards many aspects of life.

Based on this theory, these are the Seven Archetypes of Fear: fear of inadequacy, joyfulness, worthlessness, unpredictability, privation and omission. In each new life, the soul selects two of these seven to formulate its *Basic Fear*. By learning to deal with them in any way a person chooses, his soul grows. The specific composition of fears is not readily discernible. But once their peculiarities are understood, it will be quite easy to recognize them. They each cultivate two ugly masks that are perceptible in the behavior of a human being. We call these the *Primary Symptom* and *Secondary Symptom of Fear.*

The concept of »symptom« means: It characterizes the specific fear. But that mask constitutes only the surface. The actual fear lies concealed behind it. There are seven distinct masks: Self-deprecation, Self-sabotage, Martyrdom, Stubbornness, Greed, Arrogance and Impatience. These are easy to recognize. Some of them conform to one of the seven vices of antiquity or the seven deadly sins of Christianity.

The Symptom of Arrogance, for example, is easily detectable in a person's haughty, vain, disdaining or proud attitude. Hidden behind this, however, is a deep fear of vulnerability. This fear of being injured or slighted in any way, determines the life, the convictions, the impact and the existential learning process of arrogant persons. It makes them oversensitive to the most innocuous forms of criticism; they feel insulted, derided, they become offensive themselves, and need to feel high above others – more intelligent, beautiful, gifted, precious; they are condescending and revengeful. Combined with a Secondary Symptom like Stubbornness, they will insist on being always superior and right and will never change. Combined with Greed, however, they will never get enough of admiration, compliments, praise, applause, approval – they are simply the best. But underneath all those airs they feel poor and small and skinless like a newborn mouse.

The fear structure of human beings is comparable to a tree. The *Basic Fear* – that combination of *two archetypal fears*, active in all humans – constitutes its roots. »Root« has a double sense: first of all, it is invisible. Accordingly, most people are unaware of their Basic Fear, as it is hidden in the depth of the subconscious. It is the essential objective of this book to raise a new awareness of it. The text will provide spade and torch for unearthing and exploring it; using them you'll find a treasure.

Secondly, that root nourishes the whole fear tree. This means that there are many big visible branches and plenty of smaller fear twigs that seem innocuous and unimportant. There are blossoms and fruits, too. People deal more or less well with them and do not take them too seriously, but are not basically determined by them in an essential way. The Basic Fear marked by the combination of any two archetypal fears feeds the many small individual fears. Small fear twigs can be cut off. Often they are just a nuisance and can be treated successfully by insight or psychotherapy, whereas the roots and large br anches of the big fear tree will never be eliminated. First, they are what we call »our character« or »our personality«. No one really wants to part with them, as we are inseparably identified with their characteristics. They are absolutely necessary to make our life significant and to provide occasions for learning. Humans learn by opposites.

Our book *Archetypes of the Soul* (Munich 1993, available in English translation), based on teachings by »The Source«, an entity from the causal plane of consciousness, illustrates the entire soul structure (Matrix) with its seven elements: Soul Role, Basic Fear (= Primary and Secondary Symptom of Fear), Goal of Development, Mode, Mentality, Centering and Soul Age.

In *The Seven Archetypes of Fear*, we now resume and further explain the partial aspect of human fears. We are aware that in the more than twenty years since the publication of *Archetypes of the Soul*, we learned much by discussing with and applying the system to many thousands of clients. Thus we acquired a new and deeper understanding of many issues. As a result, you will find certain contradictions or alterations in small details compared to earlier statements. Our mediumistic work is an organically growing research project which requires being open to corrections on the way. The work on hand represents our present level of knowledge. We do not believe in absolute truth. Varda as a trance medium transposes pure energy into words and meaning. Reading the chapters of this book you will notice that the message is clear enough. Its non-oracular wording needs understanding, not interpretation. We assure you that the text here presented is given to you exactly as it was given to us, with minimal stylistic alterations.

This book is divided into three sections. The first section introduces the seven archetypal fears, each with three of the most frequent sub-types. It includes a discussion of the typical physical features and complaints specific to each sub-type, as well as concrete suggestions for the psychological treatment of each sub-type. We have selected succinct names for the sub-types, which are commonly used in colloquial speech. Some of the names are taken from the famous Fairy Tales of the Brothers Grimm (Germany) or Hans Christian Andersen (Denmark). Most of you will know them from childhood. These designations make them illustrative, immediately conjuring up an associative image. They help to quickly understand and communicate on the various types. Everybody knows what is meant by a Have-not, a Busy Lizzie, a Spoilsport, an Avenger Angel, a Miser, a Valiant Little Tailor or a Kindly Soul and so on. In our numerous seminars, the names prove not to be offensive. They are quite happily adopted even by the individuals affected, provided their interest in investigating their own fears is sincere.

So the Basic Fear of every human is constituted by two archetypal fears, the Primary Symptom and the Secondary Symptom of Fear. It is only this combination that creates a special dynamic and thus becomes a prerequisite for the existential human learning process. In the second part of this volume, we outline all 42 possible variants of the Basic Fear, that is, the various combinations of Primary and Secondary Symptoms, each with suggestions for gradually reducing the fear level. Once someone has identified his or her Primary Fear Symptom (ask your relatives and friends!), the description of these combinations can help identify which could be your Secondary Symptom of Fear.

The third section answers further questions on the Seven Archetypes of Fear and related topics. This discussion among members of our research group, twenty psychotherapists and psychiatrists who were present during the many channeling sessions and the entire genesis of the book, is designed to deepen the understanding of human fears. Their thoughtful and practical questions represent an initial effort to investigate partial aspects of this gigantic topic in more detail. We invite our readers to continue this kind of research.

In our view, founded on the theoretical assumption of an individual Soul Pattern Matrix), archetypal fears and experiencing them are essential to human development, the objective here being the evolution of the capacity for love of an incarnate soul across many corporeal existences. Human beings need a pulsation and oscillation between love and fear to be able to learn. In this sense, fear should be understood as a »contrast agent« to love, which every soul deeply longs for. Without consciously or unconsciously dealing with the Archetypes of Fear, however, the longing for love cannot develop. This is where, in our opinion, the central importance of fear lies for human beings. The Seven Archetypes of Fear as components of experience in any human life are indispensable for our spiritual and emotional learning process.

Now if the Archetypes of Fear are part of the incarnation plan and the Soul Matrix of all human beings, should one attempt to influence them? And if they are existentially significant in this sense, that is, essential in order to learn to live and love, what purpose can this book serve?

To understand the dynamics of the basic fear, a distinction should be made between *necessary* and *redundant* aspects. Fear itself, being an Archetype of the Soul, is necessary as an engine of human development. Redundant, however, are many of its superficial manifestations, the automatism of fear reactions, their too distressing, segregating and exaggerated aspects. The necessary part must remain, but everything superfluous can be diminished, positively transformed or treated therapeutically. In fact, only that amount of fear which is unnecessary for our spiritual and emotional learning process can be reduced at all.

Let us give an example: Someone – be it man or woman – with a basic fear of Stubbornness plus Martyrdom, will time and again experience situations in which he or she will respond with almost stereotyped reactions to his unutterable fear of the unpredictable and his panic of being deserted in the end, which is subconsciously connected with his imaginary lack of worth and his victim role. If they become aware of this mechanism and observe it diligently without fighting it or wanting to get rid of it, they will evolve and grow. They can't change anything about having this Basic Fear; that's part of their form of existence and their character. But emotional maturation processes, therapeutic interventions, an incontrovertible discovery of inner correlations or even the true patient and observant love of a fellow human will change the way they deal with this Basic Fear. They will learn to recognize their terror of being forsaken as just a fear and to distinguish it from reality. They will be able to look with humor and understanding at his recurrent feeling of being a helpless victim of circumstances or of people. They learn to lovingly see through their usual behavior patterns instead of regarding them in dead earnest as the only ones possible. What they gain from this process is something new: the freedom to react differently than usual. Their fear tree will be pruned, but the root and trunk still remain.

Self-recognition mitigates the rougher shapes and ramifications of fear. He who can observe himself gains freedom, and this book provides a modern tool for it. Our »Source« never threatens with punishment, judgment or damnation and never offers false promises. Someone knowing about the existence of the Archetypes of Fear will accept both himself and his fellow men with more understanding. It is also very enlightening to be able to distinguish apparent strengths as »false virtues« spawned by fear. For example, those »much too good for this world«, overly modest or selfless, often act out of Self-deprecation or Martyrdom, while those who are extremely efficient and audacious will be spurred by Impatience. Yet the most resolute people are also the most obstinate and stubborn, afraid of change.

The portrayal of the Seven Archetypes of Fear addresses all those who would like to experience their personality and their true being more thoroughly. People who wish to embrace the immortal soul as an essential aspect of humanness in their conception of the world or in their efforts to support others in whatever healing capacity, will start to distinguish it from the mortal psyche. Fear makes sense! Dealing with the Archetypes of Fear gives meaning to human life. With patient observation and broader consciousness, the widely ramified and distressing manifestations of those fears unnecessary for inner growth become gradually mitigated because they are more distinct. And zest for life will automatically take its place, just like a green meadow emerges when the snow is melting in March.

This intense new joy of life is felt much more strongly than if it had been there always. When your inner snow starts melting, you experience the first rays of sunshine more gratefully than those people who have always dwelt on the isles of eternal Spring.

We wish for readers who are prepared to query the quality of this information unbiased, and to vet it for its worth and significance. It conveys very practical knowledge. In our seminars, we have been graced to witness how deeply upsetting, but also how liberating it can be to recognize one's subconscious fear pattern. Those approaching these novel teachings of the soul with interest, openness and readiness for self-perception have greatly benefited from them. Being more tolerant of themselves and their fellow beings takes no effort. To know that all humans experience fear and act accordingly generates love and understanding.

Further information about the Soul Matrix and the Archetypes is available from our works published in German by Goldmann Verlag (Random House):

Worlds of the Soul (1993), *Archetypes of the Soul* (also in English, 1993), *Wisdom of the Soul* (1995), *The Soul of the Papaya* (novel, 1999), *The Soul Family* (2001), *Paths of the Soul* (2002), *Soul Elixirs* (2006), *False Virtues* (tales and stories, 2013).

For more details, visit www.septana.de and www.vardana.de., or write to

mail@frankschmolke.de
mail@vardahasselmann.de

Our postal address is:
SEPTANA GbR
P.O. Box 70 08 11
81308 München, Germany

Part I

The Seven Archetypes of Fear

Chief Characteristics of Fear

Greed
Fear of Privation
− insatiable   + demanding

Self-Sabotage
Fear of Joyfulness
− self-destructive   + self-sacrificing

Expression Level

Arrogance
Fear of Vulnerability
− vain   + proud

Self-Deprecation
Fear of Inadequacy
− self-abasing   + modest

Inspiration Level

Impatience
Fear of Omission
− intolerant   + audacious

Martyrdom
Fear of Worthlessness
− victimizing   + selfless

Action Level

Stubbornness
Fear of Unpredictability
− obstinate   + resolute

Assimilation Level

Universal Energy 1

Self-deprecation: Fear of Inadequacy

General

It is not an easy business for the soul to have a body. When a soul enters the worldly, physical sphere, it isn't surprising that it should be afraid. Living up to the requirements of the incarnated existence represents an enormous challenge. Standing helpless and incompetent in the face of this new form of existence creates great fear. The soul needs to live a life the way it was planned; it is necessarily afraid of being unable to cope with all the demands and circumstances. This anguish can produce the archetype of Self-deprecation. The cause of this archetype is a deep fear of inadequacy.

Dealing with this archetypal fear is painful but important and necessary. It must be explored and experienced again and again in the course of different Soul Ages, because a Young Soul will experience it differently from an Old Soul.

A rich treasure of accumulated experience is already available to the soul from some or even many former existences on earth. This comprehensive experience ensures that all difficulties of a new incarnation could be mastered, given some preparation. Knowledge and knowing are securely stored in any human being based on his existential history, which often encompasses many thousands of years. If somebody, out of fear to fail in this new life, denies his inherent potential, he also denies the history of his soul. At the same time, the newly aspired for Goal of Development will be shadowed by the fear of failure, although this goal has also been repeatedly pursued and successfully mastered in the course of a long existential history.

Anyone troubled with the denial of his best, most beautiful abilities and qualities and with the negation of knowledge gained in previous lives, will painfully experience failure time and again. Everything he believes himself unable to achieve will unconsciously be confirmed by others thinking him incompetent as well. These reflections will enhance his own subjective feeling of being incapable, inadequate, of not knowing enough – of being simply not good enough for this life. It is important though not to confound such helpless self-assessment with a lack of self-worth, because the Self-deprecating person, unlike someone with the archetype of Martyrdom, has no problem with his worth as such. He may have a big question mark about his ability to prove himself valiant towards life, but not with respect to his intrinsic value as a human being, which is essential and will remain so for him.

Self-deprecators will understandably try to deny or compensate their feelings of inadequacy in one way or another. That is why they develop a rich methodology which, despite their apprehensions and deep fear of failure, will enable them to actively construe and master their life. It is striking how people with Self-deprecation as an archetype of fear are often able to cope with the challenges of life much better than those not tantalized by fear of failure. That's because they make an infinitely greater effort in order to avert feeling this inadequacy and inability. They'll do anything to prove to themselves and their fellow men that they are more than good enough: clever, competent, intelligent and diligent.

This line of justification, of course, mustn't ever lead so far as to make their achievement stand out in the pattern of their self-programmed role of modesty. Because, if this should incidentally happen, the feeling of inadequacy they are so used to, will immediately be re-engaged and put in its place, so that the fear as preset in their individual soul pattern can calm down and feel satisfied:

»Yes, it is true, I am incapable.« The person is reaffirmed in his self-assessment that he is indeed not as clever, as skilled, as smart, as hard-working or as successful as he has optimistically imagined himself in order to fend off his basic fear.

The Poles of the Fear of Inadequacy

| – Self-abasing | ←→ | Modest + |

The modesty of a person with Self-deprecation is rarely a natural unpretentiousness innate to his character, which, satisfied and benign, radiates into the world. It rather conceals a false modesty, because the individual is not modest in a true expression of his natural way of being, but from fear of making demands. He takes the back seat to avoid attracting attention. He renounces for fear of rejection. He modestly remains in the background because he lacks confidence and is afraid of embarrassment, refusal and failure.

If he could, as in the way he sometimes fantasizes in his omnipotent dreams, he would be anything but modest. He would demand, he would take, he would claim what is due to him, and even more than that. Instead though, he retreats behind his disguise of a righteous modesty. He abides in the half-shade of his unpretentiousness so as to remain inconspicuous lest he should be called upon. He trembles at the thought that he might be given a commission he doesn't feel up to.

When someone jestingly says to him: »Modesty is a virtue, but you get further without it!« the Self-deprecator winces. For he feels caught in his megalomaniac fantasies, beguiling him that he would get ahead much further without his primal Fear of Inadequacy. But he retreats behind his façade because he believes that morally, modesty is to be rated much higher than immodesty of any kind. Obviously, he draws a significant mental benefit from this imaginary ethical supremacy. The Self-deprecator likes to profit from a code of ethics coined by Christian virtues, which has conventionalized modesty to a high-value commodity, without consideration from which source it is fed – from fear or from love.

Modesty is a code of behavior generally attributed to the female gender, that is, to show a demure demeanor as the male's servant in an environment dominated by the masculine principle – regardless of the given capabilities or needs. In most human societies, females are supposed to act with modesty, thereby giving a feeling of superiority and power to males. If, in any incarnation, a woman wants to explore the archetype of Self-deprecation, she usually corresponds to a femininity ideal that puts her in her place and with which she tries to identify. It is not surprising that false modesty, rooted in Self-deprecation, is actually interpreted as a praiseworthy female virtue. An overly modest male, however, is regarded as weak and helpless. It is more difficult for him to retreat behind the conditioning of his archetypal fear. Men, therefore, often experience their false modesty more painfully and will, if possible, fight more fiercely against it, because it yields little benefit, especially in professional life.

It must be kept in mind that Self-deprecation is a phenomenon of the universal energy 1, which is an inspirational energy (as in the Soul Role of Healer/Helper). Thus, in terms of the connection of this fear to the supernatural and celestial, to transcendence and recompense »in heaven«, self-deprecation plays an essential role. The Self-deprecator, whether he is aware of it or not, is willing to make great sacrifices and certainly no great demands on life. He projects his hope for reward to some faraway day, when he is no longer subject to worldly existence with its taxing efforts, but has returned to the sphere where the question of »being able or unable« no longer counts. As for the rest, he hopes for late gratification like a maiden from a fairytale. Out of desperation over the inadequacy ascribed to her by her stepmother, she throws herself into a well like the fairytale maiden. Only in the otherworld can she reveal her true qualities, and it is there that she will be richly rewarded.

When Self-deprecation is expressed in the negative pole of self-abasement, it leads to a submissive attitude and servility, an aura of sycophancy or subservience, which, in an almost biologically programmed gesture of humility, signals to the environment: »Please don't hurt me. Don't assail me. Don't reprimand me, I promise to be good. I'll do anything you want. I am ready to serve you, but please be kind to me. I can't bear any criticism or rejection.«

The energetic result, however, of such an attitude usually isn't what the self-abasing person has hoped for. He will, on the contrary, find that he gets kicked because he has proffered himself as a doormat; that he is despised because he doesn't respect himself; that he is humiliated because he acts humbly; that he is treated like a servant and sometimes even like a slave, because he has offered himself as such in his anticipatory obedience. This offering by no means occurs as a calculated act or an act of volition. A subservient Self-deprecator ducks from fear of those he considers bigger, stronger, more intelligent, more powerful, more important or worthier. Especially when he tends to act not only modestly but obsequiously, he seeks to be close to people who are self-assured or strive for power, to the highly gifted or the prominent and beautiful. It gives him a chance to at least reflect in their glory from afar while standing in the shadow himself.

The person in the pole of modesty enjoys his modesty, he is even a little proud of it, although he senses that fear stops him from coming out of the half-shade. The self-abasing person in contrast hides in the shade and feels no joy, but rather kicks himself if there happens to be no one around to do it for him. In both cases, the person develops a more or less subtle self-hate and a fearful form of non-sexual masochism, which has an unpleasant effect on people, evoking incomprehension and disdain.

That behind all these ways of behaviors, in the positive and in the negative pole alike, lurks the naked fear of being unable to cope with life and its requirements in terms of work, assertiveness, the ability to build and maintain relationships and much more. However all this rarely surfaces to the consciousness of everyone involved. Strong Self-deprecation can cause considerable suffering because the discrepancy between actual capability and self-assessment of this capability is immense.

The Released Potential

The potential concealed behind Self-deprecation, but usually inhibited by the consequences of this primal fear, is an amazing, overall competence in most areas of life. As this self-denying form of fear is gradually released, competence combined with increasing self-assurance creates a quiet aura of capability, knowledge and responsibility, as well as a realistic assessment of one's possibilities and abilities. Since both an under- and over-estimation of the self are similarly expressions of this archetype, an almost automatic balancing at mid-level will occur when the fear diminishes. The self-conception becomes more realistic.

It gets easier to admit occasionally that one cannot do or doesn't know, or has to find out first. Such an avowal is linked with lesser shame and distress than before. Even the admission that there are areas which – due to outer circumstances, lack of talent or unsuitable physical conditions – are simply unattainable, no longer inevitably leads to the helpless, shameful feelings of failure and inadequacy.

Likewise, a balanced, realistic self-conception no longer triggers the need for self-aggrandizement, either in fantasies, dreams or in contact with one's fellow men. To boast with pseudo-knowledge or to show off with a newly acquired skill becomes superfluous.

Self-assured competence spreads like oil on water in the same measure as the fear level drops. The inner certainty of this competency assuages the anxious feelings of obsequious modesty. The body no longer reacts as violently with somatization symptoms to the threats posed by requirements one believes oneself unable to cope with. It's not such a big deal anymore to admit: »I don't feel up to that, I don't know how to do that.« Such an admission becomes a calm, reality-based statement, ceasing to threaten the Self-deprecator's world to collapse.

Great joy arises at the discovery of these capabilities, talents and competences which had long been guessed at or noticed as a potential by the people around. Only the Self-deprecator himself grieved at the thought that he wasn't up to the demands of the job, the family or simply everyday life. This joy is like the bliss of a little child discovering that it can walk without help or hold the spoon, learning that it doesn't run into mortal danger at its first steps trying to explore its surroundings, but rather feels a great gain in the conquest of its little world. A new learning, which aims at life competence, builds up swiftly. And even the Self-deprecator, when he finally realizes he has only imagined his innumerable inabilities, bubbles over with delight at his skills he may now show without fear of being punished. He can even accept praise without blushing or fending it off timidly.

Fear of Inadequacy: Three Types

1. The **Wallflower** doesn't dare show itself and therefore won't be seen. It looks deliberately grey, keeping a low profile in the background. It is pushed also by others to stand at the edge or in the corner. This is a special problem of self-perception owing to a lack of mirroring. The Wallflower feels only its fear, not its own Self.

2. The **Kindly Soul** is so modest and so nice, it couldn't harm any living creature. This quality, however, is characterized by fear. The Kindly Soul feels incapable of defending itself or asserting its interests, of attacking if necessary or standing its ground. The Kindly Soul is kind mostly from fear of being confronted with life and its darker sides.

3. Like a diligent bee, the **Busy Lizzie** buzzes and whirrs and works at belying her self-image, marked by the fear of inability. Through untiring, unremitting effort and a modest over-estimation of her strength, Busy Lizzie manages to handle an enormous workload, wondering only why all of this never really gets noticed and praise is unheard. Yet if she should get praised for once, immediately Busy Lizzie would bashfully or even gruffly refute it.

Type 1: The Wallflower

The Wallflower-type of Self-deprecation starts to tremble and shake at the mere thought of emerging from the twilight or the half shadow of its self-image and step into the sunlight of attention. The idea to be seen, to be noticed, to be commended, admired or even loved will trigger a more or less serious panic. The Wallflower type is particularly shy and believes itself capable of nothing at all: no attractiveness, no skills, no resonance in fellow men and only insignificant competences. A Wallflower therefore abides under a veil of half visibility. It dreams, however, of one grand day sometime in the future, if possible rather later than sooner in life. Then it will be dragged by some wonderful person or by a large applauding audience from the shadow into the light, because, lo and behold, at last! all the qualities, the beauty and glittering facets of its personality, which the Wallflower hasn't ever seen in itself, are finally discovered by the world.

The Wallflower suffers from a problem of reflection because it hopes that others see what it cannot see itself. It appears so grey and inconspicuous because it doesn't dare look at itself in the mirror – out of sheer fear of discovering only a small heap of ashes there. As long as it keeps its eyes shut and tries not to see itself, the Wallflower feels a certain peace. With eyes closed, it can dream of a glamorous »coming out.« It's this dream, whose fulfillment would be intolerably frightening, that largely upholds the weak emotional stability.

A Wallflower – be it man or woman – is also what is called a »still water.« Due to an intense inner life of which so little seeps to the outside, a great wealth of feelings and sensations builds up over the years. Because the Wallflower finds scant resonance in its environment, it must develop all strength and abilities from within, and bury all talents and vocations deeply inside itself, so that nobody ever finds out about them. They are, nevertheless, existent, albeit the Wallflower seldom manages to open itself up to a loving, patient and tenacious person and allow him or her to take a look into the depths of this quiet lake with all its sunken, mysterious and hidden treasures.

The Wallflower keeps up an illusory façade of inability. This façade is like a painted Japanese paper wall: he who carelessly passes by will not see what is behind. To do so, one must come really close or even bore a hole into this non-transparent but very thin membrane of under-estimation of the self.

When a Wallflower, male or female, enters a room, it almost seems as if it wasn't really there, as if a shade or silhouette had approached, without a live, solid aura. A Wallflower will do and try everything not to attract attention. Men and women alike make themselves look unattractive in an inconspicuous way, yet without being strikingly ugly, since that, in turn, might also evoke attention or comments. Everything about them is sort of unreal, their movements restrained, the eyes often lowered; they seem to direct any looks away rather than command attention. They emanate the inaudible message: »For heaven's sake, do not see who I really am!« All this happens without the self-denying person being able to actually define this »real being«; because that is exactly what he or she hasn't yet discovered.

A complaint which can often be heard from a Wallflower is: »It seems I'm invisible.« Yet a certain satisfaction about this excellent strategy can be discerned behind this statement. To be seen is exactly what the Wallflower associates with horror fantasies of exposure or challenges, with feeling unprotected and helpless. The well-practiced inconspicuousness serves as a magic cap to help bear the permanent feeling of failure in human relationships.

As for the rest, the Wallflower type is convinced that it has not the slightest sexual appeal and therefore likes to keep clear of the other sex. If, however, a partner has been found, the Wallflower in cautious modesty and submissiveness believes it will find fulfillment in a homebody-fashion, unobtrusive dedication, or else as the family man industriously laboring in the background. Such Self-deprecators will frequently find out sooner or later that the partner turns to someone else who has fewer problems with being attractive.

Features

A Wallflower, finding several free seats available, will always opt for a place all the way in the back or at the edge. The voice is restrained and low-key even to a whisper, the bearing appears contracted and well behaved. When accosted in the most harmless way such as: »Well, how are things?« it will respond with vacant verbiage such as: »Well, so-so« or »oh well, getting along.« It takes special effort to find out how he or she really feels, and that's not because they try to hide something, but because they actually can't feel and tell themselves.

The skin is rather pale with a greyish sheen. There's an impression of low vitality about this person. Either he or she hasn't ever done any sports and doesn't enjoy going for a breath of fresh air, or else it's a kind of lonely, excessively practiced kind of sport, serving not so much to increase vitality and health but to discipline one's feelings. Jogging or swimming for example is a good way to get tired or offer a socially accepted pastime not requiring contact with others. Parties or large, fun events are preferably avoided.

Such a person is often a true bookworm because in books he can experience life the way it could be and can identify himself with literary figures who are less shy and mouse-grey than he is. At times, however, the Wallflower may experience unusual outbursts and breakthroughs, e.g. during the carnival season. Under the mask, everything is permitted, or during a trip to some foreign country where one is unknown and can, like in an experiment, act differently from one's usual self. Also at the football stadium or at mass events, which the Wallflower visits exactly because it hopes to disappear in the crowd, certain ecstasies of liberation from the usual inhibitions might be experienced.

Typical complaints of the Wallflower

The type of the self-denying Wallflower often has skin problems such as severe acne, urticaria, psoriasis and neurodermatitis. Contact allergies on the hands or a fungal attack of the skin, feet and genitals are the body's shy measure to avoid meeting with people to the extent possible. Various unspectacular and non-specific complaints which only seldom require medical consultation limit the zest for life of a Wallflower. It is frequently short-sighted or visually impaired. At the same time, one can't help feeling that the thick glasses don't serve primarily to perceive the outside world, but to hide and cover up the gaze. The eyes look out shyly; they hardly turn to their interlocutor. Hardness of hearing, which sometimes is purely psychogenic, can also be observed. Migraine, permitting the Wallflower to retire from the tormenting interaction with its fellow men for a while, for hours, days or completely, is not rare.

Psychiatric forms of this archetypal fear can be found in people who not only have the strong desire to withdraw but to live like a recluse, not talking to or seeing anyone for weeks. And there's an even stronger version of the Wallflower-like misanthropy, which tries to solve its problems by imputing to its neighbors all kinds of bad or magically-harmful practices.

A person stricken with such pathological fear sees only enemies and overpowering miscreants in people who would like to get close to him, threatening him in his extreme self-consciousness. Other manifestations are delusional ideas or hallucinations bordering on megalomania and exercising one's power or telepathy to influence others. What the Wallflower doesn't act out in reality is delegated to a split-off imaginary personality, who by proxy aims to intimidate and master others through developing an awesome, oversized self-image. Sometimes, such a Wallflower also follows a community which practices satanic rites, develops special, mysterious games or dangerous collective fantasies on the Internet to hurt or even blot out the society which is allegedly so hostile towards them.

Indications for treatment of the Wallflower

A Wallflower looking for help to cope with oversized inhibition and bashful modesty requires a comprehensive treatment. It also implies that some tricks be lovingly applied to help the Wallflower get over the high thresholds of self-restraint. As soon as a trustful relationship has been established, the therapist should express some kind of praise at each session. Later he needs to assert, by once bringing up the subject, that this intervention has been processed in the patient's system.

If legally possible, the therapist may also prescribe a placebo which purportedly provides the timid patient with more courage, more candor and reduces shyness. It is also important to set small tasks for the individual concerned, always building up on the previous one. At an initial stage, these refer to dress, hairstyle and adornments. For example, a male client could be asked to purchase a colorful sweater, bring it to the session and actually wear it. It doesn't have to be a red one; also blue, green or yellow will do for a start. It could be suggested to the client to bring a ring or precious stone to the session, perhaps one that's been lying in a drawer somewhere, inherited and never yet worn. A next step could be asking him to buy something, in keeping with his financial means, perhaps assisted by a female friend or even the therapist. For a Wallflower, a shawl, a scarf, a handbag or just new shoes often represent a considerable challenge when it comes to self-image.

At a later stage, mirroring techniques can be applied. These can be fashioned in such a way that, for example, the therapist takes the role of a mother who is enthusiastic about her child. The idea is to compensate for the Wallflower's early-childhood, preverbal hunger for reflection in its mother's eyes. The »mother« can look into the client's eyes with great joy and tell him how glad she is to see him again, or how pleased that he already looks much happier, and likewise. Similarly, individual body parts can be focused on and made an issue of discussion, e.g. the legs, the hands, the skin and hair. This will help the disordered self-assessment change into a more realistic perspective of the self. The therapist should be careful, of course, not to sweet-talk bad teeth or declare thin, unkempt hair to be a splendid mane. A hand-mirror or full mirror can also be used as a tool to carefully encourage the patient to look at himself in order to uncover his self-criticism and bring to the surface the good and beautiful aspects of his nature.

Type 2: The Kindly Soul

The Kindly Soul has struck a deal with life which says: »I won't harm you so that you won't harm me« and »If you don't hurt me, I'm not going to hurt you either,« or »If I see only the good and beautiful in everything, the bad and ugly just doesn't exist.« The Kindly Soul shies away from conflict and hates all complications which arise when interacting with people or confronting the realities of life. It seeks peace and harmony at all times, because, as a general rule, it doesn't feel up to coping with anything that is not beautiful, peaceful and harmonious.

It's as if an immunizing factor was missing from its genetic code, which simply makes it impossible to subject itself to the aggressions of the world. The Kindly Soul thus lives in isolation inside a bubble. He or she believes that aggressive acts would afflict them like a deadly virus or bacillus. So it endeavors to strengthen its defense by exuding an enormous amiability and a disarming, naive, almost simple-minded kind-heartedness, all the while gladly accepting that it is being exploited, laughed at and cheated on. What counts is that it doesn't suspect anyone capable of wrongdoing; its world is perfect. The Kindly Soul just doesn't get why others aren't the same.

Self-deprecation here is expressed by believing oneself incapable of meeting life any other way than with this almost super-human guilelessness. The feelings of incapability concern primarily situations of conflict, rather than one's own abilities in terms of talents or the capacity to cope with everyday life like the Wallflower. With its radiation of goodwill, the Kindly Soul disarms anyone likely to be critical or reprimand it, and so makes it impossible to do such a thing. Instead, a lot of talk goes on about how this sweetish goodness is really insufferable for everyone around, even though no one would say so directly because the Kindly Soul signals: »Any criticism will instantly kill me.«

The Kindly Soul can also be recognized by its rather sentimental reaction to any wrong, harm, criticism or bad luck happening to others. Like all Self-deprecators, it has secret dreams about one day banging its fist on the table, yelling at or really crucifying someone. These fantasies can go as far as wanting to kill those who ever wronged, criticized or confronted it. The Kindly Soul thus harbors a potential of violence which must not be underestimated, a violence which may fuse when a less inhibited person rashly releases these pent-up aggressions.

Features

The phenotype of the Kindly Soul appears childlike, soft and vulnerable, eyes gleaming with a mild gaze, hoping for compassion and demanding sympathy. This person likes to flatter and admire others, as by protective magic, for he or she has found that once they have showered someone with kindness and praise, the other person will find it hard to give anything but kindness and sympathy in return. The Kindly Soul preferably dresses in soft pastel colors; men too like to wear a pink jumper or a light, delicate yellow shirt. The Kindly Soul stands out by the permanent, loving smile on its face, which appears almost chronic, causing a mask-like wrinkle formation on the face even in younger years. The eyes are wide open in amazement about »such wonderful« or »really really terrible people.« Conversation will soon turn to topics showing how nice the Kindly Soul treats family, animals or colleagues, or how it always thinks up something nice in order to cultivate and ensure everyone's affection. In extreme cases, one may even hear remarks such as: »When I think about how good I am, tears come to my eyes.« The general attitude and statements are played down, mildly excusing or frantically harmonizing everything. The home is adorned with childlike comfort symbols. There are cuddly toys and ever so many keepsakes from infinitely grateful, kind people; also little dolls, frilled throw pillows in rich-pink and sky-blue, as if stepping into the nursery of a never born baby or a child who died in infancy.

Men are often the good-natured, teddy-bear type, while women tend to be sort of motherly-bosomy. Both will report that they are often told: »You are much too good for this world!« All this is based on a denial of aggressive impulses which are quite strong, although the Kindly Soul rarely acknowledges them. They should be brought to its attention carefully and cautiously. True kindness isn't lost if one defends oneself or backs up one's point of view or attacks an aggressor. Even a Kindly Soul can gradually be made to understand this.

The voice is a little high and child-like or, usually in men, soothing. Because they couldn't harm a fly, Kindly Souls prefer a vegetarian diet. They also hope that renouncing meat makes them even more peaceful. This way of life isn't founded on health considerations but on fear-ridden ideology. The Kindly Soul seeks activities and professions in which it can be »good« or at least politically most correct. One will easily meet them in health stores selling organic foods, and, of course, in counseling centers. Kindly Souls are on the spot whenever toads need to be carried across the road at night and they support whale protection programs.

Such Kindly Souls spoil and pamper their children and others in their care. They don't set any limits for fear of resistance and so rear offspring who act up with them and treat them with a certain sniffiness. It follows that Kindly Souls complain about insubordinate children, mobbing at work or, in later years, about being exploited by everyone and finding little recognition.

Typical complaints of the Kindly Soul

The Kindly Soul often loses quite a few teeth at a relatively young age and is sometimes unwilling to replace them because, at heart, it feels somehow comfortable with a toothless nibble-mouth. A low immunity is reflected in frequent colds, constant nasal congestion due to chronic sinusitis or auto-immune disabilities such as arthritis.

In terms of somatic ailments, a slow pulse can be observed. The heart beats slowly, getting excited only at the sight of injustice and the sorrow of others. Oftentimes, a pacemaker is required already in middle years because of severe bradycardia. The habitual inhibition of aggressive impulses causes a stiffening of joints and arthrosis, since energy cannot flow freely and acid deposits inside the joints. A continuous increase in weight is also frequently observed, intensifying the infant-like or teddy-bear impression, with a spongy tissue quality like soft rubber, for the Kindly Soul often can't think of anything better than to revert to a good, consolatory piece of cake or a hearty meal as a means to quench any aggressions timidly trying to surface. It is also characteristic of Kindly Souls that they always need something to eat, because, due to their renouncement of animal proteins, their food intake is of little substance, leaving them with a constant, unsatisfied appetite.

If this archetypal fear gets out of hand, leading to pathological forms, the Kindly Soul sometimes develops an almost compulsive urge to hurt, especially those most dear. Because it forbids itself any emotion that might trigger a murderous impulse, it is afraid of knives or anything that could be used as a weapon. Also, a panic-stricken fear of injuring or killing a pet can assume proportions requiring treatment. Religious delusions may culminate in imaginung oneself an »Avatar« or a saint returned to earth, a Bodhisattva – the incarnation of pure love and kindness, sent to show people what they must do to attain an eternal state of peace.

The abuse of tranquilizers to addictive levels can be observed when a person cannot adequately handle his natural liveliness or his need to defend himself and hit back when attacked. Acts of self-punishment, even suicide, can be the consequence if these impulses are not suppressed. For example when, in despair, the Kindly Soul has badly beaten up its child. This is unforgivable and results in permanent feelings of guilt, distorted to a pathological degree, which make severe self-punishment seem inevitable.

Indications for treatment of the Kindly Soul

A therapist must put up with it and learn to endure that the Kindly Soul initially praises and eulogizes him or her beyond measure. At a later stage however, there arises a notion that, all things considered, the therapist is by far not as indulgent and kind-hearted as the patient himself. Unspoken criticism becomes audible when, in the course of the therapy, or as gleaned from the therapist's life story, there is some indication that he or she is disinclined to let peace, harmony and unconditional love be the imperative in their interpretation of the client. Little by little, the therapist will feel impelled to convey to the patient the validity of the dark sides of life, the necessity of aggression without resorting to violence, but also the potential love inherent in a hearty dispute. At first, this attempt will meet with bitter if silent resistance. It is therefore advisable to proceed carefully but persistently, by using examples which, through the resolution of conflicts, have resulted in something good. It is important also to point out time and again the relation between the ability to put up a fight and a healthy immune system of the body.

Small tasks, such as drawing the attention of a smoker in a non-smoking zone to the non-smoking sign, or effectively stopping a family member from eating up on Friday the cheese intended for the week-end, are part of the therapeutic duties. These tasks must be set very gently but unrelentingly. Their accomplishment should not only be supervised but thoroughly examined and discussed in their emotional effect on all parties involved. The therapist mustn't lose sight of the actual background: a feeling of incompetence and the perceived inability to face the less pleasant aspects of life. The search for traumatic childhood experiences will yield little result here, because the origin of this existential fear is not an isolated event but the need of the soul to deal with this existential, archetypal Fear of Inadequacy. Each small success will contribute to a stock on which the client can lastingly rely upon.

As for the rest, the therapist should refrain from knowingly or unconsciously signing a non-aggression pact. There should be agreement from the start that he or she has permission to build up, by cautious resistance, a kind of callus skin, which will enable the client to better cope with life and its aggressive sides.

Type 3: The Busy Lizzie

If an individual's fear of inadequacy is so immense that it must under no circumstances surface to the conscious mind, it gets redirected into a need for evidence of extreme competence and almost perfect control of the self, the professional field, human relations or the living environment. A Busy Lizzie strives for perfection in all aspects of life.

Busy Lizzie, man or woman, imagines that she is able to achieve anything and is up to all challenges, if only one would leave her alone and not throw any obstacles in the path of her ambition. Busy Lizzie needs time to study in the quiet of her little room, hitting the files or taking work home from the office, stay at the lab late at night or develop and increase her proficiency by night school or adult education courses. She would like to demonstrate to herself and all others that, if she only gave it a little effort, there need be no limits for her.

For this goal, Busy Lizzie foregoes a lot of things other people indulge in in terms of private life, entertainment, leisure time and fun. Busy Lizzie has little interest in that. All she wants is to acquire more and more skills and attend to the task at hand with all her ambition and industriousness, in order to prove to herself that she is capable of achieving anything she sets her mind to. Irreproachableness is the aim. Failure is the death-dealing nightmare. The nightlight of perfectionistic control must always remain on to ward off this terrifying ghost.

That this fear of failure, this anxiety of incapability and inadequacy of any kind is actually the engine of this infinite diligence and ambition mustn't be acknowledged because it would threaten to make the whole construct fall apart like a house of cards. By the same token, Busy Lizzie wouldn't like it if somebody noticed how much trouble and perseverance she applies to acquire these competences. Much of this, therefore, happens unobtrusively or goes on in secret. It remains hidden so well that her social environment not only doesn't know how it was done, but that the result, too, often remains a private matter.

Busy Lizzie has the tendency to hide her light under the bushel, hoping that the excellent results be perceived only in part – if at all – so that they seem to have materialized as if by magic power. Since the people around her never suspected how these accomplishments, this success actually came about, it may happen that one day an attic full of excellent paintings is discovered, without anyone even having noticed that Busy Lizzie bought paints and canvas at all.

Busy Lizzie seeks satisfaction primarily in the feeling: »I can do it and I know I can, but I don't have to tell everyone else.« Outstanding novels remain hidden in a drawer until after death; research work doesn't get published and language talents are activated only when no one is around to hear that one is able to converse with Chinese tourists in their mother tongue.

Everything about Busy Lizzie is moderate except her ambition; everything is reasonable, restrained, but intellectually and practically permeated by perfection. The Busy Lizzie type will never kick over the traces because it needs all controlled strength to achieve the goals it has targeted. It will not waste its energy elsewhere. Moderation and hard work, being a very decent person and otherwise keeping a low profile – that is what Busy Lizzie strives for. No matter what position in life she holds, be it a cleaning lady or head of department, her basic attitude is: »I must be satisfied with my own work. If someone else eventually notices that I'm a true gem, it shall suit me fine.« The longing for glory, attention and love is focused primarily on a situation in which one day she will be sadly missed, having changed jobs or even died. Busy Lizzie hopes that at least posthumous fame will finally do justice to the efforts she has invested in her task of diligence. The obituary is more important to her than the present-day resonance.

Features

What is striking about a Busy Lizzie – be it man or woman – is the absolute correctness of appearance. Tautness, neatness, conformity, and a general no-nonsense attitude can be observed in the demeanor and attire of a Busy Lizzie. Women prefer a conventional hairstyle, twinset and pearl necklace; men like to wear a correct suit with an unobtrusive tie. This suit has often seen a number of years and the twinset too seems scuff-proof.

This phenotype always appears a little hounded and unrested, as if the person hadn't gotten enough sleep for nights on end, which is actually often the case, from sheer concern about asserting its claim to perfection. Modesty is paired with a certain condescension. To the fellow men this remains a bit of a mystery, since these most impressive capabilities seem to be no big deal. However, people in her environment feel that Busy Lizzie somehow signals that they, too, should make a greater effort, or that they simply didn't try hard enough. »Effort« is the keyword that never fails to fill Busy Lizzie with joy and understanding.

She has made such a great effort with everything she takes out into the world that it infuriates her when someone else abstains from doing the same; yet it evokes her anger when someone tries to be as perfect as she is. Others are often regarded as rivals or competitors.

A Busy Lizzie likes to ask whether she can be of help. During a conversation she will fiddle with her clothes, finding fine hairs or threads which have inexplicably settled there, pulling the skirt over her knees all the time, or adjusting her collar. She repeatedly straightens her hair. Men keep a small comb in their breast pocket and like to use it surreptitiously. Women's hair is frequently cut so short, it gives a boyish impression. It's practical and time-saving, and the hours other women spend on their hairdo can be better employed for other things.

Typical complaints of the Busy Lizzie

If there comes a time when, due to total exhaustion, efficiency slackens, Busy Lizzie will resort to stimulants such as cocaine, followed by sleeping drugs; consumption of coffee and coke may be high. »Hanging in there« is her dictum. A Busy Lizzie will only seek counseling when she feels that her way of being and acting causes increasing rejection and discomfort; when she realizes that she really can't cope either with praise or reproach, and that any criticism of her laboriously constructed building of perfection seriously shakes the foundation walls. This abatement of her incessant efforts leads to sleeplessness, great anxiety and a lifelong rebuff of the person who dared to chip away at Busy Lizzie's perfectionist image.

As a result, the body reacts with high blood pressure, stomach aches, spasms and gastritis, raucous vocal cords threatening to fail completely. Shoulders cramp up and the appetite vanishes or increases excessively. To face the world, even though the world seems to threaten Busy Lizzie with evidence of failure or inadequacy of some kind, she must resort to various emotional mechanisms: fantasies which culminate in punishing the company, the family or herself, which, under specific circumstances, may in fact result in just such acts. In that state, a Busy Lizzie will defy everyone, retreat into herself, grimly refuse to speak and silently cancel her unacknowledged and, from her point of view, unappreciated services, and temporarily do no more than work-to-rule, including her housekeeping; all of this in the hope that others will at last realize what they have lost and painfully miss the usual self-sacrificing dedication of Busy Lizzie.

Since this tactic is also self-punishing, involving agony and much inner pressure, her silent refusal causes Busy Lizzie great pain. The anxious strain increases when she asks herself when it will be noticed at last that she has curbed her usual commitment? She will find that her collegues' reactions are quite often rather positive than negative. Then her world comes tumbling down, and behind the unutterable effort to render unassailable and hard work, surfaces a helpless yearning for recognition and love. Those gigantic efforts often serve to prove to father or mother how lovable one really is, even after they are dead.

Other distinctive features are: chewed nails, torn and nibbled cuticles, excessively scrupulous personal hygiene, a certain obsession concerning schedules and punctual meals. A desire for perfection designed to dominate physical appearance by dieting, fitness exercises or strict abstinence from sweets or other indulgences will uphold strong self-control. The outer appearance is subjected to an idea of perfection. Sometimes, trichotillomania, the tearing out of hair, can be observed and, if the perfection impulse becomes compelling already in puberty, anorexia. The latter doesn't originate from the same source as anorexia arising from the archetype of Greed (Fear of Privation), but is the expression of despair over the uncontrollable impulses which during puberty threaten to dominate the self-image. They maintain the fixed idea that the only way to be attractive to the other sex is to be perfect and attractive also in their own eyes, i.e. by exerting complete self-control.

Since control over one's fear of failure is crucial with this type of Self-deprecation, many feelings, sensations and impulses must be constantly suppressed, because they potentially lead to other forms of self-harm, such as excessive smoking or swallowing considerable amounts of painkillers to smother the body's natural warning signals from permanent overexertion.

Occasionally however, a Busy Lizzie will look anything but perfect: overweight, unkempt, even sloppy, badly dressed, and in terms of objective, factual knowledge, not too well educated in the usual sense. Still, she herself feels that she is always striving for perfection and will long to control and master her life. But the nervous system of this Busy Lizzie variety reacts mostly with refusal, and she will complain that, with all the effort she is giving it, she doesn't have a handle on her life. Daily chores, family, work or health aren't the way they should be. Things just slip from her hands like a precious coffee pot from her finest Sunday china and shatter on the kitchen floor, even though she took the greatest care.

When her compensated Fear of Inadequacy gets overwhelming, Busy Lizzie will become suicidal. The reason is her belief that she is no longer able to cope with her imaginary failure or any criticism. So she opts for a self-determined, controlled suicide or secretly longs for it, because she cannot see any other escape from her situation: hasn't she made every conceivable effort all her life to avoid this worst-case scenario? The relational dimension will also come into play here because a patient who, in his own judgment, has done everything humanly possible to contribute to the relationship and earn lasting love through assiduousness, utter modesty and an undemanding position in the half-shade, suddenly feels deceived and abandoned. Secretly though, a Busy Lizzie has guessed that any partner would find such unpretentiousness and constant, hungry demands for praise boring rather than attractive. Suicide, primarily as punishment for the disloyal partner, seems to be the obvious solution here. Busy Lizzie is also given to fall in love with someone who is unaware of her feelings or completely out of reach. She will then suffer from chronic lovesickness or even turn to stalking. Also other forms of self-punishment for failure, which are chiefly intended as an instrument to punish others, will sometimes be applied. The desire to retreat from the world into a monastery or join a spiritual community promising perfection in other ways, for example through purity or survival of a catastrophe by acts of mercy, accommodates the wishful thinking of a Busy Lizzie. The permanent overexertion by family or work is then diverted to a desire for self-mortification and grateful recognition for her exceptional piety and diligence by the members of the group. The psychiatric disorder concealed behind these aspirations surfaces only when the religious group refuses to prolong the novitiate, or when the sect tries to rid itself of the proselyte, having recognized the inauthentic motivation.

A patient of this type quickly adjusts to the ward community, immediately starting to help, doing more than is required and seeking the role of mediator between those who, in his mind, are the really sick ones, and the staff. If Busy Lizzie is fairly well educated, one soon gets the impression that doctors, nurses and guardians are wanting in their performance, and that she could handle things much better and more efficient. When her excessive commitment is stopped for therapeutic reasons, Busy Lizzie will at first fall into a deep hole of powerlessness and incapability, from which she can only resurface when she feels that her true personality, now buried, helpless and in need of recognition, is actually appreciated and valued.

Indications for treatment of the Busy Lizzie

Behind all the buzzing activity and work, a Busy Lizzie seeks praise, recognition and tender devotion more than anything else, also and especially when she demonstrates the opposite. The therapist should therefore offer plenty of it. Each time, for even the smallest of reasons, Busy Lizzie should be praised, because praise mitigates the pressure of having to do something, subduing her fear-based diligence. It is holding back praise which generates Busy Lizzie's impulse for modest submissiveness and wearing herself down in busyness. When the therapist notices that praise merely leads to the patient squirming, fending off, playing it down and starting to denigrate himself, this should soon be made an issue of discussion.

The second measure is to caringly perceive and actually express these observations. The atmosphere, the client's appearance and the way he or she acts or reacts to the therapist – all that can be provided as feedback and a clear sign that the client has actually been noticed, which in turn will soon make him feel seen. It may occur, however, that at first the client feels unmasked or exposed as phony, because a Busy Lizzie, on the one hand, wants to be noticed, yet on the other hand tries hard to hide behind a façade of unassuming industriousness. In no case may the therapist give in to Busy Lizzie's offer of applying her skills or acting out her need to do something in this relationship, too. When he or she offers to babysit or repair the water tap, to somehow assist or help out with the income tax declaration, it must be kindly but rigorously rejected.

In this therapy, Busy Lizzie should be provided the opportunity to experience what it is like to be appreciated for her own sake and not because of her modest and industrious devotion. The bustle, which usually offers an outlet for her smoldering fears, should be effectively stopped. The client may, as a result, become quite restless because he is prevented from doing anything to please the therapist or get his attention. This may easily lead to the misconception that a more active therapy would be more appropriate or favorable here. But that is definitely not the case, it would rather aggravate the client's fear structure.

Small tasks, to be undertaken between sessions, should primarily be dedicated to introspection and the motivational analysis of behavior. The standard ploys of modesty the patient uses to belittle himself should be addressed and their accuracy questioned. Examined superficially, they seem to correspond to a social convention. For the Self-deprecator however, they conceal a fearful, painful truth. What he feels behind these casual statements is: »Basically, I am incapable. I have failed again.« When this client says for example: »Oh really, that was nothing special,« or »you don't have to thank me for that,« the therapist should always ask: »But why ever not?«

A last note of advice: If the client unduly praises the therapist, the wonderful atmosphere or the therapy method, this usually encodes a great fear of not being loved otherwise, or else a masked criticism, which is paradoxically expressed in excessive eulogizing. This should make the therapist prick up his ears and not simply accept or shrug off the praise, but rather reflect about whether something sounding unreal veils something real. A second approach is to somehow convey the message: »I'll be there for you even if you don't shower me with praise« or, though expressed in a kind way: »I'm not so dependent on praise as you may think.«

Self-sabotage – Fear of Joyfulness

General

Self-sabotage is the attempt to inhibit or subvert the elementary joy of an ensouled body. To suppress the liveliness of physical existence means to sabotage it. Man, like any living creature, enters the material world, ready to make the best of his existence. And each individual attempts it in his own way. When someone tries to dampen the joy in this venture, it is out of fear that his vitality might overwhelm him. He needs to keep his life energy in check and therefore sabotages situations and the people around him. It's a frantic, fearful and restrictive control, a deep fear of his own liveliness.

For illustration, a self-saboteur can be compared to a Tantrik who, based on his religious convictions, makes every effort not to reach an orgasm, yet at the same time doesn't want to give up sexual intercourse. It's trying to live without being joyfully alive. Holding in an orgasm can make sense occasionally. However, applying this practice all his life will ultimately keep this person from experiencing an orgasm at all. Yet this is just what someone with the archetype of Self-sabotage is doing: He tries, out of fear, to let no unchecked zest for life or real joy arise in himself or in the people around him. In the end he will lose the simple faculty to rejoice.

Self-saboteurs always look quite gloomy and somber. They are afraid they won't be taken seriously if they are jolly, let alone silly and tomboyish. They aren't much inclined to get any exercise either and invent various measures to keep their liveliness in check. Lightheartedness makes them suspicious.

Now a person with only little interest in sexuality will hardly become a Tantrik. The same principle applies to someone struggling with Self-sabotage. He or she has a greater potential for exuberance and joy of life than others. This cheerful vitality could bubble over, and the sheer joy of being alive might carry this person away into realms he can no longer control. But just as one can learn to hold back an orgasm, one can also learn to release it. And this is what's recommended as a therapeutic and also practical method to help someone with a pronounced archetypal fear of Self-sabotage. There are different ways to teach him to go for something big making small steps. Small joys can become big, fun becomes delight. Liveliness can be fostered instead of being restrained.

The Poles of Fear of Joyfulness

– Self-destructive	⟷	Self-sacrificing +

If a Self-saboteur takes a self-sacrificing attitude in the positive pole of this fear archetype, he doesn't behave like a selfless Martyr trying to enhance his worth by not making any demands. A Martyr initially gains a certain amount of life energy from his constant busyness and readiness to suspend his own interests beyond those of his fellow men. The Self-saboteur, in contrast, sacrifices something else. He renounces his zest, his vitality and his ability to take pleasure in life. When he does that, he too feels seemingly better at first. He withdraws into himself, hardly making any demands on the joyful and positive aspects of his existence. He feels virtuous in giving himself up. The Martyr also gives himself up, but with senseless activity on behalf of others.

The Self-saboteur's sacrifices are rather on an energetic or mental level; no one benefits from them. His energetic sacrifice has no value for himself or other people.

Usually this attitude isn't even noticed by the outside world. The saboteur's sacrifice is self-referential. It isolates, segregates and gradually kills his vitality. Nevertheless, it passes as an apparent virtue since the Self-saboteur neither really feels nor expresses his own needs or wishes, thus suppressing his potential for happiness. So it happens almost automatically that other people's wishes are more likely to get fulfilled than his. They will enjoy while he stands back with a sour face.

The seemingly positive pole of this archetypal fear is renunciation of merriment and vivacity, for example by workaholism, over-exercise or strict vegetarianism. If it's a pity, it doesn't really harm anyone. Still, this auto-aggressive willingness to sacrifice oneself in the name of austerity is and remains a false virtue.

The negative pole of Self-sabotage, in contrast, has a clearly destructive note. It affects both others and the Self-saboteur himself. Everyone gets to share in the depressing atmosphere, in damaging actions and destructive behaviors. Typical examples are drug addiction, alcoholism and pathological gambling. Also apparently harmless versions of this negativity, such as ›spoil-sporting‹ happy situations, habitually raining on other people's parade or an undying pessimism have destructive effects. They act as energy killers. The negative pole results in a general dampening of joy and delight all around, often to the extent of destroying the most beautiful moments life has to offer. Occasionally, it is even applied with purpose. For example, by obsessive gambling, the Self-saboteur endangers or destroys not only his own professional career, his fortune, his old age pension and much more, but also the trust of his family, their basic subsistence, cohesion and affection.

He sacrifices his lifetime and his opportunities to indulge his addiction, or he sacrifices his health, wealth and, in extreme cases, ultimately his life as the last way out of a desperate situation. And even this last act is in no way constructive but solely destructive. His death benefits nobody. His life-insurance will find a way not to pay. The harmful quality of such a way of practicing self-sabotage is demonstrated just by the fact that no-one gains from it. Everything lies in tatters in the end.

The Released Potential

Bound as a potential in every form of Self-sabotage is a great love of life. It can be unraveled stratum by stratum from its bonds again, changing into a manifestly positive quality. Joy of life is a primeval and innate need of any creature. Being afraid of joyfulness, happiness and aliveness will manifest Self-sabotage in a more or less pronounced way. So once the inclination for self-sabotaging diminishes, meaning that this archetypal fear eases off, love of life will automatically occupy the vacated space previously held by fear of vitality. Just as a greening meadow emerges when the snow melts and the wintry cold gives way to the spring sun. And this budding of joyfulness is felt much more strongly than if it had been there from the start. Someone whose inner snow starts melting experiences springtime more consciously and more gratefully than those who dwell on the isles of eternal spring.

A Self-saboteur can learn to live largely without destructive actions and attitudes and to rejoice in life. He is able to wholly accord others their pleasure, too, to fully enjoy his aliveness for no particular reason. If he manages to reduce his archetypal fear by a small amount, he may turn into a pleasant, peaceable contemporary. He can then laugh about his defeatism, and raise rather than paralyze the general atmosphere with his presence, feeling gratitude for his natural vitality.

Three Types of Fear of Joyfulness

1. The **Spoilsport** ruins carefree moments by remarks that destroy the atmosphere. He stops any childlike, naive playfulness like a ball in mid-flight. So the Spoilsport intercepts the colored balls of fun and aliveness before his fellow men can catch them with open arms. Then he keeps them safe in the cellar like a grim janitor.

2. The **Grouch** spreads ill-humor without intending or noticing it. There's always something for him to niggle about; it's hard to please him. He has a chronically dour face, making the jaws of any onlookers spontaneously drop. When confronted with good news, a success story or some beautiful experience, he'll be quick to think of something to deflate them. He himself finds no reason to report anything nice. Life doesn't have much to offer him.

3. The **Mope** calls on his fellow men's sympathy. He has innumerable sad or bad stories to tell; he is never well and never feels good. Should his life for once seem easy and positive, he will soon dig into his terrible past to downgrade the moment of contentment and destroy it.

Type 1: The Spoilsport

The universal energy 2 is merrily playful, childlike, unconcerned and sunny. It is connected to the Soul Role of the »Artist«. Self-sabotage represents the dark side of this light-hearted energy. This explains why to a Spoilsport, anything easy and light and filled with unconcerned cheerfulness feels suspicious. In his eyes, such merry-making looks superficial and dubious, even morally open to attack in its apparent carelessness. Life is a serious business, after all.

The Spoilsport has a certain awareness of his ability to cause atmospheric disturbances. His energetic effect is like a cloudburst on a beautiful summer's day when people enjoy themselves out in the open air, having ice-cream or splashing about in the water. When he shows up, people's faces suddenly drop. The fun is over now. Everyone has the impression of behaving in an inappropriate way.

When the Spoilsport appears, they make an effort to restrain themselves. They start to tidy up and turn the music down, disappointment and ill-humor spreading everywhere. One critical devastating look of the Spoilsport suffices to call everyone around to order, signaling that they must stop being silly now, that they should pull themselves together and bring their uncalled for cheerfulness under control.

This type of Self-saboteur isn't only a Spoilsport for others; he also keeps spoiling the atmosphere for himself. When he plans some fun event, something always comes in between. He prepares to go on a journey, but a few days before falls ill so badly he can't go and moreover has to pay the full cancellation fee. While he celebrates his wedding, he already suspects that it's the wrong partner and won't make a happy marriage – which is just the reason he has chosen him or her.

Being sick, he consults the wrong doctor and subjects himself to unreasonable methods of treatment, just to insist on his point of view that nobody can help him anyway. He also tends to lose his purse or damage his belongings. At precisely the moment he has plans for a good time or just enjoys a pleasant and agreeable moment, something foolish or harmful happens. At a party he had actually looked forward to, he inadvertently drops his burning cigarette onto the expensive wooden table. He knocks over a precious vase or breaks the wine glasses on his way to the host's kitchen, but of course, he only meant to help.

He always means well, wanting the best, yet he often can't manage to feel an unbroken joy in any event or a get-together with other people. He lives under the compulsion to spoil the fun for others and the free play of his energies for himself.

Typical features

A Spoilsport likes to report with mild pride that he is quite an unlucky bird. As he tries to spread his feathers stuck together by ill-fortune, he almost relishes, relating all the terrible or embarrassing things which happened to him, that went wrong in his life or didn't work out the way he had planned. Of course, it's never his own fault. He has nothing to do with it. It's other people or some mysterious fate which destroy his happiness.

The Spoilsport radiates a subliminal unrest, like when someone has an itch but doesn't dare to scratch for reasons of etiquette, or has the urge to sneeze and desperately tries to suppress the impulse, even though it's going to happen anyway. It's the unrest before the outbreak that marks the Spoilsport. He frequently taps his foot or drums his fingers. His demeanor is sometimes meant to signal to his counterpart that they still haven't come to the point. His face shows ill-temper at this loss of precious time and energy. In this way, everyone in the room starts feeling guilty. In a laid-back atmosphere, when people horse around, he merely grimaces and – should there actually be cause for laughter – unknowingly sends admonishing looks around the room. He seems sulky and bad-humored. When he is on a visit someplace, his unspoken criticism of the lack of cleanliness, orderliness or furnishings is all too obvious, although he believes it's not.

His nasolabial grooves are very distinctive, even in younger years, the corners of his mouth drooping. No matter how tired he is, he always gets up at the same time and won't indulge in another half hour of cozy slumber. In the course of a conversation it is revealed that discipline and the need to deny himself »superfluous« things like having fun, eating good meals or wearing good clothes, play an important role in the everyday mastering of his life.

Typical complaints

Our Spoilsport often has a blotchy, ruddy complexion. He watches his diet carefully, insisting on food that is supposed to be healthy but doesn't taste good. Yet he has a knack for picking out that to which he reacts with difficult digestion or allergies. When he is invited to some party or happy get-together, it serves as an excuse to say: »Sorry, but I've eaten something which disagrees with me. I can't come.« He is extremely sensitive to a number of interference factors such as noise that others hardly register; he gets vexed at things he can't change and wastes his energy ranting against red traffic lights or laws he considers unreasonable.

Frequently, he has bad breath and carious teeth since he is terrified of dentists. He prefers to be chronically ill or suffer non-specific complaints rather than do something about it. To »somehow« be ill or permanently unwell serves to stabilize this sub-type of fearful Self-sabotage. After all, what would happen if he were to feel better or even well? The answer is: he would be flooded by joy of life, happiness and vitality, and he would feel threatened. To him, life is a difficult and sorrowful business.

When the fear level of a Self-saboteur is very high, it may lead to compulsive, controlling personality disorders, but as a rule not to severe psychiatric illnesses. Because his ability to control is so pronounced, it is in itself controlled. The Spoilsport rather tends to develop an increasing coldness and self-control which has an isolating, alienating effect. The Spoilsport complains that others avoid him, that his relations die down after a short time or that people suddenly turn away from him. What he needs is help to recognize that this can't be the fault or deficiency of his fellow men alone, but that human relations are a complex structure of interacting effects – something the Spoilsport has almost forgotten. He is so used to broken friendships or partnerships, either completely or at least energetically, that he has rarely experienced relationships in a positive, inspirational way. That is why, deep down, he doesn't believe happy relationships exist at all.

Indications for treatment

When the therapist feels that his attempts at establishing a playful and trusting rapport are immediately fended off by the Spoilsport, sensing a cloud of cold and sadness in the company of this client, it is particularly important to give him a cautious feed-back, like: »You know, I feel quite depressed now. I meant no harm in telling that little joke and didn't suspect it would offend you.« The Self-saboteur needs to become aware again and again of his effect on other people. »I feel sad now, I am suddenly depressed« is not what he normally hears. His usual experience is that the other just drops his visor, cuts the flow of energy and turns away. It is crucial therefore, especially in a therapeutic relation, not to do this, either energetically or verbally.

This patient should furthermore be assigned a small task between sessions. For example, he or she should report of some pleasant, happy experience or event, no matter how insignificant. Since there is usually an interval of several days between therapy sessions, the real problem, namely Self-sabotage and the Fear of Joyfulness, will become all the more evident if the patient shows up saying: »There was nothing. I just can't think of anything pleasant at all.« Then the next step could be to scrutinize each single day with him and draw his attention to the one or other episode which really wasn't all bad or even quite nice. If he remonstrates, trying to play it down, the therapist can gently and cautiously help him to change his attitude towards these little joyful events in his life. In less serious cases, a joy diary is a helpful tool. In it, the patient should record even the smallest pleasant moment and at the end of the day strike the balance. Was it really so bad today?

After an appropriate length of therapy, when his stiltedness has softened up, it is also possible to discuss specific interventions on his part which have spoiled the atmosphere in the past. Toward the end of the therapy, when intimacy has been established, even the funereal expression he often wears could be playfully mimicked or referred to: »Oh dear, the face you're making again today! What has bitten you? Did anything terrible happen again you'd like to tell me about?« The intended goal is to exaggerate a little, to raise the energetically destructive perception to the client's consciousness. It must be remembered that the entire syndrome is connected to the playful Energy 2. The therapist should specifically avoid yielding to the client's interaction rules and inner regulations. Conversations should be kept buoyant and light-hearted. The biggest trap in the treatment of a Spoilsport is to cater to his dead seriousness and allow him to determine the atmosphere of the therapy session.

Type 2: The Grouch

The Grouch is morose through and through. In his view, life is colorless, exhausting, senseless and joyless – that's exactly how he feels it to be. He experiences reality like a person with advanced eye cataract, hardly able to see colors anymore. Or like someone who spends his time in a room with frosted windows, never letting in the bright sunlight with a view on people, grass and trees. Everything seems blurred and indistinct. The outlines of his life aren't clear but spongy, which is why the Grouch can't get a handle on it. People for him are like lifeless shadows. He has long given up trying to reach out for someone who might establish a solid or even satisfactory relationship with his environment again. The Grouch takes a pessimistic view on his own just as on the life of his fellow humans – all grey in grey without bright colors. The Grouch spreads an aura of hopelessness within and without.

His faculty to criticize however is in no way underdeveloped. He cavils about everything and everybody, considering it a positive and necessary measure of correction. But he forgets that it's his own eyes needing cataract surgery in order to recognize the colorfulness of the world again. Instead, he loves to poke in the eyes of others – in their attitudes, positions and ideologies -- and take them apart. He also likes to put his nose into things that are none of his business, because to him anything that interests or satisfies people and makes them happy is either suspicious or simply incomprehensible.

There is so little joy, so little color in the life of a Grouch. He suspects that others only imagine their joys, that they are actually kidding themselves about the real character of existence and life as such. To him, life is a vale of tears, and someone seeing things differently is just a dreamer. Without hesitation, he can list hundreds of examples why his view of things is the right one. When he goes for a walk in the forest, all he sees are ill trees and areas destroyed by forestry workers. He visits places but notices only dirt and noise, ruins and poverty or other things which displease him. He goes to a restaurant and wonders why everyone looks so content, because he is sure to find a hair in his soup. He has a knack of attracting the adversities of life.

Only when he has reached a certain age and hasn't much time left to turn his life to the better will he notice that he himself spoils his days with his constant grumbling. So it rarely happens that a Grouch calls on professional help before his fiftieth year.

Typical features

The Grouch expresses the greyness veiling the psyche and appearance in his shallow complexion, shrouded look, thin lips and dull clothing. A Self-saboteur of this type is rarely corpulent. Why eat much if he doesn't enjoy his meals? Besides, gluttony is unhealthy and what's more, expensive.

A Grouch usually lives below his means. He rather saves up for a rainy day because he always expects the worst. He is often over-insured and warns others of events which might occur any time. He sees dangers looming everywhere against which one should hedge and insure if possible. In general though, he is restrained and careful. His flat is furnished with the most basic necessities. If his partner wants to purchase anything smelling even faintly of comfort or luxury, a relationship crisis will ensue.

It is characteristic of the Grouch that he doesn't care much about the opinion of neighbors and relatives. They only serve him in their role as objects of criticism or rejection.

Typical complaints

The Grouch type is often a heavy smoker, also frequently resorting also to hard liquor, usually without turning alcoholic because of his habitual self-control. Heavy smoking and drinking can cause complaints in the gullet and throat, like a burning pain, as if he had drunk acid. Other than that, psychosomatic complaints are infrequent. This man or woman sleeps well. They don't suffer from stomach trouble since they are moderate in everything except smoking and those quick shots of liquor. This drinking happens almost secretly, not because the Grouch tries to hide it, but because he pours down the alcohol so fast, he is hardly aware of it himself. A little schnapps, swigged fast, helps him to be in a better mood for a little while, a mode which even to him seems pleasant – to the degree of pleasure, of course, that he can tolerate.

In rare and distinctive cases, the Grouch may develop a pathological defeatism and fear of catastrophes leading to panic, though more often it manifests in anxiety fantasies and nightmares. In these dreams, something devastatingly dreadful will invariably happen: a flood, an earthquake, a bad accident, a fire. It's usually something really destructive, annihilating or threatening to destroy not only the dreamer but also everyone else around him.

Due to his fear of catastrophes, this grumpy Self-saboteur may avoid leaving the house. While this is phobic behavior, it's not a classic agoraphobia. The Grouch's anxiety doesn't primarily relate to people, to talking, showing or having to prove himself in front of others. It is rather based on the irrational idea of something awful happening to him or in his surroundings as soon as he leaves home.

Indications for treatment

A good way to help the Grouch – after an adequate phase of getting acquainted and building up trust – is to encourage him to go on imaginary journeys. These should primarily focus on childlike pleasures, colors and colorful events. The excessive grouchiness is in fact based on unfulfilled childhood dreams. There once was a child who wanted a little dog and was forbidden to have it. He wanted to go on the merry-go-round but he wasn't allowed to for no apparent reason. His parents were overcautious and prevented him from cycling and swimming – from fear that something terrible might happen. Presents from other people were either rejected or locked up in the cabinet so that the child couldn't play with them. The chocolate an uncle had given him was allocated in tiny pieces or eaten by others. Seldom or never did the child, who later developed into a grumpy adult, have the chance to feel an uninhibited, carefree joy in anything.

Nevertheless, during imaginary journeys or regressions, the focus should not lie on mourning past sorrows. Instead, the patient should get the opportunity to ride the merry-go-round at last, as often as he wants, to eat up a whole box of chocolates in one go, or to dip into the jam jar without being punished.

With the therapist's permission to ride a pretty pony, just as he or she had wanted to do as a small child, soon a new kind of memory will place itself over the old one. The brain will begin to restructure the memories, leading almost automatically to a considerable reduction and dissipation of grumpiness. If he feels like it, the therapist could tell a joke at the end of each session or look at some cartoon with his patient. The key here is the sheer childishness of the joy. Therefore, such a joke or cartoon should be »silly«, that is, close to the laughing criterion of a three- or four-year-old child.

Type 3: The Mope

The Mope basically looks at his life backwards, no matter whether he is twenty or seventy years old. He regards his past with deep mourning, worry and self-pity. He feels his whole life overshadowed by irreversibilities. Indeed, many sad and mournful events may be found in the story of his life. Early death of one or both parents, flight or prosecution, destitution, misunderstandings, alienation, the role of scapegoat and exclusion from the family occur frequently. But also medical conditions or heavy responsibility too early in life can produce the Self-sabotage type of Mope.

Striking about this phenotype is that he can seldom or never be fully in the moment. As soon as the atmosphere is relaxed, he will automatically turn his thoughts to something depressing, dreadful or unalterable from his life story or from the recent past. If, for example, this individual is in a good relationship, he or she will not enjoy it properly but be secretly reminded of all those negative experiences from earlier partnerships which did not turn out well and led to bitter disappointments. He loves to talk about how he was deceived or deserted, cheated and fooled.

Typical features

Typically, the Mope has a sunken posture, his shoulders drooping. When he tells a terrible, true story, he frantically clasps his hands, as if trying to rally his last bit of life energy. Actually though, this gesture is a way to prevent his hands from covering his face in despair, or raising them in lament or accusation.

His eyelids are often heavy. The skin is a little doughy since this person rarely feels the urge to be out in the open. Fresh air may be dangerous. (Hasn't he had many bad colds before?) He doesn't move around a lot because he usually feels queasy and feeble, so his muscles are weakened. He waits for the next opportunity to tell his bitter life-story at length and gets restless when he finds none. Yet he'll fend off any compassionate questions with a tired gesture, even though he longs to be asked for more. He actually hopes that the innumerable sad events will be little by little wormed out of him. Then one story opens up behind the next, stratum by stratum; there is no end to his litany of grievances.

Typical complaints

It's not surprising that the Mope is given to depressions. Curiously, they often become all the more intense the more he tries to analyze and come to terms with the past. He desperately searches for more experiences he would like to uncover in all their bitterness and sadness, and over that effort misses actual life.

In his presence, his fellow men will inevitably get sad too. They constantly feel compelled to show understanding or to excuse the Mope, since, after all, hasn't he gone through so much, and isn't it a known fact that such experiences will indelibly stamp the personality for good? There is nothing to be done about it; he just had to learn to live with it. That's simply ill fate.

Tears will come either easily or else they haven't been cried since childhood. A deep sigh will escape from the Mope's lips from time to time. He often breathes only haltingly and must take a deep breath to be able to speak normally again, the burden of life weighing so heavily on his chest.

Psychosomatic complaints are primarily concentrated on the heart and lungs. Patients report of a great weight on the chest, as is frequently the case with depressions, and tightness in the lungs resulting from flat breathing. The metabolism is sluggish, the blood pressure low, the skin pale. In many cases, adult Mope's have been diagnosed unable to work in their trained profession, or they are on early retirement at the end of a long treatment history. It all boiled down to the pathology having gotten rather worse, in particular the depressive part.

The type of Mope in need of psychiatric treatment is recognizable by the fact that he or she is no longer able to talk about their past. But chemical medicine won't help. They simply can't lament, complain or accuse any more. They can no longer relate any details or give the therapist a proper account of their complaints. This person seems blunted, fallen silent. He sinks into an almost catatonic condition, completely sealing himself up and, as he sees it from his inner perspective, »protecting« himself against anything that could hurt him again. Silence is his last resort.

Such a Mope – the strongest form of Self-sabotage – having completely lost and dissolved himself in the pains and wrongs of his life history, feels skinless and defenseless. Above all, he looks for some last remnants of security he can somehow get hold of, either in his own frame of mind or in his environment. Frequently, this is achieved by amnesia, permitting him to split off and block out the intolerable. This in turn leads to a number of conversion disorders (transformation of unresolved issues into physical symptoms), accompanied by paralyses, loss of speech or sudden deafness.

Indications for treatment

A Mope turned mute must, first of all, be given permission to curl up for a while, wrapped in blankets, to be solitary and not speak or establish any rapport with the therapist. In group or individual therapy, he should be allowed to hide away in a corner or under a blanket. Only after this respite has been granted him and he has gratefully felt that his mourning is duly respected, a slow and very careful approach by way of a gentle contact can take place. For example with some soft spoken words meant just for him, one hand resting on his shoulder protected by the blanket; or by expressing the wish to shake his hand, then holding it a little longer than is usually normal. Later, the therapist's hand may touch the cheek. All this, however, must happen very cautiously, concentrating on that one patient at that particular moment. What he needs is silent understanding and comfort through physical contact, because he feels so terribly alone in a hostile world.

A conversational therapy should focus on current distress if possible (preventing the patient from sliding back into the unalterable past) and generate his identity from that source. The woe of the day will provide sufficient material for discussion, and it is important that his misery be truly acknowledged by the therapist. It is not recommended to try and change the patient's perspective or direct his attention to the smaller or greater everyday joys too early. This method would be advisable with both the Grouch and Spoilsport. But the Mope's sorrow should be taken seriously and met with sympathy and compassion, yet without both patient and therapist wallowing in it.

At the same time, a greater distance is required here than with the other two types of Self-sabotage. It takes an inner distance plus sympathy without getting entangled, but one must not get entangled because, over the years, the Mope has firmly developed his social ability to infect other people with his sadness and grief. Special care must therefore be taken that this doesn't happen in therapeutic interaction.

The general line of argument should somehow contain the message: »You don't want to let your sad past spoil your future too, do you? I'll help you break free from it, so that these horrible things don't need to happen again.« And yet, a true change of perspective can only occur when, one day, the patient sees his therapist spill tears together with him or her. It is from that moment on that the Mope can at last let go of the past.

Universal Energy 3

Martyrdom – Fear of Worthlessness

General

A soul incarnates into the physical existence intending to learn how to act in time and space. It wants to find out about the cause and effect of actions – no action of whichever kind is without resonance or consequence for the greater whole. And only a soul which animates and inhabits a body can act and integrate the consequences of its actions into its accumulated experience.

It is an unquestionable truth that any living, acting human being cannot but become guilty in some way or other in the course of his numerous incarnations. Culpability is inherent to each life as the direct and irrefutable consequence of being incarnated, at least on a micro-scale. It is this guilt issue as an essential experience that Martyrdom is based on. Once a soul has decided to explore Martyrdom as a fear phenomenon in the course of an incarnation, this axiom of physical existence leads to a fearful misunderstanding. The experiencing of a person with this fear of worthlessness is governed by the firm idea that only the feeling of existential or actual guilt makes his life worth living and warrants his right to exist. This in turn creates the illusion that it were possible to increase self-worth and life-worth by a declared willingness to take on more than one's own share of human guilt, while simultaneously feeling compelled to constantly apologize for everything one does, is, or is not.

The intrinsic worth of a human being can be raised to question by no one and nothing at all. This is something not even the Soul Family or other superior powers can do. Even God – if we may say so – wouldn't dream of calling the existential worth of the least of his creatures into question. The Martyr, however, is more than ready to take on this mission. He queries himself and his existence from a value perspective. And his answer to the query is always: »Since I'm not really worth anything or at least don't know whether I am valuable enough and worthy of life, I have to do anything in my power, from my first to my last hour, to prove to myself and others that I haven't come into this world for nothing. I must understand that I, more than other people, am obliged to behave selflessly – so selflessly that, in the end, everyone is happier than I am. This is the only way I can justify my existence.«

The fact that this fundamental attitude, this kind of self-image, makes suffering unavoidable actually meets the Martyr's disposition. He hasn't expected anything else. The seemingly inextricable and yet illusory relationship between his existence as such, the presumed culpability of his existence, and the lifelong effort at debt-relief he incessantly makes in thought and deed is hard to explain to him. It is almost impossible to talk him out of it. Still, there is a way to mitigate the suffering of Martyrdom and its innate willingness to endure feelings of guilt and selflessness up to self-abandonment.

The relentless readiness of the Martyr to sacrifice himself for his fellow men, a social group or a cause – be it for a company or the survival of the killer whale – and to devote himself to a noble aim up to exhaustion is a »martial« attitude of the universal energy 3. This attitude can be molded into an acceptable, salubrious form once the Martyr learns to understand that a natural energetic law exists which sets certain limits to his noble efforts. And this law defines that no one can benefit from an act that leaves the benefactor worse off. Revealing this energetic interrelation to a Martyr is the basis for progress in his self-awareness. It will also be necessary to address the guilt-ridden feelings he has felt from day one of his existence and examine them in their absurd over-dimensionality. Furthermore, the self-sacrificing behavior and the infinite selflessness characterizing this fear should be exposed in their grotesque exaggeration. Martyrdom wants release from guilt. It's just that the guilt-ridden methods it applies are unsuitable to the goal.

But the Martyr will readily and gratefully accept it when guilt is taken off his shoulders. Martyrs need others who formally – sometimes even in writing – acquit them before the tribunal of life. Their insecurity in terms of self-esteem is so great that all debt-relief must be announced in bold headlines; otherwise it won't sink into the depths of their unconscious.

Since all Martyrs already carry a considerable measure of guilt feelings within, any further accusation, even the slightest criticism, discussion or conflict, could be the straw that breaks the camel's back. Their excessive burden becoming insufferable, it may lead to a sharp defense or profound depression. This doesn't mean the Martyr should be guarded from exposure to the world and his fellow men with their social structure. Because even if he manages to keep himself blameless and free of guilt for decades, a scrap of fresh accusation will suffice to cause his unstable self-confidence to cave in.

To lovingly show and reflect to the sorely afflicted, suffering Martyr his intrinsic self-worth, validated by existence itself, will do much good and will in turn be rewarded with existential gratitude.

The Poles of Fear of Worthlessness

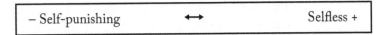

| – Self-punishing | ⟷ | Selfless + |

In our generally accepted understanding, selflessness is equated with generosity, the willingness to make sacrifices and the notion that one must not think of oneself and one's own interests first. Those who truly and unselfishly give ample room to the needs and woes of their fellow men, act from a source of inner freedom and a considerable ability to love. When we talk about Martyrdom, we imply that such inner freedom and great love-ability are not the true motives of selfless behavior, but are guided by an illusion aiming to increase self-esteem. The Martyr is oblivious to the fact that he or she thinks and acts out of an attitude of fear. We do not encourage selfless generosity if it's bought at the price of low self-worth.

While ego- or selflessness in an ethical-moral sense may indeed contribute to the meaningfulness of a physical existence, it remains a rare exception in an incarnation cycle. Striving for total egolessness would be tantamount to an attempt at suicide. Egolessness only exists in a non-incarnated state. The human »I« has an implicit reason to exist in any incarnation, and a natural right to the best possible self-fulfillment within the structure of the current incarnation. Talking about selflessness in connection with Martyrdom, however, we mean the efforts to deny one's legitimate needs, instead upholding the illusory idea of acting selfless and egoless out of fear of loss of love, in favor of the needs of others. Losing the self in order to win someone over can't be wholesome.

While the false virtue of selflessness is attributable to the seemingly noble, positive pole of this characteristic, self-harming by self-punishment – in whichever form – must be described as the minus pole of this fear phenomenon. Such Martyr's inner maxim is: »I really wanted to prove my noble spirit, but nobody thanks me for it. Seems I must have made a mistake. I haven't contributed enough to the human community. Consequently, I must expiate and chastise myself so that I may survive under the burden of my guilt feelings.«

The Martyr fights for reward. He punishes himself to be praised. He behaves selflessly to reap gratitude. He hopes for just pay in the afterlife for all the things he is denied gratitude here on earth. His need to put himself last, to deny his just interests or even punish himself for his misdemeanor, generally aims at recompense in whatever form by an illusory up-grading of his self-image or the grateful recognition by his fellow men. From fear of otherwise becoming guilty, a martyr-like behavior proffers more fearful selflessness than is beneficial for one's own good, granted all love and freedom of decision. It will lead to an emotional and energetic deficit, like someone always living above his means and still generously giving alms from a bank loan he can't pay off. To the ones benefitting from it, but also to the Martyr himself, this extent of selflessness or self-abandonment seems like a great, almost superhuman virtue. We call it a false virtue because the energetic source of his willingness to give more than he has got is not fed from free will and love, but out of fear of loss of worthiness, criticism and withdrawal of affection.

The admonition written on the selfless Martyr's forehead is »I mustn't think of myself and my own.« Often, he isn't even able to feel his own needs anymore. And if ever someone should suspect the Martyr of having acted selfishly in some way, despite all his selfless efforts, he will tumble into the abyss of his guilt feelings. Moreover, he is obliged to suffer all the disadvantages of his habit to appear noble, generous and forgiving under any circumstances. The Martyr seldom realizes that his assumed selflessness and his ingratiating willingness to make sacrifices of which he is so proud, basically just serve to boost his self-esteem.

As long as a Martyr basks in the positive pole of his selflessness, he still feels quite good, filled with a great measure of satisfaction and relief. He basks in his false virtue. If, however, he slips into the negative pole of self-punishment, his life becomes sad, manifestly agonizing and constrained. The gown of penitence the Martyr has donned himself in is webbed with self-devaluation and self-reproach. He is thrown ever deeper into the precipice of his fear of worthlessness, hardly seeing any chance to prove his worth again, not even by an immense effort. Usually though, the people around him will notice; the person affected can talk about it or seek help.

In the course of his life, the Martyr learns that such selflessness nurtured by fear and laden with guilt feelings will earn him neither respect nor gratitude. So it's no wonder that nobody complains as much about the ingratitude of the world and the egotism, the inconsiderateness and insensibility of his fellow men as the Martyr, who does his utmost to suppress such behavior in himself. Now if someone not suffering from such disposition – being focused on another primal fear and obviously not considering this selflessness a virtue but a weakness – rightly asks him: »How can you be so stupid not to pursue or defend your interests?« the Martyr sometimes simply doesn't understand. He feels misunderstood in his infinite efforts for self-upgrading by selflessness. Such criticism will make him feel unloved and unappreciated in his value-increasing endeavors.

If, on the other hand, he feels a whiff of truth in the reproach of having behaved unreasonably and stupidly self-damaging, earning him the ingratitude and lack of respect of the beneficiary on top of it, his first reaction won't be to change his behavior. Rather, it will result in profuse apologies and possibly self-punishment for something he must have obviously done wrong. He lapses into bitter self-recriminations, self-mortification and habitual denial or derogation of his qualities. If none of this helps to restore his inner balance, he will interpret some ailment as the just punishment for his factual or moral misconduct. So-called bad luck in life or some accident without obvious causal reference to one's actions are also attributed to a heavenly punishment or as atonement for some impalpable evil, or even for alleged karmic debt. All this serves to establish a martyr-like justice and emotional relief.

Optionally, self-punishment may occur by the Martyr indirectly fashioning his current life in such way that, as just reward for his putative offences, he feels really bad financially, socially or health-wise. He only feels better when his well-being is impaired by pain, poverty, or loss and solitude. These usually completely unconscious forms of self-punishment are credited to his account of self-worth; and yet – to keep with this image – the Martyr with his fearful magnanimity pays no more than the debt interests, his tendency for self-punishment driving him always deeper into the debt trap of the bank of life.

The Martyr succumbs to the illusion that he can actually pay off guilt. If he is versed in esoteric matters, it will relieve him to imagine that he has been quite bad in former lives, given to violence or hunger for power, of having incurred a great amount of guilt he can expiate by self-harming actions and an egoless attitude in this life. This is a misconception of karmic laws. The Martyr must understand that one can make up for karma only in direct contact with the human being whose soul one has harmed in an earlier existence, but certainly not by self-derogation.

The Released Potential

Martyrdom is a basic fear of the »warrior«, martial energy 3. So despite all weakness in saying No – it holds a powerful, militant component which, given a phase of insight and transformation, will be highly beneficial to the individual suffering under his self-sacrificing and self-punishing behavior. When a Martyr learns to look after himself, to ascertain his interests, to refuse and to counterattack instead of ducking and remaining on the receiving end, if he learns to accept criticism and deal with it realistically, he will soon be able to turn to new tasks. These don't primarily serve to restore his chipped self-esteem; rather, this invigoration of his energy system can be used constructively for himself and the people around him. He will be able to really feel his strength and be at one with himself. He will actively use his power for the good of the whole and pursue new, promising deeds without denying or forgetting his own well-being. He will be able to hear that inner voice again which had ceased to warn him when he was just too dutiful and self-sacrificing, when he generously abstained from defending his rights, living on credit energetically. And he will reclaim the joy in his doings by the same degree as he carefully listens to any feelings of listlessness, which occur when he is about to do too much, too early or too selflessly. He will gratefully follow this voice now, instead of silencing it, embarrassed.

The pleasure in applying his powerful strength to interesting, important and emphatic objectives rather than to suppress feelings of guilt will increase by the day; and without effort, his fellow men's laudatory appreciation he missed before is now bestowed him at every occasion. Instead of ingratitude, the Martyr reaps thankfulness, instead of getting kicked, humiliated or mobbed, he now finds that people will respect his honest Yes or No.

His new ability to refuse an unreasonable burden or reject unhealthy commissions instead of willingly letting himself be exploited, no longer acquiescing to any humiliations but actively rebelling against them, genuinely serves the growing self-esteem of the Martyr. It will help him to inwardly upright himself and come into his »warrior-strength«, using it not only to defend others but also himself. He no longer offers himself as a victim but becomes the master of his actions, utterances and wishes.

Three Types of Fear of Worthlessness

1. The **Scapegoat** takes upon him the blame of the whole world without even noticing. He proffers himself to be trampled on, as the one who is always at fault, willingly accepting the responsibility for culpable events, no matter that he has little or nothing to do with them.

2. The **Little Sunshine** has a constantly kind and cheerful nature. It beams and worries; it doesn't want to burden anyone. Its concern is to make everyone around happy and content, not noticing that it is drained of all energy and can no longer feel happy itself unless everyone else is radiant and rejoicing. The Little Sunshine wants to keep others warm while feeling cold itself.

3. The **Valiant Little Tailor** suffers from such feelings of un-worthiness and smallness, that he is fulfilled by a boisterous impulse to exalt himself, to aggrandize himself beyond the boundaries of his humanness. He tries to accomplish the superhuman or denying his humanness. The Valiant Little Tailor aims to be more magnificent and noble, but most of all stronger and braver, than his fellow people.

Type 1: The Scapegoat

The Scapegoat is infused with a victim mentality that taints his whole self-concept and self-feeling. He believes that a devoted attitude and the willingness to suffer is the only truly loving and noble lifestyle. He always shows himself understanding and forgiving.

Whatever you do to him, be it ingratitude or even bodily injury, he will still be ready to excuse and defend the perpetrator and to offer himself as the one who probably – unknowingly and without noticing it, perhaps even in a former life – has done something that justifies the treatment he is subjected to.

In his eyes, all human beings are bad; yet the scapegoat simply cannot but forgive them. He alone, so he is convinced, is good and noble; sadly this was something his fellow men simply wouldn't understand. His victim attitude arouses anger and indignation in others because it monopolizes responsibility and sense of guilt in the social structure, almost automatically prompting his fellow men to offload their emotional rubbish, vent their aggressions and conflicts, their dark sides, misgivings and fears on the Scapegoat. The reason is that he offers his shoulders – perceived to be a mile wide energetically – for the relief of others, and his backside to be kicked with impunity. In all of this he feels quite good, finding his right to exist strongly confirmed. The function he takes over for the greater whole seems to prove him right, as others feel indeed better and relieved of fault when they could clobber and kick him around. This happens in families, in companies and many other social groupings. This person may complain, but the docile willingness to suffer nevertheless prevails, as if he or she was born with this fateful purpose.

That this is a massive fear phenomenon remains hidden at first, because the Scapegoat doesn't feel his fear as such. He is often aware though that others pick on him and abuse him out of fear of their own impulses. What he usually realizes only later in life is that he has an energetic share in this. Through his selfless readiness to take everything on himself he makes them an offer, which, in the interest of social balance, can hardly be rejected. In a best case scenario, the Scapegoat then finally activates his »martial« defense and typically turns towards the opposite at first: into a compensation attitude which induces him to create a Scapegoat of his own, on whom he can dump all the weariness and surplus of fault and pain and rage of his life in turn. Only in a second stage comes the day when he feels: »This is no solution either.« It's at this point that convalescence can begin, removing the supposedly fateful part from this social position of blame.

Features

The Scapegoat unconsciously signals that one may treat him less considerately than others. He can take a lot. He is prepared to excuse and forgive everyone – except himself. He defends the culprits of this world, shows sympathy with wrongdoers and torturers. He argues that the evil in this world must manifest someplace and somehow, and that it was appropriate to hold out the other cheek and offer himself as a catalyst.

Sometimes his eyes have a feverish gleam derived from an inner glow, which is rooted in the satisfaction of an almost masochistic social behavior. His posture is often stooped or marked by crooked shoulders. The shoulder blades are pulled forward as if he were expecting to receive blows and simultaneously protecting himself from it. This picture of a beaten dog conveys a strange impression of double cowardice: first, because others wouldn't be prepared to endure so much and bravely suffer all the humiliations, and second, because the Scapegoat doesn't defend himself, which is taken as weakness.

The Scapegoat complains a lot about the evil of the world and that, his whole life, he has suffered many bad turns. Yet at the same time he shows indulgence for those nasty people who cannot help themselves but to let their rage out on him. A longer conversation will reveal that he has developed a certain pride in the fact that, despite the social abuse, he still hasn't perished. A kind of need for revenge seems to be lurking in the background, which ultimately manifests itself in some illness or invalidity of the Scapegoat. This contrasts the badness of his abusers even more vividly, since, obviously, someone who tramples on a defenseless, ill or elderly person is undoubtedly a brute. For the Scapegoat, this strangely balances the distribution of burdens and his sense of justice and order is restored.

Typical Complaints

The Scapegoat typically suffers from disorders of the spinal column, ranging from severe backaches or a slipped disc, scoliosis, Bekhterev's disease, cramped shoulders and cervical spine syndrome up to tormenting headaches. Also major digestion disorders such as Crohn's disease and colitis ulcerosa are common. These ailments can be explained by the Scapegoat's permanently weak immune system. He doesn't defend himself against anything. He also doesn't »digest« what's dished out to him, but simply pushes it away or – spoken symbolically – tries to excrete without having metabolized it.

Someone experiencing again and again that he is made the scapegoat by his fellow men and cannot see how to change it, will frequently develop high blood pressure, cardiac arrhythmias, constricted vessels, convulsive states or psychogenic paralyses, but chiefly also damaged teeth due to his habit of clenching them in fury. Scapegoats often have a high cholesterol level and false teeth at an early age.

When the Scapegoat can no longer carry and suffer the burden of the blame ascribed to him, he turns it against himself by punishing himself for everything he feels worthy of punishment or valueless in him. He does it in various ways, for example by criminal acts which land him in prison, where in turn he becomes the scapegoat of his fellow prisoners again. Preferably, however, the self-punishment occurs by harming his body with alcohol and drugs, by scoring his skin and other kinds of self-inflicted wounds or by accidents caused almost willfully. When he sees his own blood or bruises, something inside of him seems to mysteriously set things right. His emotional balance attains a pseudo-stability.

People with severe auto-destructive behaviors – be it by self-mutilation or alcohol – need very long-term therapeutic support and established, solid human relationships to truly experience that they have an existential human worth, that they are appreciated and valued, even without bloodshed or physical pain.

The self-punishment expressed in this self-harming also pursues another purpose, namely to draw attention to himself as a way to bail out of a difficult and dodgy situation. Because once the Scapegoat is in a clinic or psychiatric institution, he can temporarily escape the role of the family scapegoat, the bullying at work or being the one to be called to account for any failure.

Scapegoat syndrome as an expression of Martyrdom may vary. One is that the Scapegoat, in order to finally throw off the rocks of guilt feelings from his shoulders, develops delusional ideas of himself as the world's savior or saint, pure and innocent as a new-born baby. This self-exaltation serves to convert fault into innocence, or make others feel guilty for being allegedly sinful, wicked, or actually planning crimes. This type of Scapegoat seems exceptionally mistrustful and might develop a persecution complex, believing that they are out to kill him or destroy him in order to thwart his mission.

Also critical are cases of Martyrs who have been sexually abused and maltreated in childhood. Unable to assimilate the infantile guilt feelings and the dismay at not having defended himself, such Scapegoat might convert his anxieties into a need to torment or abuse children, elder people or animals himself now. Another subtype is the Scapegoat who accepts the oppression, derision and maltreatment by his fellow men for the longest time, until his measure is full. And since he has never defended himself before, he now feels forced to kill someone who tormented him in particular. Also serious alcoholism can be a manifestation. At first it seems to calm the mind, opening up ways of escape into a dream world, it soon gets out of hand, resulting in acts of violence.

Indications for Treatment

Physical therapies are particularly effective for the Scapegoat. The physical treatment of the pectoral girdle, spinal column and teeth helps him to upright his inner self. It helps him learn how to snap back when threatened, keeping his eyes straight on his opponent instead of sheepishly averting his gaze. The more his back straightens up and the shoulders return to an anatomically correct position, the more visibly grows his self-esteem. He is no longer ready to burden himself with whatever is thrown his way. In parallel, specific abuse situations should be addressed. Present-day events are best suited to cause a change of his inner attitude and subsequent behavior modification. Sometimes however, negative or traumatic experiences from childhood, early adulthood or a first marriage must be dealt with. However, it is crucial that this should lead neither to an interminable lament, nor a resigned assessment of the self as being basically defenseless and helpless.

A firm, almost severe therapy concept is the right approach for Scapegoat type Martyrs, provided they aren't enmeshed either in self-injury or violence, and who don't drink too much alcohol. It consists in curbing – after only a few sessions – the flow of lament over the evil of the world, the terrible childhood, the bad parents or the uncomprehending partner. Because if given free rein, the endless litany about his helplessness in the face of wickedness, followed by excuses, justifications and accusations will be unhealthy for a salutary turning point. That is why a classical psychoanalysis is less suitable than a conversational therapy. The therapist may often be called to verbally intervene and try to give the conversation a positive turn, to forestall sinking into a quagmire of guilt feelings and helplessness along with his patient. Otherwise it may happen that the therapist feels first a vague, later a more pronounced climate of accusations spreading, aimed also at him, and gradually turning him into the substitute Scapegoat should the therapeutic efforts appear not to work out.

The deeper, and, to all involved inexplicably free floating guilt feelings, do not in general originate from childhood and cannot be causally derived from it either, although often manifest already at an early age. They should rather be attributed to the soul's prenatal willingness to experience the fear characteristic Martyrdom as part of its plan for this existence. Nevertheless, it relieves and comforts the Scapegoat when childhood and adolescence memories get uncovered and assimilated. These were frequently so hurtful and damaging that he had no choice but to duck and let himself be kicked around; resistance wasn't an option. One sure measure of support is to little by little teach such a discouraged patient how he can defend himself. This can also be accomplished by behavioral therapy. A priority goal should be to practice adequate resistance and response that doesn't degenerate into fights or bodily injuries up to killing in self-defense. Other efforts should focus on converting the tormenting feelings of having failed in the face of humiliations into some degree of self-esteem and inner dignity. Also necessary is teaching him to bravely face his torturers, at least in his imagination.

A special regime also applies for women who let themselves be abused, ready to forgive their brutal partner and staying with him over and again. In fact, these women often only feel their love and emotions when they are physically or verbally assaulted. In such cases, a relationship restriction period must – as a rule – be observed. Because as long as the relational structure remains outwardly stable, they are seldom able to disentangle themselves or change the situation, despite all the help available. The partner will continue to imbue them anew with feelings of guilt at the least occasion which they – willingly and grudgingly at the same time – feel justified. For example, it suffices that the soup is lacking salt and made an issue of reproach. The expression this produces on her face is justification enough for the partner to smack her.

Martyrdom being a primeval fear of the »martial« energy 3, it may be a useful means of relief to allow Scapegoat patients to formulate their feelings of revenge or fantasies of violence and defense. They can be occasionally encouraged to bitterly punish – in their imagination – those who did them wrong, and returning to them all the blame they have so willingly taken on. Particularly counterproductive in a therapy of the Scapegoat syndrome are, however, any well-meant attempts to invite the patient to forgive the culprits, or at least show some loving understanding. The only way to healing for the Scapegoat is to understand and forgive himself, and to grant himself permission to defend himself.

Type 2: The Little Sunshine

The Little Sunshine endeavors to justify its existence by making other people and especially its parents and other siblings happy, trying to give them the feeling: Although circumstances were difficult, the effort to have given birth to and raised this child was worthwhile after all.

The Little Sunshine is always happy and always ready to lend a hand. It is on the spot to take care of mother who has fallen ill, to manage the household for her orphaned brothers and sisters or look after the old father, even when there are many others who could take on those chores. It never allows itself to be morose, ill-humored or feel weak. It always makes an effort to appear upbeat and positive. This attitude serves to hide its sorrow and feeling of unworthiness under a kind of shiny golden dish cover. The Little Sunshine's fearful idea is that when – figuratively speaking

– this dish cover is lifted at a festive dinner, it should suddenly be revealed that there's actually nothing on the plate, which would infinitely disappoint everyone at the table. So this must be avoided at all cost.

The Little Sunshine is convinced that if it doesn't make the utmost effort to show itself lovable and always happy, mankind will fall into a state of deepest disappointment and bitterness. Such efforts to always appear cheerful, comforting, helpful, generous and self-sacrificing, and of coping with the most difficult tasks with a smiling face, are quite welcome and respected socially. So the Little Sunshine doesn't even feel how infinitely exhausting it is to uphold such a compulsive attitude of happy selflessness.

But the Little Sunshine will hardly ever permit itself to be ill or tired. It gets by on a minimum of sleep and time for recovery, and never even considers taking a longer holiday. Indispensability is its most favorite illusion. Someone indispensable must be worthy – that is self-evident. A proper holiday can only be justified if it offers the chance to feed hungry children, tend to an elderly aunt or house-sit for someone. Something good and selfless must come out of it. The Little Sunshine must under all circumstances continue cultivating its noble and infinitely lovable and caring image.

The Little Sunshine doesn't ask for gratitude, it doesn't even realize that its incessant efforts to earn the appreciation of its fellow men aren't properly noticed or valued. The Little Sunshine's contributions to the fabric of society in terms of activities and generally supportive attitude are usually taken for granted; its unsolicited little favors are sometimes even considered a bit of a nuisance. Yet everyone likes to fall back on the services of the Little Sunshine, thereby seemingly confirming the right to exist and intrinsic value of this martyr-like person.

The Little Sunshine doesn't make any demands. It hates to ask for something, especially for any service in return. All it ever wants is to serve and be there for others. Should a crumb of praise drop at its feet from time to time, it will gratefully pick it up, thinking: »One gram of praise is already a lot. Although, I really could do completely without, after all, I don't give love to be praised, but to go to heaven.« The Little Sunshine is convinced that the greater an effort it makes and the less it asks for, the more valuable and greater is the love it gives.

The Little Sunshine, be it girl or boy, man or woman, likes to please. It reads any wish from the others' lips before it has been voiced, yes, before the wish has even been conscious in their mind at all. A Little Sunshine will frequently think up activities, kind gestures or deeds that are totally redundant, just to be active and busy, giving it the feeling of selflessly supporting the wellbeing of the family or its fellow men. Its ability to anticipate other people's needs is so pronounced, there is no room anymore to feel its own needs. Little Sunshine works itself to the bone, even when no one asked or circumstances called for it. It bends over backwards to show itself as a lovable, sensitive, self-sacrificing and valuable member of society.

It's just odd that this selfless, kind-hearted and caring individual must ultimately realize with bitterness that hardly anyone appreciates its efforts; or worse, people don't even notice what he or she has been doing for them. The reason is simple: because the Little Sunshine itself considers its cheerful industriousness a given, it is taken for granted also by others. Even worse, when the Little Sunshine cuts back its efforts just a little bit – all the while racked by guilt feelings – it will earn reproaches rather than recognition. And, as we already know, the Little Sunshine is susceptible to guilt feelings. Someone so overly zealous will rarely reap gratitude – on the contrary, he or she will be thoroughly exploited.

The non-fulfillment of unvoiced desires for emotional closeness and attention, added by the Little Sunshine's unsatisfied personal interests, will lead to a misguided fulfillment of wishes »in proxy«, that is, in declaring the interests of others one's own. This usually ends up in more work, squeezed into the few leisure hours of the Martyr. For example, a woman accompanies her husband to a motor race because it really means a lot to him, even though she thinks it terribly boring. Or a man gets into debt up to his ears to offer his wife a home she didn't ask for. Charity appointments or onerous jobs such as preserving unreasonably large quantities of fruit harvest from the garden are popular evasive maneuvers of the Little Sunshine to avoid having spare time.

This type of Martyr is usually prepared to forgive humiliations and insults unblinkingly. He also magnanimously ignores when there is no Christmas present for him under the tree or his birthday has been forgotten. He pardons and justifies other people's mistakes and blames himself that in some mysterious way, things have gotten this far, thinking that he probably wasn't selfless or caring enough.

Yet there are limits even to the resilience of a Little Sunshine, because its psyche is highly susceptible and sensitive to accusations and criticism: »Haven't I done just everything humanly possible? This is how I'm rewarded for it!« When the ingratitude and lack of appreciation by the partner, parent, supervisor, child, or colleague are getting too much, it will one day turn away, outraged and embittered. It doesn't realize that others are unconsciously reacting to the fact that it doesn't defend itself against disrespectful treatment but, on the contrary, tries even harder. But the Little Sunshine's system only functions as long as it can make itself believe that the relationship – be it love, work or parent – is based on loyalty and common bonds. Martyrdom as the expression of the »Warrior« energy 3 doesn't bear disloyalty or too much ingratitude well. When this happens, the emotional state of the Little Sunshine can switch to hardening, desire for vengeance and an inner retreat. For any uninvolved onlookers, such »unusual« emotions still remain within the bounds of decency and kind-heartedness. The Little Sunshine will justify and excuse its so-called »negative« feelings on the grounds that the ultimate goal is to advance the emotional development and inner growth of the person to be punished. It is very important to the Little Sunshine that its image as the forgiving, noble, understanding and, despite it all, untiring soul shall not be tarnished. It serves to stabilize its self-esteem, which had been temporarily challenged by the openly humiliating and debasing treatment by its partner, family, friends or colleagues.

The Little Sunshine likes to gather people around itself who need help and, without being aware of it, makes sure that by and by, they become even more helpless. Or it seeks out sick, disadvantaged, handicapped or persecuted individuals as its friends from the start. The Little Sunshine tends to exhaust all possibilities of relieving these people – for whom it's obviously hard to provide for themselves – of the last remains of autonomy and self-responsibility. So over time, they will become totally dependent on him or her. This indispensability serves the Little Sunshine as confirmation of its boundless strength and unconditional love. It has filled all positions and all space for compassion and care, and therefore gets hardly anything back.

The vague feeling that a coffee-break, window-shopping or a therapy session – in short: anything offering some rest – somehow represents an outrageous, unjustifiable, actually almost blame- and sinful luxury serves to confirm the Little Sunshine's problem of self-worth. What's really hard to take for the Little Sunshine is when someone refuses to be supported or comforted, seeming evidence that its every effort has been in vain. So it turns away disheartened: »It's of no use, my love is unwelcome. This person doesn't want any help; I'm not needed here. Nobody appreciates me.«

Features

Men and women alike, but also teens of this type, tend to neglect – if not the personal hygiene – albeit their outer appearance. It's not about looks but the inner worth that counts, right? This often makes Little Sunshines look a bit unattractive. Elegant clothes, a nice haircut or expensive jewelry will be avoided or at most endured. The Little Sunshine wants to be appreciated for its undemanding, selfless character, not for its attractiveness. It likes to wear clothes in bright, gentle and happy colors. It tends to put on weight – satisfaction must, after all, be derived from some source – but also because it serves up too much food out of over-protectiveness and someone has to eat up the remains.

A Little Sunshine tries to be always cheerful. Even when it narrates some sad or unpleasant event, it has a shining, almost transfigured, but in any case down-playing facial expression and a cheerful voice. Any difficult situations it has encountered are made light of; the willingness to suffer is considered natural.

The fact that the Martyr provides an immensely impressive moral and factual support to his fellow men will usually be played down – or else greatly exaggerated. Little Sunshines do like to talk about how much energy and selfless support they have bestowed on their fellow men at numerous occasions, and that this is where they find the greatest happiness and satisfaction. Yet gratitude or compensation are unwanted really.

The Little Sunshine might also offer its therapist to help out at home if need be; it would even love to clean the consultation rooms or provide some other selfless support. It is happiest when someone is ill and actually needs help. Then its whole system thrives. The beatifying thought »I am needed« gives the Little Sunshine a sense of worthiness that comes next to none.

A Little Sunshine often looks back on a more than unhappy family background, for example having to cope with a stepparent, always ingratiating itself. Or it married an alcoholic it tries to convert and reform by its excessive readiness to love and forgive. It also suffers any infirmities with stoic cheerfulness, hardly ever complaining or talking about its misery. It preferably compares with people who are even worse off. Whatever the situation, the Little Sunshine makes itself believe that there are no grounds for complaint. In fact, one of its common sayings is: »I really can't complain.«

The Little Sunshine speaks with a with a high, childlike, happy, although somewhat pressed voice or rushed, because, while it is sitting there telling stories, it incessantly thinks about what it could be doing in terms of meaningful, selfless and helpful activities instead.

Typical complaints

The Little Sunshine tends to suffer from chronic diseases such as neurodermatitis or bad eyesight which, exactly because they are a permanent infliction, it considers not noteworthy. It is often of delicate physical constitution, ultimately leading to a chronic state of exhaustion as the consequence of its self-sacrificing and selfless activities. Feeling drained is also considered normal, despite the obviously overtaxing demands. This state of exhaustion too is ignored and only taken seriously in the event of a nervous breakdown or a major traumatization due to an alarming diagnosis – incidents which overtax even the stoically merry mind of a Little Sunshine. Also heart conditions, i.e. cardiac insufficiency, are frequent, brought on by the Little Sunshine's refusal to admit sadness, tiredness and disappointment for the longest time. Normal compensatory functions of the body can't take effect due to its constant effort to force itself to be cheerful.

The characteristic feature of psychosomatic strain with this type of Martyr is usually physical exhaustion up to chronic fatigue syndrome. Because at the point where other people feel and say: »I'm exhausted«, the Little Sunshine will only just start to step up its efforts. Its emergency energy tank seems to be inexhaustible, until it is, quite suddenly, empty.

Backaches and general pain syndromes are also frequent, as are severe headaches, used by the body as a last emergency brake so that the Little Sunshine may from time to time retire from its busy schedule. In case of a breakdown, the ulterior motive is the hope that, just for once, it might receive some support and commitment from others in return – though this rarely happens.

This type of Martyr will see the doctor only in an emergency. »It's alright, I'll manage, don't bother« is the usual line. The Little Sunshine tends to postpone any indicated medical treatment. It really needs a good friend or family member to call up the doctor and make sure it gets thoroughly examined. The excuse is that it doesn't have time for it – while in truth it fears that the medical diagnosis will force them to rest or slow down. These people are seldom off sick. Even with a temperature, they'll still go to the office or manage the household instead of having somebody take care of them. To lie down in bed is an admission of failure and worthlessness. Should this ever happen though, the Little Sunshine is likely to lie in bed embittered and lonely. Its monopolizing caretaker position has almost smothered any empathy and care efforts on the part of immediate family and friends. The disposition to chronic pains – be it back pains from spinal column problems or arthrosis and arthritis – is an indication that the Little Sunshine doesn't properly look after itself, not respecting its own limits. Totally immersed in work, it also forgets to drink enough fluids. It firmly believes that two aspirins will suffice to make it go to work again, or that pains should simply be ignored because it's not good to take oneself too seriously. This in turn will often lead to a high consumption of pain killers or abuse of tranquilizers and sleeping pills, because the psyche constantly needs to repress, forgive or ignore insults and debasing situations. Together with the physical pain, it has an adverse impact on the ability to relax and go to sleep.

The Little Sunshine is seldom found in psychiatric institutions, unless there is a hereditary disposition to the disease. Should psychiatric treatment be required, this type of Martyr will be exceptionally popular at the ward, pityingly taking care of others in need and always ready to help. Even then, it always keeps a happy face and struggles to handle its depression, making it an effort of diligence. Since the Little Sunshine feels better when it can do something, it will soon support the staff and relieve it of all kinds of jobs. Yet, larvate depression is the most commonly diagnosed disorder in a disappointed and embittered Little Sunshine. This is – as said before – reflected in sleeplessness, an unspecific feeling of being unwell or in overweight. Initially, this doesn't impact its work effort. As the depression deepens however, a profound feeling of hopelessness and meaninglessness will spread, turning any assignment for the Little Sunshine into a mechanical performance; it no longer expects any praise, recognition or gratitude.

Its worst fears relate to feeling totally useless and unworthy as a human being. At this stage, the accusations the Little Sunshine doesn't dare direct at others will turn against itself. Serious delusions of guilt up to self-incrimination or self-punishment for presumably unpardonable omissions or crime can be observed.

Indications for treatment

As said earlier, the Little Sunshine will not often see a doctor or psychotherapist. What for? Isn't it always doing just fine? When it happens, though, the following is sound advice: Already early on in the treatment, the therapist should give this patient specific permission to come to the session in a morose, gloomy or depressed state.

But it's not easy to convince a Little Sunshine that it doesn't lose in worthiness but rather gains when it allows its range of emotions and reactions to expand in a seemingly negative direction. It can be considered a success if the therapist manages to lure this person out of his cheerful reserve while simultaneously reducing the workload he has imposed on himself in conscious, targeted and small steps. Ultimately, it will be possible to provoke an »ignoble« rage, elicit an »egotistical« impulse or gradually dismantle the chronically loving attitude or excessive selflessness of the Little Sunshine. Also the eternally cheerful face might be commented on and uncovered for what it is – a protection mechanism.

It may temporarily happen though that the Little Sunshine meets the therapist in silent reproach, implying, out of the need to save its convictions, that the therapist simply doesn't know true selflessness and unconditional love, or what it means to sacrifice oneself for the family or dedication to work. It is therefore important to remain vigilant and firm on this issue and to uncover the huge effort this selfless, renouncing and always forgiving attitude requires.

At the outset of the treatment, the Little Sunshine will portray the matter-of-factness of physical or emotional strain beyond any beneficial limit as a high value and noble duty. The correlation of this selflessness and self-obliviousness with the idea of virtue should therefore be carefully but effectively ruptured. What must definitely be avoided is that this Martyr offers help or consolation to his helper, trying to cheer him or her up when feeling unwell. If ever it should happen that the Little Sunshine is ill or forgets the appointment, it can almost be rated as a positive performance, a softening of the unhealthy structure. Any criticism of this patient must be expressed extremely carefully, because even the least disapproval is taken as a serious slight and devaluation in general.

Since the Little Sunshine makes no great ado about its ailments, often consulting the doctor too late, diseases may be protracted, also as a disguised self-punishment by pain or incurable conditions. If the condition has evolved this far, the therapist should make sure to address the erroneous idea of being able to expiate or pay off some imagined karmic blame, or to obtain a reward in the hereafter by such suffering, and hopefully put it at the right inner perspective.

As the Little Sunshine feels guilty when it can no longer accomplish the usual scope of work, it is also important not to neglect the resulting self-incriminations and self-accusations. With adequate attentiveness, rather than simply relegating the issue to the realm of the absurd, these sentiments can be turned into helpful insights.

Type 3: The Valiant Little Tailor

The Valiant Little Tailor is a martyr-like individual with a weak self-esteem, given to compensate through self-exaltation and fantasies of grandeur. The sensation of his own paltriness is so overwhelming that it would create an unbearable self-image. In his efforts not to face it, he designs a construct of his personality, of his achievements and deeds that lies far beyond anything real or factual. A Valiant Little Tailor has, on the one hand, an unusual courage to selflessly face circumstances and situations that would have everyone else turn pale with fear. That's because he can neither feel his self properly, nor the danger he is exposing himself to. On the other hand, he develops a need to talk about it for the rest of his life, boasting of all the great challenges he has mastered, of how many people he has rescued from direst situations, how many children he was able to save from drowning or companies from bankruptcy. It's always about great, noble deeds, accomplished solely by his brave and unrelenting commitment. Without the Valiant Little Tailor, they would not have gotten anywhere.

At first, this attitude will deeply impress his listeners, soon to make them feel small and unimportant in the face of such magnificence. This extraordinary, incomparable bravery designed to upgrade the self has a devaluating impact on the audience, dwarfing them in comparison. The effect is that the listeners will temporarily adopt the Valiant Little Tailor's deep doubt of self-worth, and it will take them a while to recognize this strange humbug for what it is.

A Valiant Little Tailor has developed a strategy to increase and stabilize his sense of self-worth by reaping admiration. He will always be looking for a new audience ready to admire and fancy him, and before whom he can preen and prance about his superhuman deeds. So this type of Martyr will wander on as soon as he notices that his audience is getting a bit tired or starts to express any skepticism. That's why his personal relationships are often brief and fade out after a short time. Fellow men avoid his company in the long term since it makes them feel quite inferior. They are obviously not prepared to suffer this sensation, which is otherwise unknown to them, for any sustained period.

Features

A Valiant Little Tailor type Martyr looks rather puffed-up and peacockish. He carries his flashy self-esteem around as if on a hawker's tray. Everybody shall notice and admire him. He won't relent until he gets the feedback in some way: »You are the *king*!«

This oversized need for reflection of his self-worth in the listener, combined with a panic-stricken fear of being unmasked as the miserable worm he deep down feels to be, produce an immense inner tension. It is comparable to what someone might experience whose house is just getting searched by the police. That's exactly how a Valiant Little Tailor feels at the thought of being exposed, and that there isn't much more about his fantastic heroic deeds than on a herring bone gnawed off by a cat.

The flashiness of a Valiant Little Tailor also manifests in his clothing and behavior: golden chains, precious fabrics, expensive gifts and exaggerated offerings at every occasion. This guy or girl boasts loudly of daredevil adventures, always making them look good. They take up so much space, their interlocutor hardly has a chance to get a word in edge-wise.

The Valiant Little Tailor doesn't know pain. His medical conditions often go unnoticed until the bitter end, or at least he himself hasn't noticed anything. A case of cancer may be advanced to a stage where anyone else would have long consulted a doctor. But the Valiant Little Tailor saves others instead of himself. This individual will bear suffering silently and bravely, because in contrast to the Scapegoat, who will eventually offload blame on someone else, he hides it from his own feelings in »warrior fashion«.

Typical complaints

It's a striking phenomenon that such a seemingly assertive character often loses his teeth or has them extracted at a young age. The latter, so he willingly believes, is the best way to prevent pain syndromes, rheumatism or other autoimmune diseases. Behind the toothlessness, however, is a hidden desire for self-punishment or self-maiming, expressing his true helpless- and defenselessness.

Conversely, the Valiant Little Tailor type of Martyr tends to dramatize the least somatic disorder, whereas – as described before – he will hardly register any grave conditions. So if he's got a bit of a stomach pain for example, he suspects stomach cancer, expounding on it in detail before his friends and family. A slight headache is interpreted as a potential brain tumor. Simple diarrhea is likely to be dysentery. When he has overexerted himself, he might dramatically clutch at his heart, convinced he is suffering a coronary attack. Important is that there are always spectators to show sympathy. This type of Martyr consults one doctor after another, giving a theatrical account of his complaints. But as soon as there is any indication that it really might be a serious condition, he refrains from seeing one because he is afraid of the truth. For example, his blood pressure is frequently so high, he might have a stroke or a heart attack at any time without warning.

Usually, however, the Valiant Little Tailor is only a hypochondriac. The complaints serve to garner attention and to nurture his self-image as the hero bravely bearing pain and disease, no matter how severe or serious. At closer examination, a therapist will be able to assess that the suppressed feelings of inferiority and guilt, vented in exaggerated fantasies, lead to such an edgy, tense state, that they may well cause psychosomatic disorders. Typical is a high degree of »nervousness« which may suddenly turn into aggression. They are also given to such phenomena as frequent clearing of throat, involuntary eye twitching or unconscious movements like hand-rubbing, knee-slapping, running their fingers through their hair and occasionally also making somewhat obscene gestures.

In women, this tension between self-perception and the image projected to the outside is often expressed in provocative clothes, too heavy make-up, extremely high heels, a pronounced desire for jewelry and constantly twinkling her eyes or stroking back her hair. As they get older, these women seriously suffer under their dwindling attractiveness. They try to compensate for it by an almost manic search for sex partners to maintain their self-image as being erotically attractive. Typical syndromes in this context are frequently localized in the genital area. A recurrent fungal attack or itching of the vagina can often be attributed to a psychosomatic disorder. The nervousness may also reflect in hectic smoking, contributing to premature ageing. An added problem may be a slight chronic intoxication due to excessive coloring or bleaching of hair.

When the fear of a Valiant Little Tailor or Tailoress aggravates to a psychiatrically significant condition, a histrionic (theatrically narcissistic) personality disorder can be observed. It is often manifest already in youth, with bragging, bluffing and an irrefutable need to take center stage. It no longer suffices to blow ordinary events and experiences out of proportion and turn them into genuinely spectacular stories designed to boost his weak self-esteem; now the Valiant Little Tailor makes up almost unbelievable stories. These are narrated time and again with dramatic language and gestures, until the individual himself believes they really happened, and countering any corrections by »unbelievers« with iron resistance.

The serious cases found in psychiatric institutions are those individuals whose self-esteem has been trampled on so badly by neglect, early injuries and abuse, that they cannot survive any other way than by an amplification, embellishment and exaltation of the self.

A special variety of this disorder may be encountered when the person has suffered lasting injuries, such as a missing limb or clearly visible scars from an accident. Sometimes, this may even be the result of a self-instigated, highly dangerous, dramatic situation. This pathology will be thoroughly exploited now. Obviously, hardly anyone can resist asking the Valiant Little Tailor how this happened, thus triggering a dramatic account of the brave and selfless course of events. That the physical injuries are owing to an unconscious desire for self-punishment, the observer will rarely surmise. The Valiant Little Tailor – be it man or woman – is so very dependent on his compensation mechanisms, that the treatment of difficult cases of histrionic personality disorders will seldom lead to success.

Especially female Valiant Little Tailors often carp about their inadequate physical features, notwithstanding that their partner and others are perfectly happy with how they look. But it just doesn't sink in with the person affected. She develops the need to actively change something – not from a superficial discontent that could in fact be considered founded on something tangible (»my nose is definitely too big, my breasts too small, my belly too big, my eyelids droopy«). It's out of a much more deep-seated motivation, a desire to achieve something fundamental, that is, to be valued and noticed, admired and considered perfect at last. So this Martyr might develop a virtually compulsive preoccupation with insignificant physical irregularities, concentrating his feeling of unworthiness on one single physical feature, finding a valve in its rejection.

Such diversion of self-hate on a body-part based on feelings of worthlessness and an extreme longing for appreciation by his fellow men may result in not just one, but several plastic surgery interventions. These basically redundant, but supposedly aesthetically motivated interventions serve to satisfy a deep desire both for suffering and for love. The longing for perfection is an expression of the fear of worthlessness. It often incurs lasting physical damage, like tissue rejection reactions and irreversible disfiguration as the manifestation of an unconscious self-punishment. The need of a Martyr for quiet, secret pain is expressed in the proverb: »No pain, no gain.« The Valiant Little Tailor's own definition, however, makes it even more poignant: »No pain, no love.«

Indications for treatment

Such disorders of self-image and self-esteem can only be improved with great patience in a long-term, trusting conversational therapy. The Valiant Little Tailor's sense of worth is dependent on so many factors outside his range of influence, or so he believes and projects, that it requires some effort to redirect this sense of value back into and onto the self. Those two needs – to suffer quietly and in secrecy on the one hand, and to show off with all kinds of exploits on the other – appear to be totally unrelated at first. Access can only be found by dealing with the problem of self-worth buried under these behavior patterns.

Even more deeply hidden are the guilt feelings, covered up by a bold, irrefutably brave and noble demeanor – and this is where the root of the whole problem lies. This person will stubbornly refute and declare these guilt feelings as absurd. They aren't, of course, based on facts, but on the imaginary fear that his existence in itself is already culpable and tainted as by an indelible original stigma. If he faced these feelings instead of compensating for them, his system would collapse. So the therapist must work his way up from the depths and darkness of this buried sense of guilt, to the light of the basically superficial symptoms like the flashiness, the striving for ever more selfless acts and also the redundant surgery or cosmetic interventions. It will not suffice to make him understand intellectually that the existence of a human being as such cannot be worthless but simply is because it is. He also needs to catch up with the emotional insight into his own existential worth connected with this knowledge.

Early in the treatment, the therapist may feel called upon to tell the Valiant Little Tailor repeatedly how he treasures and admires him for his great deeds. Unfortunately, this will sustain the disastrous but well operating system of his client. Little by little, he must withdraw the admiration from him. But there isn't much ground gained as long as the client doesn't openly dare oppose the therapist with proper indignation, insisting that he is very worthy indeed, even if the therapist unfortunately hasn't recognized it. This is an exhausting and dangerous tightrope walk between a certain reluctant austerity and a refusal strategy, to not be pulled into the Valiant Little Tailor's system. Simultaneously, it takes an unspoken, deep emotional appreciation, an inner willingness to praise the client and the ability to express nonverbally all the things the patient believes he needs to hear for his survival.

There's no getting around though that initially, the therapist must subject himself to the Valiant Little Tailor's exhaustive self-display and account of his excellent deeds. These may in no way be taken at face value on the mere communication level. They must, however, be taken very seriously at the level of emotional helplessness and profound suffering from his sense of guilt and lack of self-esteem. It may be required at regular intervals to conclude a new pact with the client, such as, for example: »Promise that you will have no medical interventions done for the duration of our therapy, unless I have discussed it with your doctor.« Or: »Are you prepared to tell me about even the slightest guilt feelings you feel towards me?«

The treatment may be long-term and laborious. With the right approach, however, a self-contented person will emerge from it who accepts his existential self-worth. He has developed a new balance between the natural desire for praise and natural modesty. It is the patience the therapist musters that helps the Valiant Little Tailor learn to lead a positive life, contented with himself, without dramatic suffering or theatrical self-exaltation, and at peace with his fellow people.

Universal Energy 4

Stubbornness – Fear of Unpredictability

General

Souls opting for the specific experience of Stubbornness as their primal fear in this life intend to deal with the incarnated soul's need for safety. It is founded on the desire to tie a planned incarnation to a sort of guarantee that it won't be terminated by premature death, e.g. some fatal threat or circumstances occurring so violently and unexpectedly, that the incarnated human being has neither time to prepare for it nor to fend it off. All measures a stubborn individual develops to deal with or check his fear of the unpredictability of life serve only one need: to not have to accept any unforeseen event as an irrevocable change or even the termination of his incarnated condition.

When a soul has embodied to remain on earth for a while in this physical state, it must submit to various conditions and physical laws. We will only mention three of these here, which are, however, of particular significance for a stubborn person. The first is that anything which exists and takes a material form, including human beings, is subject to continual change – if not always obvious or visible to the naked eye. Secondly, it is a fact that time and space play an irrefutable and extremely important, all permeating role in any incarnation event, causing a continuous interaction with any changes happening within time and space. While this is something that affects all human beings, a stubborn person feels particularly painfully exposed to it. If only he could, he would love to suspend this law. The third law concerns the conjunction of cause and effect. The principle of causality related directly to the physical conditions on earth provides that any individual – stubborn or not – is always in danger of something unexpected happening that could take his life. Now how does a stubborn person, in contrast to people with other forms of fear, deal with these facts applicable to all living creatures? He develops a survival strategy based on – symbolically speaking – clenching his teeth, pulling himself together, tightening up his energy into a solid block and bundling all his strength, as a way to brace himself and survive any unpleasant and unpredictable life situations as best and unharmed as possible. Stubborn people usually develop this behavior very early in life; the reaction pattern sets in as soon as any kind of unexpected, sudden threat is looming. Even an infant will become quite rigid or is given to cramps, trying to somehow survive the experience that something unforeseen has happened which is not in line with its ideas, its fixed notions of how life is supposed to be. All his life, a stubborn person would like to enforce that people around him behave predictably, to ensure that his incarnation shall be successful.

The parents of a recently incarnated stubborn child cannot – given all the love they have – save it from the necessity of experiencing this specific fear; they cannot do or desist doing anything to avoid what its soul has chosen as a program for mastering fear in this life. Whichever way they act or behave, there will always be, and usually early on, a moment when the primal fear of loss of safety, of change and unpredictability manifests itself, leading to the tenseness, obstinacy and hardening which are so typical of stubborn people for the rest of their lives.

Stubbornness is a feature of the Universal Energy 4, that is, of »neutral« effect, which means that it cannot really be felt as a fear emotion. Stubborn people often believe they have no fear and defiantly reject any insinuation that they must obviously be afraid of something.

But they have, of course, developed different approaches to cope with their primal fear. Usually, stubborns become incredibly practical-oriented, savvy and skilful people, seemingly always finding a solution for any difficulty, in the firm belief that they are able to deal constructively with the imponderability of existence at all times. A stubborn person adapts, after a short phase of bitter resistance, to anything new, making his feelings of solitude equate to a kind of freedom, standing unwaveringly and solid as a rock amongst the general unreliability. The world may perish before him; he won't perish before the world!

A stubborn person experiences the highest degree of threat when he believes himself deserted. This fear of abandonment, a sudden falling out of emotional safety, triggers the greatest insecurity in him. This, in turn, prompts a number of coping mechanisms, which ultimately have a more or less obstructive or harmful effect on his ability to master his life and relations with his fellow men.

The Poles of Fear of Unpredictability

| – Obstinate | ←→ | Resolute + |

Most people find it easy to make decisions and invite new situations without much hesitation. But a stubborn individual possesses a special ability – one he generally doesn't recognize as part of his fear – and that is a remarkable, sometimes almost hell-bent determination. It gives him an instrument to quickly get a handle again on anything unexpected happening or sudden changes doled out by life for which he has not provided. The stubborn person considers this determination a high virtue and hence is impatient, even condescending of people who can't make up their mind, not knowing what they really want. It's just such feelings of uncertainty that the determination of stubborn people is trying to avoid. Their fear knows only one single goal: provide or maintain safety at all cost. Determination helps them to have every new situation under control again as quickly as possible.

It won't be easy to protect a stubborn person from his false virtue, the wild determination, because to him it's not obvious that this should be a fear phenomenon. In his perception, his resolution and decisiveness is something very positive. It will require some logical persuasiveness to point out to him, at least theoretically, that decisiveness isn't a goal in itself and that determination can also pursue the wrong aims.

When a situation arises which confronts a stubborn person with uncertainty, illustrating numerous factors which might impair his life and on which he has no influence, he'll become very insecure and nervous. Ambiguity is a sensation he can hardly bear. If he can't rely on the world around him to be predictable and safe, he must find a solid anchor at least in himself. His propensity towards fast, but mostly too rash decisions, leads him to believe that he merely needs to get either the old or the new situation under control again. And no sooner has he decided in favor of one or the other direction than he relaxes, because he temporarily feels less fear and unsafe. We would like to recall that Stubbornness is a fear form which aims to forestall any alarming emotions. Every effort of the psyche, mind and body of a stubborn individual is targeted at averting any feeling of insecurity or fear of the unpredictable. The contraction of energy, the hardening and stiffening, the defiant insistence on a decision once taken, all serve to relieve him of having to endure the seemingly fatal threat of uncertainty any longer.

When a stubborn person becomes afraid of a new situation and hasn't decided on a solution yet, that is, when he hasn't yet been able to apply the false virtue of his single-minded determination, he gets plunged into a very unpleasant interim phase in which he is forced to actually live through the sensation of not knowing what life has in store for him. Issues that don't particularly bother people with other types of fear, thrust a stubborn person into strangling emotions, making the floor sway under his feet, confusion clouding his mind; his body reacts with tension, stiffness and muscle hardening, which sometimes become extremely painful. Such phenomena fall away once a decision has been taken, i.e. when he applies resolve as the positive pole of this fear and pseudo-contribution to the solution of conflict. Then relief sets in; the neck pain, the back tensions ease up, the fog in his head clears. He no longer feels like a whimpering infant let down by God and the world, but can get his life, his goals and his behavior under tight control again. His jaw muscles loosen up; his furrowed brow relaxes and he can start thinking about new prospects again. Because they can make up their minds so quickly, stubborn people often believe they are particularly flexible, oblivious to the fact that this is out of fear of the new and unknown.

Since resolve represents only an emergency measure in the psyche of a stubborn person, such decisions taken out of fear of the fear are, for the most part, of rather adverse or obstructive impact on his future. After the short-term relief, an often lasting, perennial insecurity lurking deep in the unconscious sets in, namely the negative pole of obstinacy. Having felt so much relief resulting from his decisiveness and fearful determination, however, the stubborn is grimly intent now on adhering to the course adopted, and no one can get him to stir from his resolve, unless life forces him to. Such a dogged person can often be recognized by his particularly pronounced jaw muscles.

As mentioned earlier, this obstinacy manifests on an unconscious level. The stubborn individual doesn't feel it emotionally, nor is he mentally aware of it. It rather expresses in somatoform disturbances: chronic muscle tenseness, uptight stomach and general abdominal discomfort, gradual decline of visual and hearing faculties, tense forehead and much more. Most typical though, stubborn people who, during the day can hold their fear at bay, will start to grit and grind their teeth at night as a way to grimly express their defiance of life.

These phenomena will become particularly severe when a stubborn person feels insecure and threatened not only by the vicissitudes of life, but fears being let down or deserted by someone – be it partner, friends, siblings, parent or colleague – or even by a body part! This represents the ultimate threat to him or her. To pre-empt any such thing happening, he tends to apply his hell-bent determination to initiate himself the process of being abandoned, even before the other person has made a decision. He hands in his notice, files for divorce or submits to surgery. However, until such an often arbitrary and redundant separation actually occurs, the frightened stubborn person gets locked in a hold-on position. This clinging and controlling has such a wretched, needy notion, it expresses just the opposite of what the stubborn supposedly wants – notably his independence – but rather his total dependence on the lasting, loving affection of his spouse or those around him.

Illustrating the suffering, the doggedness in the negative pole to a stubborn individual is easier. He is usually aware of his obstinacy, the petulant striving for stability, steadfastness and safety, both on a material plane and within relationships, his defiant adherence to the old so there's no need for change. He sticks to the new, in which he has just arranged himself, or the plans for the future, which he'd love to write in concrete every step of the way if he could. He is familiar with it as part of his character and often quite proud of it. But his pain, his physical condition and the rigidity of his muscle armor are giving out clear signals, no matter that he claims not to feel any fear, and that the pain wasn't really as bad that he'd need professional help. Over the years, however, the stiffness as an expression of his obstinacy worsens, leading to severe afflictions. It's from this level of suffering that the chance for alleviation arises.

The unfortunate stubborn individual now finds himself in a predicament. If, from insight or better even from physical closeness, warmth and muscle relaxing treatment, he loosens his rigid armor of fear, he'll get overwhelmed by a whimpering insecurity. Understandably, he'll wonder whether it wasn't ultimately better to remain rigid and numb instead of being subjected to this earthquake of emotions. But the softening of these stubborn manifestations is the ideal way to inner growth. The more a stubborn person keeps away from the trap of his determination and obstinacy, reducing the defiant reactions of his body, all the more free, truly independent and loving he will feel and also come across to others.

But if he gets locked in his grim attitude towards people and life, he'll grow increasingly lonely. Life is simply unpredictable, and so are people. He can't abstain from life, and even while he's trying, he also knows at heart that it's illusory. But he can, to a large extent, protect himself from the unreliability of people, leading inevitably to loneliness: »If I don't let anyone get close to me, then no one can desert me. If I don't rely on anyone, I won't be disappointed.« The obstinacy with which stubborns in the negative pole of their fear cling to lifestyles and habits once adopted, seemingly also keeps them from unpleasant changes. But in truth, as they grow older, it will make them lose touch with the times. In the end, they appear old-fashioned, their ideas obsolete. Not keeping up with the times, they shut themselves off from the dynamics of natural change.

An interesting variant of obstinacy is the willful and determined search for high risk and permanent threat of life, e.g. as a parachutist, career soldier or extreme climber. This reversal of the basic fear into its seeming conquest is experienced like a great challenge, designed to produce an apparent relief from the unpredictability of existence. So the more impressively the permanent physical threat is staged on an outer level, the more clearly visible becomes the doggedness and hell-bent determination of a person wanting to prove to life itself that it is indeed calculable and can't harm him.

The Released Potential

An individual with the primal fear of Stubbornness needs much safety, but he also provides it for others. As his fear of uncertainty and being abandoned subsides, he takes confidence in life and his fellow men, gradually evolving into a personality notable for its faithfulness, persistence and reliability in emotional relations. If his fear of unpredictability is mitigated, the stubborn person will become a loyal friend, a reliable business partner and dependable companion in all situations of life. With the lessening of his inner tension, his fearfully overreacting resolve turns into decisiveness based on a just consideration of all relevant facts which respects the feelings of all involved.

His fear decreases by the degree that he finds sufficient physical exercise, relaxation and diversion, which in turn has a positive impact on his obstinacy: the more loose and relaxed his body feels, the less fear he has. The potential bound and caught up in the hardening of his whole system – stiffened muscles and joints, ossification of intentions, contents and attitudes, the clutching to old situations and relations, the propensity to take rash decisions and the obstinacy with regard to preserving his safety – becomes pleasantly undone. By unfettering from the necessity to become distraught and tense at each and any threat of the unpredictable, sovereignty prevails in dealing with the vicissitudes of physical existence. It is interesting to also discover an astounding share of flexibility and adaptability in the freed potential. Astounding because the stubborn person himself usually doesn't think he's got it in him, and the people around him react perplexed too when they see this habitually rigid individual moving through life with more ease, willing to go with the flow instead of swimming against the current.

Three Types of Fear of Unpredictability

1. The **Autonomist** banks on his principal life strategy as the reassuring solution to all conflicts related with safety and unpredictability, namely his belief: »I manage perfectly well on my own. I don't need anything or anybody. If I only rely on myself, there won't be any problems.« The Autonomist solves his troubles by retiring to an island of pseudo-liberty.
2. The **Hardhead** drafts a concept of life for himself and the people around him which mustn't be changed. It's as incontrovertible as a law of nature. In the face of change he is apt to lose his footing. However, he will immediately draw up a new constitution to which he will commit again. He also places everyone else under this law and woe if they infringe on it!
3. The **Survival Whiz** applies all of his energy to simply circumvent any vagaries or incertitude. He just bobs and weaves over the everyday changes of his situation, his relationships, his feelings. He's got a strategy of numbing himself as best he can and, due to the ease in which he takes everything in stride, believes himself invulnerable. He can cope with everything and everyone. He takes his decisions within seconds. He finds his security in the belief that nothing could happen to him that he hasn't wanted himself.

Type 1: The Autonomist

There's one thing the Autonomist wants above anything else: maintaining control over the extent of closeness to his fellow men. This regulatory process takes up a lot of his energy. He needs to keep other people – as close as they may be to him – at bay and not let them get any nearer than is absolutely necessary. For lovers and family this is often incomprehensible, as it can change from one day to the next, now a little closer, then suddenly far away. They don't understand at first that it's not their fault when he distances himself, that they didn't do anything wrong, but that this type of stubborn person has to keep this back door to independence open to remain emotionally stable. He is the type who wholeheartedly subscribes to the saying »distance makes the heart grow fonder.«

The Autonomist always needs the certainty that he can pull out of a relationship unscathed at any time. This also applies to a job or his residence, his native country or his family of origin. The Autonomist believes that he is best off without any ties, not bound by any obligations, so he can indulge at least in the illusion that he lives best alone and without any interferences by demands from his fellow men. Concealed behind this need is an extremely painful feeling of a permanent, latent threat to be suddenly abandoned. No matter how intimately the Autonomist may be associated with others – he will nevertheless always feel alone and moreover believing that it's better that way. But he isn't alone of his own free will; it's rather under the sword of Damocles of being deserted. When in doubt, this fear of an unpredictable future induces him to leave rather than be left. Before anyone can threaten to break off a relationship of whichever nature, he will end it himself, usually far in advance of any real danger.

It will take many years, if not a whole lifetime, before the Autonomist can see the absurdity of his behavior. Only when he begins to recognize the fear of being deserted hidden behind his strong independence effort, can he allow himself to really feel his desire for fearful autonomy without turning this urge immediately into reality and sever relations. But there will always be a number of areas where the Autonomist cannot bear to be dependent on anyone, to submit to regulations or yield to someone else's needs. He or she vehemently fights any »shalls« and »musts.« Only in a relationship with someone dear can he temporarily suspend this defense because as the years go by, two options become quite obvious: He either spends the rest of his life as a kind of hermit, or, despite all fears, he lets others get closer, accepting their warmth, affection and care.

This acceptance will initially make the Autonomist feel helpless and weak. The sensation of being loved makes him contract and stiffen, because it upsets his conception of the world. It invalidates once more everything he had previously established and relied upon – namely that there is basically no one except himself to take care of him, to be around when in need. This softening, the warmth, coupled with the sensation of somehow disintegrating in the other person, of being usurped, feels very menacing to the Autonomist. He must approach this test of courage warily, no matter that this is actually what he had so ardently hoped for and desired as a child, before his initial hardening.

Closeness and disintegration in the love of a companion takes him back to the time before his original affright, which may have occurred during the first weeks of his life or even earlier in the womb. Hence, when he lets himself in for intimacy, he justly fears a massive regression at first. And if he doesn't get bolstered in this process, the old trauma will repeat itself, creating another layer of rigidity, a new armor of pseudo-liberty and pseudo-autonomy. So the Autonomist must feel very safe emotionally and situational – with the assurance that this safety isn't going to be withdrawn from him again at any moment – to be able to really let his hair down and trust in someone. Though one mustn't expect this to happen often or even become a permanent condition; this is something the Autonomist just can't manage. Given his nature, it would make him a miserable, timorous creature.

At this point we would like to speak about another characteristic of the Autonomist: jealousy. The Autonomist doesn't want to get too involved with others emotionally, yet demands of every partner and those close to him that they should be totally, one hundred percent and absolutely at his disposal. They cannot turn to anyone else with friendly interest, be it a sibling or the other parent, another friend and least of all another potential partner, without the stubborn Autonomist feeling threatened. This absoluteness in his claim for emotional safety is hard for others to tolerate. But unless they yield unconditionally to this demand, they'll be punished by his flight into cool autonomy. Loneliness is easier to bear for him than agonizing dependency.

Yet, even when he is honestly assured every day and every hour »I won't leave you!«, the Autonomist will still expect it to happen at any time, because he can't believe that he could *not* be deserted. Now this is exactly the Stubbornness of this vision of fear: that it is unshakeable. But only the Autonomist himself can struggle free from the prison of his view of the world; anyone else would have the hardest time of it. Their line of justification would always be jeopardized by the Autonomist's conviction that being abandoned bitterly confirms his basic attitude of life.

Features

The Autonomist shows himself upright, independent and confident. He truly believes that, if necessary, he can do without help and support, without anyone to talk to, without comfort and warmth. He is completely self-sufficient. In conversations, he signals that it's actually unnecessary to discuss his problems because they really weren't of substance. He also couldn't see that they were creating any problems. He'll concede that, of course, it might not hurt to hear someone else's opinion now, though in the end he would do or not do what he felt right.

All circumstances of his life are organized and neatly arranged. Nothing can get out of hand or run riot. The Autonomist will neither drink too much alcohol nor eat too much. He doesn't live above his means. He plans everything in detail. He is well aware of his needs – with the exception of his need for intimacy of course – and he can provide for himself. He is able to manage his household on his own or go on vacation on his own without feeling lost. He seems extraordinarily solid and brave. When someone tells him that it looks like he has got everything under control, a smug little smile will dart across his face.

The facial expression of the Autonomist too is »controlled«. His face shows remarkably few lines also at an advanced age. His outer appearance is typically very correct.

The Autonomist is usually successful professionally. When his company plans to lay off people, he has long taken precautions with another job at hand; it will certainly not happen to him to be left standing in the rain without a job unexpectedly.

On the contrary, he is the type to save up for a rainy day. He always expects the worst – even with a seeming degree of self-mocking. In case there is a power outage, he's got a camping stove in the basement. A good stock of canned foods and various other precautionary measures in place for any emergency situations serve to calm his mind, before the mere thought that anything might happen can upset his usual pace of life or plans. If ever any truly unforeseen or unpredictable event should occur though, he's already got a plan worked out, including plan B of course, which he can resort to in an emergency. This is where he resembles the Survival Whiz. The difference is that he doesn't take things easy, but rather takes everything too hard. Autonomists actually like to make things hard for themselves, because that's how they can best demonstrate their ability to survive on their own without help or support.

When life is easy, everything going hunky-dory, the Autonomist fears triviality setting in and quickly loses interest in the situation, even in his partner. It is not unusual that he starts to get bored when the relationship is without conflict or problems, devoid of any grounds for the impulse to save himself into his autonomy fantasies. What's more, he can no longer feel the »voluntariness« of staying in this relationship, which allows him to keep up his illusion of: »I'd rather be on my own, but then again it isn't so bad either. Sometimes it's actually quite nice to have someone at your side.« That is also the tenor in which he talks about his relationships: that it didn't actually do him any harm to be in one, but that it wasn't anything he really needed either.

The Autonomist is not inclined to crack his teeth on life's adversities. If something doesn't work out, he will shrug it off and change his strategy. His false virtue of determination helps him find another solution that will deliver him from the dependency of circumstances in no time. Dependency is a key word, and he often talks about how he hates being dependent on anything or anybody, and how he devises ways to resolve this condition or avoid it altogether. To him, dependency is synonymous to entrapment and helplessness, which he shuns like the devil shuns incense.

Autonomists often live on their own, usually having done so for an extended period and settling well into the situation. Unlike other people who find themselves alone, e.g. following a separation or the children moving out, the Autonomist will rarely get a pet, because that too means dependency and responsibility.

Everything in his life has its order. Sometimes, the apartment is fitted out like a hotel room, with few personal objects. He believes that it's better for him that way in case he feels like packing up his few belongings and moving out. Whereas other stubborn types try to find security by holding on to material things, the Autonomist would also be content to live out of two small suitcases if need be. When asked for his personal view of life, a typical answer might be: »We must all die alone, and besides, we are only guests on this earth.« His autonomy effort ultimately aims at being able to let go of his attachment to anything material and this world in general, should the threat of dependency or unpredictability get too crushing.

Typical complaints

The Autonomist always has his back covered. To be able to do this, he develops a dorsal armor like a turtle. His massive, but poorly circulated back musculature is designed to ward off his fear that someone might attack him from behind or take him by surprise in a kind of ambush, leaving him unprotected.

The Autonomist's endeavor to remain independent in all life situations results in a progressive induration of the complete musculature. He finds it hard to trust in someone or let himself go. Furthermore, he is prone to numerous complaints which ultimately limit and inhibit his mobility. A number of rheumatic diseases, e.g. arthrosis, arthritis or multiple sclerosis, as well as some rare sclerotic disorders leading to ossification can often be attributed to the stiffness and obstinacy that come with Stubbornness.

The greatest problem and challenge for an Autonomist is a condition that renders him helpless, be it due to old age or any medical condition forcing him or her to ask for help, support or care from others. Such situations will create a conflict between his often absurdly exaggerated and seemingly unreasonable need to remain as independent as possible, and the longing he secretly fosters beneath all this fearful rigidity, notably: to be able to let go, to trust in someone, to be pampered like a baby and no longer having to be strong or cope all alone.

Should the autonomy capsize into complete dependence, a psychiatric condition requiring treatment may be the result, because this formerly inordinately autonomous individual is suddenly reduced to a frail, whimpering bundle of fearful helplessness. In this regressive state, the previously over-independent person is totally devoid of the least bit of self-confidence. He even believes himself unable to hold his fork or spoon to eat alone, sleep alone or get dressed without help. At that stage, all he wants is to curl up under a blanket and just doze in some corner. It's important to understand this condition as the attempt to return into the protecting, all embracing and nourishing womb.

A different kind of psychiatric disorder will manifest when the need of the Autonomist for total control, letting no one and nothing interfere with him, turns into obsessive-compulsive disorders, reflecting for example in compulsive orderliness and isolation. This kind of isolation occurs from a situation where the patient feels relief when there is no one around to disrupt or even destroy his inner order. Such condition will occasionally show traits similar to some social phobias, though it's of different origin, notably Stubbornness. A deliberate, obstinate social isolation, that in later years can sometimes also manifest in self-neglect, is another expression of stubborn autonomy.

This neglect is due to the rejection of co-human contacts on the one hand, and a growing collecting mania on the other, which develops as the control mechanisms begin to slacken. The Autonomist wants to hold on to whatever promises to provide a feeling of security. When there is no one left to leave him, the fear of being abandoned funnels into an inability of parting with objects. So this formerly well organized and orderly Autonomist, always keeping everything under control, turns into a person whose habitat becomes cluttered up to the ceiling with neatly bundled magazines, superfluous objects and collections. He'll never become a »messy« though, as this would be counteracted by his need for clarity and control. But his fear of separation has shifted from people to material objects. The only way to check this fear is to hold on to hundreds of neatly folded and sorted wrapping papers, gift bows and buttons, their »nearness« being the only thing seemingly providing warmth and safety.

Indications for Treatment

To help an Autonomist who has lost his footing and slipped into a state requiring treatment, one must offer and grant him two things: structure and physical contact. An Autonomist trying to find himself again needs a framework of rules, temporal order and processes to hold on to. So it is important to encourage him to always get up at the same time, regularly take his meals and be on time for his therapy sessions. If possible, these sessions should always be scheduled for the same day and time, and not be rearranged. He should be given assignments to be completed steadfastly and on time, and he needs a rhythm to his day offering him stability. Only when he has settled in and found his bearing again, without inner pressure, yet attached to certain outer requirements, is it possible to gradually loosen the regularity and strict temporal sequence and carefully build in more flexibility. This gives the Autonomist an opportunity to get used to anything unplanned, surprising even, without feeling as if the rug was pulled out from under his feet.

The second strategy, to be applied in parallel, consists in a careful emotional and physical approach to the lonely Autonomist. At first, he should be given reassurance from outside that he is indeed coping perfectly well on his own, but that it might be even nicer, more relaxed and also more fun to undertake, cope with and experience things together with others. If he's in a clinic, it's important to suggest he participate in small groups for example, or, if he's an outpatient, to ascertain that there is a small number of people at his side to look after and give him bodily contact also outside the therapy sessions. This should, however, happen discreetly and seemingly of his own accord. If the diseased Autonomist is compelled to take part in any communal activities, the result may be that he retreats into himself again. But if he gets the impression that someone else actually likes spending time with him, now and then taking or touching his hand, putting their arm around his shoulders or just resting a hand there, he will slowly start feeling »softened up« a bit. Every single touch will be something for him to ponder about for a long time. Yet if he feels overtaxed by human contact, he'll recoil and harden once more.

At a later stage, physiotherapy can be very helpful for the Autonomist, which, under the pretext of back straightening techniques or gymnastic exercises, can gradually turn into a gentle caressing of the indurated, tensed up muscle areas, of which he no longer even feels the pain. A next step could then be initiated by recommending sauna visits or massages including heat treatment, such as mud pads. Little by little, these measures will make the Autonomist step out of his compulsive solitude. It is imperative though that all of this should seem to him as if happening voluntarily and out of his own impulse.

The therapist should encourage other treatment measures in parallel. Most favourable would be the combination of back treatment and conversational therapy, or a group therapy with some gentle touching of his hands or shoulders, depending on the degree of his or her previous loneliness and overall hardening. Once an Autonomist is willing and able to endure an embrace that is more than just chummy back-slapping, it can be assumed that he has largely recovered. He can organize his life again without getting submerged in the »boxing in« of his needs. He'll be able to feel himself and his needs, his longings and wishes again. And he'll himself initiate contact and seek to be close to others. He'll learn – to the degree tolerable to him – to ask for support and help, or accept it when offered.

It's also favorable during treatment to let the Autonomist report about what he has recently accepted or rejected in terms of help, and in the context of an exercise invite him to address another person with a small request for help, later giving an account of his experience. These assignments should initially not go beyond such innocuous requests as »would you mind handing me that blanket please« or »would you care to join me on my errand to the travel agent.« The Autonomist considers such requests, which are totally normal for other people, of far-reaching importance.

If the patient is in an advanced state of regression, he needs anxiolytic medication. Initially however, one should rather support his need to curl up and no longer have to perform. One can offer him a hot water bottle or a warm blanket and just keep him quiet company, soothing his dismal feelings of abandonment. Empathy demands that he should not be immediately dragged out of his helplessness, e.g. by forcibly appealing to his ego strength with such remarks as: »Come on, pull yourself together now!«

It is generally helpful for the Autonomist to provision himself with things warming – also for those Autonomists who aren't in a particularly needy condition. This warmth can and should be applied to the grown-up body and the childlike, forlorn psyche alike. Taking a hot bath, mud packs, hot water bottles or electric heat pads, thermal baths, scarves and a cozy cardigan, knitted socks and his favorite (security) blanket give the Autonomist a feeling of shelter and rest. A cuddly toy – ridiculous as it may seem at first – can do wonders for the Autonomist. If he remonstrates against such suggestion, a special pillow, also to be taken along on a trip, will do, or some mascot – that is, anything which conveys to him the feeling of childlike shelteredness and a homely atmosphere.

Type 2: The Hardhead

While the Autonomist is always ready to search for alternative, new solutions, the Hardhead gets so jaw-locked into what offers him resistance, he'll apply all his ingenuity to change the world instead of changing himself. The Hardhead wants to get his way. His intentions shall also apply to others, his plans must be fulfilled by his fellow men, life must turn his expectations into reality; otherwise he believes himself to have failed. He obstinately and grimly pursues his course, and where others would long have surrendered, he keeps holding on. He thinks his approach to be commendable perseverance and persistence, not seeing how he has become obsessed with something which is either unattainable or far from even a chance of realization – a fact everyone else has long recognized.

He becomes fixed on a completely hopeless goal or relationship. But the Hardhead doesn't notice and won't do so for a long time. He puts on blinkers so he doesn't see how adverse circumstances really are. He pegs his nose so as not to smell any of the good and pleasant in other places that might tempt him. He clogs up his ears not to hear any advice or accept consolation. He just wants what he wants, and he's going to achieve what he has resolved to do, regardless of the consequences.

The Hardhead bangs his head against the wall and feels no pain. Rather, he hopes that by repeatedly hitting his head against the wall he'll develop a callus or protective shell, enabling him to make a breakthrough in the end. He doesn't take no for an answer and is mighty proud of it. If he covets a partner, he can wait for years and persistently reconfirm his interest, no matter how often he is turned down. On the contrary, the more he gets rejected, the more it provokes his persistence. One can't get rid of him unless by completely cutting all ties. The least concession is interpreted as a partial victory.

Professionally, a Hardhead is able to achieve distant goals out of sheer single-mindedness. The striving for long-term objectives fills him with great strength and a sense of purpose. Should the targeted goal indeed be accomplished, the Hardhead often falls into a depression because that wasn't what he wanted! He only wanted to want it, not necessarily win it. He reacts the same way in relationships. When the partner he fancies finally acquiesces, he frequently loses interest and his covetousness focuses on a new partner who defies or eludes him.

The Hardhead appears very consistent in his lifestyle. He has strict rules to behave and live by. The Hardhead's outstanding feature is his defiant attitude. It develops during early infancy but continues beyond the so-called »terrible twos« and becomes a fundamental attitude towards life. The Hardhead defies all circumstances, all adversities, all obstacles. He wills his small and great successes into being by sheer obstinacy. He wills his health, prosperity and partnership. The Hardhead defies his son to follow in his footsteps, or the daughter to marry the man her mother would have wanted for herself. The obstinate will-power, therefore, is the central, characteristic nature of a Hardhead. And this will-power is applied without examining the final consequences; it manifests for the sake of itself. So the Hardhead is someone who permanently challenges his fellow men, be it silently or openly: »Put me under pressure and you're in for trouble. My will shall be done. Your will I don't care about. I demand that my will shall be yours too. We can only get along if we both want the same, and I decide what that should be.«

Features

The striking features of this type of Stubbornness are a well pronounced chin and jaw, an often thick and sinewy throat, hard neck, a determined, direct gaze and a deep furrow signaling: »I focus my will on what is important to me, everything else is secondary.«

His neck musculature is not only hardened, one can frequently observe a kind of bull's neck on men and women alike, because the head is slightly bent forward, as if the individual wanted to ram his forehead against whatever is in his way. He's got a rigid look that rarely seems to soften.

His build is usually stout and compact. He tends to be the tough, sporting type. With bright eyes he tells of all the things he has successfully managed to do, of his victories and goals. And when he talks about what he's going to tackle and target next, he conveys an impression of strength and unwavering confidence.

Of note is his poor physical sensitivity, but also his emotional lack of understanding of the needs and wishes of his family and fellow men. He is convinced of himself and his concerns in a know-all way. When he talks about what he considers important, you'd think these are laws of nature. That lunch has to be on the table at one o'clock sharp is as incontrovertible as the law of gravity. In a conversation it becomes evident that he likes to eat the same dish again and again, that he is highly reluctant to change any situation in his life, that he'd like nothing more than to spend his life from the cradle to the grave in his parental home, subconsciously construing circumstances that will prevent him from bringing about any major changes himself.

The sitting posture is comfortably laid back and appears anything but anxious, because the Hardhead is convinced that no-one can find fault with him. He radiates the message: »Don't you come bothering me with any of your ›ideas‹. With me, you might as well knock your head against a brick wall. We're gonna fight this out before I'll make even the slightest concession.«

Typical complaints

The Hardhead's frontal sinuses are frequently affected, e.g. blocked or inflamed, sometimes turning into a permanent cold, without the Hardhead really suffering from it. He or she accepts indispositions and illness uncomplainingly. Since the neck tendons and muscles are as hard and tense as steel cables, his eyes are affected by circulatory problems and the resulting lack of vitamin and mineral supply. He is occasionally afflicted with a strong astigmatism, more frequently though with poor eyesight, aggravating with age if the Hardhead doesn't become conscious of his absurd efforts to strive for unrealistic aims.

Since he declares his physicalness marginal, completely concentrating on his will-power and long-term goals, he tries to either ignore various small complaints or cure them instantaneously with radical measures. He is unwilling to let his softer and more delicate traits »disturb« him. This is where the panic-stricken determination will occasionally come into play, seducing him to take rash measures, e.g. surgery when it's not yet indicated, so he can »put it behind him«, or some other kill-or-cure remedy, the side effects of which he is sure to take with ease. The Hardhead also tends to develop brain problems, though not classifiable as psychosomatic disorders in a narrower sense. He typically develops aneurysms or benign tumors evolving from the high tension in the head area.

As a result of muscle stiffening and armoring around the neck and head, the Hardhead often has dental problems. He gnashes, grinds or gnaws his teeth not only at night, but often during the day, too. So his teeth are shortened from the nightly grinding, even reduced to stumps; still, he seldom suffers from a toothache. If it does happen, a Hardhead will often be strangely terrified of the dentist. Just the thought of a drill or a syringe fills him with panic for loss of control. It also has to do with the fact that he must lay back his head at the dentist's and somehow relax his neck muscles while surrendering to the treatment. He cannot really bite off the dentist's finger, as he would like to do, nor can he give in to his half-conscious wish to ram his forehead against the dentist's chest as punishment for the pains caused.

In later years, the Hardhead frequently develops tension headaches and cervical spine arthrosis. He'll find it hard to even turn his head left or right, being forced to turn the whole upper body when trying to look to the side.

The extreme discipline a Hardhead submits to with pleasure, also in terms of sports or a particular physical exercise he has once identified as healthy or helpful, may then be the reason that he overtaxes himself and suddenly suffers the heart attack he meant to avert by his »healthy« activities. Or he has a bad accident because he took on too much, brushing aside his tiredness and attention deficit to accomplish one more goal, trying to do so with will-power instead of physical power.

Psychiatric disorders attributable to Hardhead type Stubbornness can be found for example in stalkers. They just can't resist observing and harassing their object of interest.

Also typical are fatigue syndromes of the autonomic nervous system. If these go unnoticed and untreated for years, they may lead to physical and mental breakdowns, sometimes in conjunction with delusional ideas, such as, for example, believing he or she still has to finish some major, urgent and important work, while in fact the Hardhead has long retired from professional life. These imaginary tasks will often lie in the area of world politics, occasionally associated with the ambition of bestowing religious or medical salvation on mankind.

The Hardhead is particularly susceptible to psychiatric disorders requiring treatment when he becomes unemployed or is forced into early retirement, due to business failures or mergers, things he is unable to affect with his will-power. He may then be assailed by suicidal impulses, sometimes even ending up in a family suicide or running amok. His need to control, his will-power and goal orientation must find a valve: the Hardhead, robbed of his professional objectives and his always dutifully completed job responsibilities, often finds no other way out of his helplessness and quandary but to tumble into death, in the company of others if possible.

Indications for Treatment

Should a Hardhead actually need or seek help – be it from a physiotherapist or psychiatrist – it is beneficial to accommodate his particular needs for security and conclude agreements which contribute to his inner relaxation. Most of all, it's important to jointly draft treatment objectives, even though to the therapist this may seem like an inadmissible intervention. The reason is that the Hardhead must have a specific goal on which to concentrate his efforts with his usual doggedness; otherwise the whole procedure will make no sense or feel silly to him. Open therapy methods are rather unsuitable for him. Having a specific, clear-cut problem he can target helps to let himself in for this procedure in the first place, a process which he finds both unfamiliar and alarming. He simply isn't used to sensing any other will or intention besides his own. When he gains the impression that some other, unfamiliar will in fact contrasts his own, it might evoke his resistance or even dropout from the support contract.

So the therapist is well advised to ask the Hardhead right from the beginning to clearly define his objectives and problem areas. Because it's precisely this safety framework offered to the Hardhead, which later permits to step out, or at least peep out, of the too restrictive bounds of such pseudo-safety. One can also meet his need for order by arranging the therapy sessions each week at exactly the same hour and assigning him his own specific seat in the consultation room. It is also helpful to suggest accompanying measures – with some caution at first, later as a friendly recommendation – e.g. a consultation appointment with the dentist, or physiotherapy to relieve his neck muscle stiffness. Otherwise the rather conversation-oriented therapy process might aggravate his unconscious jaw and neck musculature tension. Because a Hardhead, who seeks help only for rational reasons, feels a subliminal threat triggered by the mental loosening of his life defiance, which may initially be counteracted by a reinforced armor-plating of his body. This in turn leads to a seemingly inexplicable resistance to treatment.

Useful advice for a Hardhead is also to place a hot-water bottle under his neck for half an hour before going to sleep. This will soon yield reports of dreams that might give the therapist revealing clues. The armchair the Hardhead sits in during treatment session should ideally have a headrest, and the patient should be repeatedly encouraged to recline and rest his head there. If the therapy is body-oriented, it is useful to let the Hardhead lie down on a very soft-padded treatment couch and also keep him warm with a blanket. This helps avoid any more tension from building up, which would – figuratively speaking – make a »horn« of resistance grow from his forehead. The method of treatment allowing, it is particularly beneficial for the Hardhead if one of the therapist's hands rests on his forehead, pacifying that »horn«, while the other gently massages his neck.

When in a psychiatric clinic, it would be constructive to initially offer this fear type a substitute for the goals he has set himself and not attained so far. The best way to go about it would be to assign him tasks having to do with specific areas of responsibility, rather than with daily clinic routines, for example the care of a co-patient in a wheelchair who needs to be pushed around, or checking whether the shower rooms and toilets are clean. As an added benefit, it would give him the opportunity to »make a report« should this not be the case. He should not, however, be enlisted for cleaning services. Sometimes it can even be helpful for someone in this situation to be mandated to assure the regular exchange of toilet rolls. The idea behind this is to divert the energy from his erroneous targets to a more harmless substitute. Based upon these measures and with time, a healing process can develop.

Type 3: The Survival Whiz

There is one particularly smart way of dealing with the fear of uncertainty, and that is practiced by the Survival Whiz. A Survival Whiz considers any difficulty, each unpleasant surprise, every problem and uncertainty a thrilling challenge. He or she will handle it like a circus clown, a juggler, a magician and – if that's the only way – like a lion-tamer. Everything is a charming provocation of life and his art consists in transforming a situation that is deeply frightening and rattling him to the bone into a triumph, a victory, a relishable experience within minutes, hours or just a few days.

The Survival Whiz is convinced he can cope with everything. He is amazingly flexible, hardly anyone notices the effort it takes him to turn lead into gold. He will usually claim that he never sees the dark clouds, but always the silver lining on the horizon, that out of every bad situation, something good can be gained, and that some bliss is hidden even behind the worst of back luck. He enjoys the way he manages to make the best of everything. And that's also how he reaps the admiration of his fellow men, because he seems generally content and cheerful. Occasionally though, his euphemistic talk gets on people's nerves, and his debonair illusions, when too obvious, will tick them off.

It is typical of the Survival Whiz that he doesn't know what suffering is. So he or she has little understanding for people who cannot handle difficult situations, who have woes and worries and no idea how to change their state of affairs. Such things make him intolerant. He would love to intervene or bang his fist on the table, shouting: »Now get moving, try harder! Why do you think I always find a solution? It's not that difficult after all. You just have to really want it.« This »after all« and »nonetheless« is his medicine against all ailments.

The fact that a Survival Whiz no longer knows what it means to suffer from uncertainty, or how sorrow feels caused by unforeseen circumstances, bad surprises and sudden painful changes, makes him appear floating somewhat above the human condition. It is personal suffering and appreciation of other people's misery which builds a solid bridge and creates alliances. Only sympathy and empathy from one's own experience can make the other person feel understood. So it can't be denied that the Survival Whiz appears a little condescending.

Since the Survival Whiz fits in always and everywhere, adjusting and finding his way while keeping a happy face on top of it, one isn't likely to suspect that in him, too, is rooted a deep fear of the unpredictable; all his clever measures and successful strategies being ultimately designed to keep this fear at bay and ignore it as best possible. He goes by the motto »there is no such thing as bad weather, only the wrong clothing.« And that, he is convinced, could even make him survive the Great Flood.

But there are, of course, limits – even for a Survival Whiz. Often, they manifest only late in life, when a situation occurs which shakes his perennial confidence of success (»I can't fail. I'll never perish and probably won't die either«). Even the Survival Whiz cannot tackle all bad surprises and vicissitudes of life with his bracing optimism. By the death of a child, or his business going down the drain along with all his savings, he suddenly turns dependent and miserable. Should he develop an incurable, fast-progressing illness, his optimistic conception of the world will cave in, too. In the face of such tragedy it becomes apparent that the Survival Whiz's euphemistic attitude was nothing but a fear mastering strategy. Confronted with an uncontrollable situation and – from his lack of experience in dealing with such circumstances – finding it hard to handle, he'll feel thrown into an abysmal depression, because he has no idea how to apply his skills to this situation. Didn't things always work out just fine before? Didn't he always have everything under control? – impervious as to how grimly he held on to this control. Now all of a sudden, something happens which he can't control, on which he has no leverage and can't turn around to fit into his vision of happiness and sunshine either, of pie in the sky and hidden blessings.

But in general, the Survival Whiz believes in and thinks highly of his capabilities and he is the one who – subjectively – suffers least from his Stubbornness. Objectively, however, his supremacy has a somewhat segregating effect on his fellow men because they, in contrast, aren't always successful; things will go wrong for them, they openly suffer at unforeseen developments. While they are sometimes envious of the Survival Whiz, they also feel incomprehension and irritation because he takes everything just a little too easily. He doesn't see the depths; his lack of suffering making him shallow and superficial.

So it will ultimately be of great benefit for the personal development of the Survival Whiz if, from time to time, he is afflicted by incidents on which he cannot exercise his art of control. It makes him distinctive. It adds gold to his emotional treasure chest and is a capital to draw from in later years and also in his hour of death. Those last issues, which even a Survival Whiz can't manage with an easy hand, will then be the aqua fortis for late self-recognition. The Survival Whiz will finally understand how artful and pleasant the strategy he acquired and implemented was, and where the limits of its applicability lie.

Features

The Survival Whiz simply can't see any real problems. He believes that his life is mostly conflict-free. When pointing something out to him one recognizes as a potential difficulty, it seems he doesn't know what this is all about, or he believes he is being talked into a problem, indeed lumbered with one he hasn't actually got.

The Survival Whiz always has a cheerful air about him or her, taking things easy. Found among them are also those happy-go-lucky people with their lively expression. Then there are the corpulent, jovial types, also taking things easy and getting a grip on their problems with a good meal and a leisurely way of life. The Survival Whiz radiates cheerfulness and likes to elaborate on his clever strategies that have proved successful again just recently. People talking to him soon get the impression that they can learn a lot from this person. Now this holds a certain risk, because the outward appearance is not quite in line with his inner identity.

A Survival Whiz usually has sufficient financial resources at his disposal. He will seldom strip himself to the bone of material wealth. If however, he should actually go broke, like a stand-up doll he'll soon be back on his feet again, relishing in telling the story of how he pulled himself out of the bog by his bootstraps. They are frequently shrewd business people, or people with artistic talents, generally moving amongst their own with a bit of bluffing and boasting.

A Survival Whiz thinks nothing of habitually fibbing to others and himself, or to twist the truth and circumstances a bit the way it suits him. Since he is bent on always looking on the bright side of life, he advises others to do the same, oftentimes promising or holding out the prospect of things he cannot keep in the end. His fellow men may be disappointed; to the Survival Whiz it feels good. He is generous with his wealth and possessions and likes to give, since he believes to own a kind of Wishing-table or Gold-ass.

He has often made the experience in his life that what he gives away comes back two-fold.

Even so, a Survival Whiz can easily be taken advantage of. Since he is – despite his savvy and intelligent mastering of life – naive and trusting, he will now and then meet someone who is even cleverer, ripping him off, coaxing him out of the Gold-ass or taking over the table that was set for the Survival Whiz.

Typical complaints

The Survival Whiz only seldom has any physical complaints. He typically refuses to have a blood count done, because his thinking is: »What the eye does not see, the heart cannot grieve over.« His strategy consists in denying potentially unpleasant surprises. Someone unconsciously formed and tantalized by the primal fear of Unpredictability in the particular way of the Survival Whiz is given to woolgathering and embellishing his reality, sometimes up to a dubious scale. It can make him lose the ground under his feet, float above the waters, making believe whatever whitewashes his problems and difficulties. He is ready to either ignore or convert into its opposite anything which subliminally – for others more obviously – torments him. That way he seemingly fixes his world again. He or she likes to employ affirmations or half-magical practices designed to dissolve all difficulties »as if by themselves« into thin air or sacred smoke.

To an observer it soon becomes evident that here is someone tailoring his depressing reality in a way he feels digestible. A sad childhood is turned into a fragment of memory reduced to the rare pleasant moments, or else the ability of retrospection is confined to a few facts. A vicious mother becomes an angelic figure, a raging, alcoholic father someone who was a kind soul at heart, only wanting the best for the child.

An increasing loss of reality, spreading also to his present-day ability of experience, will then lead to this individual no longer finding his way out of the illusions about himself and his world. His vision is limited to the beautiful and good, the noble and wonderful; he is unable to understand himself as a multifaceted personality anymore. He seems like a Star Taler child, collecting the blessings from heaven with big round eyes and a beatific smile, while in reality everything around him goes to pieces: be it health, family or finances.

The denial of things unpleasant, therefore, is characteristic of his more or less pronounced pathological attitude to life. This, and the repression effort it takes, may lead to some hard to diagnose conversion disorders (transformation of unresolved conflicts into physical symptoms), since the person affected no longer dares to truthfully name and depict his reality the way it is. When afflicted by such disorders, he will deny it in the usual way, declaring an inability to speak or walk not really that bad. Or he claims he can accept his loss of vision quite well, to actually benefit from it, because his inner life was now filled with so much more vivacity and colorfulness.

Another potential disorder could be seemingly inexplicable guilt complexes cropping up, because a Survival Whiz feels responsible that people in his near or distant environment don't feel just as happy, unperturbed or content as he or she does. When a Survival Whiz witnesses one of his children getting depressive, or an uncle running his business into bankruptcy, while he must helplessly watch without the chance to better the situation or take action, he will ascribe a moral blame to himself or even some involvement in the process, in order to put things into his usual perspective again. So if the daughter suffers from depression, the Survival Whiz mother will be certain it's because of mistakes she made or – taking the other example – feel guilty because she hasn't told that uncle in time of her dream which might have saved him. Also weighing heavily on a Survival Whiz can be global peace prayers which yield no results, or a general apprehensive suffering at war horrors and injustices in the big wide world, especially when he can't see any change happening despite the hopeful, euphemistic view he upheld. Such things may lead to a depressed mood that remains incomprehensible for outsiders.

When a Survival Whiz begins to conspicuously emphasize how thankful he should be for everything, e.g. for bad things always turning out to be a blessing in disguise, and other people being so much worse off, that if only one looked on the sunny side of the street and followed it, everything would turn out fine in the end – when such statements are uttered again and again like an incantation, the family or counselor should prick their ears. This is the herald of a deep-rooted despair of life, which he or she doesn't seem able to cope with any other way than by a kind of autohypnosis, painting the insufferable in gay colors as the last emergency solution.

Indications for Treatment

When observing signs that a Survival Whiz is floating in cloud-cuckoo-land most of the time, the danger of suicide must not be underestimated; he should be protected from himself in time. What he needs is a sheltering institutional setting with people who are sincerely concerned about his well-being, allowing him to fall back on the ground of reality again from his illusions and not break all his bones in the process. A lasting, wholesome cure is usually achieved not so much by pharmacotherapy, although at times quite urgently indicated, but rather by an environment providing the protective safety, warmth and comfort the patient has for so long tried to find in and give himself, without much success.

The therapist will glean informative clues as to the condition of his client, if, in a therapeutic conversation, he experimentally reports of his own difficulties to cope with life, or of critical cases from his professional practice and problematic life-stories he learned about from the newspaper or some movie. This approach will provoke a flood of solution proposals from the client, usually founded on the demand for a change of attitude from »negative« to »positive« that is, the conception of man, on philosophy, or on religious orientation. The client will shower the therapist with suggestions and behavioral recommendations which have already helped him, thus drawing a distinct picture of his own rose-tinted view of life. Just by listening, the therapist will learn about the full repertoire of his client's personal strategies, which he can then gradually make use of and later also re-function, the way one can use a claw hammer to drive nails into the wall and then pull them out again. It is important to always keep in mind the deep existential, and very real, insecurity of the primal fear of Stubbornness the Survival Whiz is trying to compensate for.

The idealizing painting the Survival Whiz has drawn up of his existence can only be touched up and furnished with the necessary depth of shadow by the therapist, if the latter is willing to articulate his feelings of compassion at each appropriate occasion, sort of a feeling of sympathy one could term »compassion by proxy.« So when the client reports of some dreadful childhood episodes he has obviously sleekened and sugarcoated, it is helpful to comment on them to the effect that these would have surely been hard to take for other children, and that, actually, they were quite sad. It's a way to gradually induce the client to take a different perspective, carefully lifting the euphemistic veils from his memory. Oftentimes, this approach will entail an uncovering of traumata that necessitated the overly pink painting of his life vision in the first place. But it is imperative to proceed with the greatest caution, because by looking at events in their stark reality, the client may easily lose a big chunk of his usual courage to face life. If the former embellishment isn't replaced by a soothing and still somewhat pleasant and acceptable perspective of the atrocities exposed, a depression is almost inevitable.

It is noteworthy that a client describing his life to be of such dreamlike quality only seldom dreams at night. And if he does, he reports of nightmares which seem so absurd, that he can't see how they could possibly have anything to do with his real life. So he relegates them either to the sphere of his lively imagination, or, facetiously, to experiences from former lives that can have absolutely nothing to do with the present. Accordingly, when this client starts dreaming more frequently than before, generating also new dream contents which don't resemble the old nightmares of this stubborn person, it can be inferred that he is on the mend. Physical »grounding« exercises from bioenergetics, yoga or the like, can help the Survival Whiz learn to stand with both legs firmly on the floor again.

Greed – Fear of Privation

General

Bodiless souls in the astral world of consciousness know nothing about poverty or wealth. They exist in a fulfillment unaffected by the duality of abundance and lack. But as soon as a soul enters the terrestrial, material world, it will inevitably experience a difference between having and not having, between taking and giving, between need and abundance. This applies to all incarnations and all human experiencing. The majority of incarnations on earth are linked with the experience of hunger, lack and need. Only about one third of all life spans are blessed by prosperity, material satisfaction and physical satiety.

When a soul decides to investigate the primal Fear of Privation as a special aspect of the incarnated form of existence, it will find that this fear exists inside itself quite independently of real material need or abundance. The phenomenon of Greed evolving from it can be investigated everywhere and any time under all circumstances of each incarnation, while the specific targets on which this primal Fear of Privation concentrates can be most individual. To understand that the fear of hunger is something else than actual, physical lack of food, is an important learning step in the different cycles of an incarnation journey. Time and again, a soul shall and wants to explore different aspects of Greed, but also the possibilities of outgrowing it in love and awareness.

Consistent with the universal energy 5, Greed is an expressive and expansive fear. It doesn't relate so much to introspection or the inner experiencing; it rather reaches for the outer world, to the other person, to material things as well as to success, to being seen, to experiencing. Greed, therefore, more than other primal fears, is a phenomenon of the relation to the environment – not only to fellow men, but primarily also to the material aspects of life.

The archetypal feature of Greed is based on a heightened sense of privation, even where lack cannot be objectively established. The Fear of Privation may quite generally relate to a feeling of emptiness and hollowness, thirst for life or hunger for food, but also – depending on the remaining configuration of the individual Soul MATRIX – on various single areas of life like money, success, beauty, satisfaction, relaxation, glory and praise, while other aspects of life remain free of this fear of lack. Or the Greed can fix on specific goals, frequently connected with the person's life history, education or early childhood patterning. Depending on how strong this fear characteristic is, the Greed causes a perpetual or even unquenchable hunger for something that is felt to be missing or is simply unattainable. This might be motherly love, prosperity or wealth. It can mean yearning for glory or political status, for specific physical features not provided by nature, and for various other, subtler aspects, such as the greed for sexual satisfaction for example.

The inner emptiness that must be filled is usually not – or hardly – registered consciously. But since Greed is an expressive, expansive fear, it creates the illusion that such need or hunger could be assuaged by reaching out and taking from the outside whatever one can get, and always more of it; it's never enough. What may happen, though, when the hope for fulfillment, this expectation of repletion, gets frustrated again and again, is that the reaching out turns into a shameful contraction, notably into the notion: »I won't ever get enough. There just isn't enough to go round, so I might as well forego completely. I'm not going to ask anything of life anymore, because I'll never get what I need anyway.«

The Poles of Fear of Privation

| – Insatiable | ⟷ | Demanding + |

When a person with the primal fear of Greed is in his fearful positive pole, he is surrounded by an aura of satiety and self-satisfaction almost resembling gluttony, as if he had just gobbled up several pieces of cream cake in one go. This complacency and satiety has something sensuous, voluptuous about it. It results when the greedy person, having finally eaten his fill, has got or taken more than enough of what he needs – even in his own subjective perception. A sort of profusion expresses itself in this self-satisfaction, feeling rather stuffed, with a little stomach ache even, because with the other parts of his non-fearful self, also the greedy person feels that it was really a bit too much of a good thing.

A complacent self-contentedness is the positive pole of this primal Fear of Privation, or the pseudo-virtue of this feature, evolving when a greedy person has taken possession of or hogged something of which he is firmly convinced that he is more than entitled to. Whatever he strives for, he covets like a bag full of coins. Self-satisfaction spreads when, finally, something materializes which he or she has renunciatorily awaited for a long time. Then their eyes begin to shine; the mien wide. Their facial expression is comparable to that of a person squatting on his bag of gold, never to be parted from it again. He doesn't want to use this gold, nor spend or exchange it for something. He just wants to own it, bathe in it like Scrooge McDuck, and enjoy his exquisite triumph. This applies, of course, also to other aspects of life, such as landing a well-paid position, obtaining a large discount, getting married to a wealthy husband, winning the lottery or fighting for an advantage or a reward. It is the plentiful, saturated, contented feeling the greedy person gets when everyone enviously eyes him, his possessions, his success. Then the demanding person temporarily enjoys a feeling of satisfaction and satiation. And although it won't last for long, it assuages his primal fear at least for little while.

A greedy person hovering mainly in the negative pole of his fear, however, is obsessed by the idea of a black hole in his system he must somehow fill, without ever reaching that feeling of satiation. His insatiability makes him a bottomless pit. If, in the positive pole, a greedy person is occasionally able to feel that he's got enough of something for a little while, he can never get enough in the negative pole. He never has the impression of ever getting, or having asked for, enough of something or from someone. That gnawing feeling of a black hollowness always remains. This negative pole renders a person insatiable. As long as his fear remains unabated, he won't even attain that bit of satisfaction which could potentially make him happy in the positive pole. The insatiability extends to food, love, success, recognition, money and many other things. There is also a spiritual insatiability, when the seeker cannot find the enlightenment he has hoped for, resulting in a kind of guru-hopping.

An individual with the basic fear of Greed can alternately observe both poles in himself. Important for his inner balance is that he doesn't habitually arrange himself in one of them, otherwise he'll forget how the opposite pole feels, although it will always remain present as a potential. Any human being, for as long as he lives, will continually oscillate between the poles of his basic fear.

Due to his chronic dissatisfaction, the insatiability of a greedy person also affects the people around him; they too become dissatisfied and unhappy. No matter how much they give or grant or invest in him, the insatiable person is always hungry and ungrateful because he can never develop that feeling of satiation. He simply never gets enough. When ultimately family, friends or colleagues realize that their strained efforts to sate the hungry person – be it with compliments, affection, with gifts of money or praise – are in vain, they'll withdraw after a while, disappointed. The insatiable, however, won't let up. He will make even greater, heavier demands, bitterly accusing the ones withdrawing from him of stinginess. This negatively polarized quality of the primal Fear of Privation has – like all negatives poles – a destructive component, leading to dissonances between people who otherwise are or might grow really close to each other.

Amongst the insatiable, one also finds swindlers and con-artists such as legacy-hunters or marriage swindlers, plus those greatly overweight individuals, hungering for the primeval need of feeding at a mother's breast. But they have, in the figurative sense, unlearned how to reach out for it. Once they didn't get enough from their mothers; now they try all their lives to make up for what they've missed. Due to that feeling of privation, insatiability also breeds forms of keen envy and avarice. Someone feeling like a bottomless pit can't give much and consequently envies others what seems to sate and satisfy them.

When it turns out early in an individual life that it's impossible to fulfill the fearful need for satiation by food and loving security, the ability to take, to reach for, to grub and stuff oneself, may in fact wither completely. The greedy person withdraws to the position of neither needing nor wanting anything at all, in order to avoid feeling that unremitting frustration any more. This in turn produces a different kind of smug self-satisfaction: someone who needs hardly anything at all doesn't have to want, yearn or ask for anything either. He is content with little or nothing, finding a certain peace therein, like someone who, with only one third of his stomach remaining after surgery, feels full from a meal much faster than other people.

The Released Potential

The potential bound in the basic fear of Greed holds a pleasant generosity. Every scrap of Fear of Privation the greedy person can divest himself of permits him, bit by bit, to be more generous, with himself and others. To enjoy life with everything it has to offer, to be content and feeling inwardly sated is the perpetual goal of a person with the fear of Greed. But as long as he targets this goal through the visor of his primal Fear of Privation, it will seem unattainably distant.

Serenity and experiencing the simple joy of being are closely correlated. The juicy fruit of the effort to look at the warped effects of one's fear is to recognize that the fearfully felt scarcity can be redeemed and replaced by a perceptible fulfillment, by satisfaction and contentment, allowing to give and take at the right measure without exaggerating, and staying in the middle between desire and renunciation. Envy and stinginess abate, as does the need for excessive asceticism. A person who, in his Greed, often had a strange aura of hunger and neediness despite his corpulence and the surrounding profusion, turns into someone who knows what he has and hasn't got. His charisma changes to a rosy abundance, allowing him to give and receive without making it a barter deal or an investment, hoping for high interest. Released generosity also yields gratitude which, in addition to the beneficial and relaxing effect on his fellow men, also creates a new closeness, new relationships, understanding and an unperturbed interchange.

Three Types of Fear of Privation

1. The **Glutton** wants to get as much as possible of everything. He is constantly preoccupied with food, which doesn't necessarily mean that he's an excessive eater, but his thoughts

always revolve around food. The Glutton also feels the need to take as much as possible of all other phenomena of his world. He can't get enough of anything nor of anyone.

2. The **Miser** tries to keep everything for himself. It's all about taking and retaining. He doesn't like to give, either of himself or of his possessions. His Fear of Privation makes him hide what he's got, so no one will come to take it away or demand something of him.

3. The **Have-not** tries not to feel his Fear of Privation by semi-consciously bringing scarcity about himself. Best if he owned nothing at all. This is a special form of fearful asceticism. A Have-not doesn't do justice to the primal urge for abundance and luxury so typical of the basic energy 5.

Type 1: The Glutton

The Glutton has an unquenchable appetite, an almost irrepressible hunger for more. It has to be more of everything. He conceives the whole world to exist only to satisfy his hunger. Whether it is hunger for food or hunger for success and attention now is less important than the »gathering« effect in itself. Also a corpulent person – as can frequently be found among this type – expresses a need for attention through his sheer body mass. He is being seen, if usually with a critical eye. But he finds satisfaction in the mere fact to be perceived at all.

More often, however, the greedy type of Glutton is found amongst people with a burning desire to become popular or even famous. From the very beginning, they try to fashion their life in such a way as to always be at the center of attention. They just can't get enough adulation for their beauty, their talents, their attractiveness or success. They are never satisfied with themselves and actually only feel themselves when they can mirror in the envy of others. This reflection must also take on a tangible form, i.e., everything around them should be as big and garish as possible: the big house, the flashy car, the bulging bank account, the enormous success, the insatiability in amassing a fortune. At the same time, the feeling remains that their emotional tummy is always empty. Many famous, often very thin, cooks, but primarily show business people, politicians and great athletes such as football players or tennis pros, can be found among them.

More than others, people with the fear characteristic of Greed who are exceptionally successful, always standing in the limelight, are often prone to a financial collapse. The more money they make and attention they get, the more often they suffer a personal or financial disaster in their mid-years. Always out for more, they invest in fantastic projects or in papers promising an unrealistic return. Also the sensational marriage with a most beautiful and successful partner is part of their investment. But they can't hold on to what they gained. They are like people walking into a supermarket without a shopping cart, then gathering up so many goods that, on their way to check-out, they must helplessly watch as everything tumbles from their arms to the floor, some of it broken beyond repair.

Features

The Glutton comes in two phenotypes. One type is very corpulent, everything about him or her gives off voluptuousness. The body is well cushioned, the face radiant and content. The flat is richly furnished, preferably with precious and striking objects. He maintains a number of superficial friendships and many acquaintances, and he can resort to a dense network of people as long as he stages great parties and generously splashes his money about. He knows that it'll get him back even more in return.

The second type of Glutton, however, might look really gaunt and lean, with an almost starved, undernourished air about him. This person has a fast metabolism and a high basal rate. He often has digestive problems – either constipation, which is why he doesn't eat much, or chronic diarrhea because he can't keep anything, and therefore eats all the more. The intake of food is of great magnitude. This overly slender type of the greedy is restless and fickle, his eyes always wandering in search of more objects of any kind, including non-material, he may possibly assimilate or avail himself of.

The Glutton often has big, wide-open eyes. Also frequently striking are his disproportionate hands – either too small, yet very animated hands, or strangely big ones, somehow incongruous with the other features. The mouth comes in two conspicuous variations as well. One is reminiscent of a thick-lipped, sucking infant, large, with massive teeth; the eyes of an observer immediately wander to this part of the face. A second, typical form of mouth looks puckered, lips pursed together, as if ready to suck, or like an anus unwilling to let go of anything.

The Glutton has an unbalanced relation to matter. It doesn't, however, attract much negative attention, since his success seems to prove him right. The Glutton nevertheless complains that he doesn't get enough of this and that, of not having enough money or not getting enough love from his partner, that he doesn't find proper recognition or hasn't enough success professionally, his financial transactions falling through, and especially that this sensation of hunger for more seldom or never leaves him. The neediness and getting possession of can also extend to immaterial subjects, for example greed for self-knowledge, for intensity or drama. Even the greed for enlightenment must be listed here.

Typical Complaints

The Glutton tends to be smitten with various eating disorders. Especially obesity is very common, due to an incessant ingestion of small meals or snacks, producing a high insulin level. But also the opposites, such as bulimia, and even more frequently anorexia nervosa, can be diagnosed. The eating disorder may also be on a less obvious pathological level, e.g. compulsive dieting or an ex- aggerated need to create – by plastic surgery or liposuction – that glamorously slender figure seemingly holding the prospect of suc- cess and attention. The lean phenotype often suffers from a thyroid hyper-function.

The Glutton is usually given to all kinds of addictions, in par- ticular to alcohol, dope, drugs, gambling and sex. Permanent dis- content is the company of this fear type. Depressions will occur primarily in people with Fear of Privation of the Glutton type who are born into this world with everything they could ever dream of already available in their family of origin. So it's rather the greedy offspring of very rich parents getting depressive as a result of being exposed to excessive affluence as adolescents, which sort of pro- grams them with a disgust of opulence.

Indications for Treatment

When treating a Glutton, the therapist will soon feel confronted with countless expectations and exigencies. While seemingly the object of desire, he or she is at the same time given to understand that every session is too short, that there wasn't enough time for conversation, not enough understanding or too few suggestions offered. That is why many Glutton type patients either abandon the therapy at an early stage, hoping to find another therapist who offers them more, or they have great difficulties winding it up, even after hundreds of sessions, deeming in their own subjective perception that they never got enough, or still haven't gained enough insight from the therapy.

The therapist cannot be successful if he tries to give the Glutton what he, in his insatiability, demands. The therapy should rather focus on the feeling of privation and despair at the existential feeling of hunger lying underneath it. When the therapy has progressed to an advanced stage, the therapist should repeatedly point out that this is an energetic hunger, not a material appetite.

If a patient or client tries to follow a diet or a strict slimming cure during the therapy, this should definitely be made a topic of discussion and not be unconditionally supported, not even with very corpulent people. When this fear characteristic is treated sensitively and appreciated as a real, panic-stricken fear of starvation, the patient will of his own volition eat less, because he'll understand that his primal fear cannot effectively be dealt with in this way.

The Glutton might also shower his therapist with presents, trying to induce him in some way to make an emotional business deal with him. These gifts must regrettably be rejected, because it projects the Glutton's own permanent need of being bestowed with presents.

Type 2: The Miser

The Miser believes that he'll never have enough, and it worries him. He worries in particular about the future – next year, old age – and providing for his family. He dresses in old or cheap clothes. He loves second-hand shops and flea markets, where he also tries to reconvert into cash what he has been given as a present or considers redundant for his family. Fearing that even minimal expenditures jeopardize his safety, he keeps his family on a tight budget. He views his life as the effort to hold on to everything he ever laid his hands on.

The Miser is characterized by a distinct lack of generosity. He can specifically be found among quite wealthy people, often having worked their way up from a humble background and seemingly so happy about what they achieved, that they keep skimping on everything and everyone as before, if not quite obvious right away. But they always live far below their means, never above. The Miser fears for his future and that he'll have to starve in old age. Even being a millionaire can't dispel this fear, as is typically represented in the Dickensian figure of Ebenezer Scrooge from »A Christmas Carol«.

The Miser actually likes to borrow from friends or from the bank – for two reasons: one is that such a loan gives him the pleasant feeling of needing to ask others for an advance; secondly, he likes the impression it creates on friends or colleagues, notably that he's in such dire situation, he has to borrow money to make ends meet.

But also the Miser has dreams he wants to see fulfilled, his longing for more prosperity satisfied. When he buys a car for example, he mulls over it for ages to work out the best deal, overjoyed when he manages to get a car – third or even fourth hand – in good condition. He is also a great bargain hunter and meticulously compares all flyers he finds in his mailbox to see whether he might not get that pound of coffee or even those diamonds somewhere for a little less, no matter that he has to cover long distances to get there. He saves on heating, wearing warm jumpers instead -- not because it's better for his health, but because »nowadays« everything is costing him too much. His conversation usually revolves around how much he has spent for what and how he has so wonderfully been able to save again on something just recently!

The Miser is also parsimonious with his feelings, with his tokens of love and affection, with praise or the time he dedicates to others. His family has good reason to complain that they don't get enough from him. Children are missing their father's or mother's affection, because no matter whether man or woman, the Miser is afraid lest he should invest in something first and then not get it back two-fold. He has high demands on others though. So he tries to give nothing or only the absolutely necessary: tenderness, attention, understanding, interest in the other. He is so needy himself that, by giving, he would trigger a torrent of feelings of lack. Subconsciously he believes he can prevent this by allotting only a minimum, a modicum of love and affection, so that ultimately those around him are also affected by this sense of privation. They withdraw instead of showering him with gratefulness or expressions of affection, which he doesn't like to either accept or return anyway.

Features

The Miser's face is often very distinctive: haggard, the cheeks sunken in. The mouth is thin, lips pressed together, even to the point that no more rosy lip tissue is visible; everything is pulled inside.

The outer appearance is notable by his oldish garments, looking faded and discolored, sometimes also mended. Both the impression this gives, and his occasional comments on the subject, convey: »But this is good enough!« Or one can sense the pride when he says: »I've been wearing this jacket for 28 years now.« Or: »My father wore these shoes before me.« Women spend little money on the hairdresser; the perm having long grown out.

The Miser sometimes has bad teeth, occasionally curving inwards, which makes him or her look like a hungry rodent. One or the other develops a wattle like a turkey early on. Misers are usually rather gaunt, however with a small, hard belly. At times they will suffer from vitamin deficiency because they live mostly on cheap, canned food and rarely buy fresh fruit. They'll rather go for the old, cut-price and almost decayed veggies at the greengrocer's, sometimes even foraging for edibles left in the rabbit box.

Typical Complaints

Chronic constipation or dehydration are typical ailments of the Miser. These people often drink very little, so they don't have to let go of it again. Also observed can be bladder cramps or an increased urinary retention, which doesn't originate in feelings of shame but is based on the unconscious fear of letting go of something they feel is part of their personality. Children who get sick due to stool or urinary retention can also be classified in this category.

Psychiatric abnormalities consist in delusions of impoverishment setting in already at a middle age, also in great distrust against people, allegedly robbing the sick person or wanting to take things from him. The patient will clutch anything he is ever given to his chest, like a child its toys. Eating disorders are rare; the imaginary fear rather focuses on some kind of loss, including family members, or on a deep fear of dying, because dying is what the sick Miser considers the ultimate robbery or essential loss.

Indications for Treatment

The Miser will react positively to affection bestowed on him by the therapist – regularly but carefully measured. Important is also that it be specifically mentioned and verbalized. At first, the patient will classify this as his due right, something he has, after all, already paid for in advance, or is entitled to, since his health insurance is covering the cost. But when the flow of deliberate and repeatedly verbalized affection doesn't get turned off, he'll realize with time that it's meant specifically for him as an individual. He'll understand that he is getting something energetically valuable, maybe even a small present now and then: a pebble, a seashell, a chocolate or something of no great material value, but nevertheless an emotional treasure he can take home and keep for himself.

The therapist will frequently feel the Miser's reservation, maybe gaining the impression that there is no response from him, no confidence or confidingness, no indication of an offer, but also no demand for help. He or she should understand that this is only superficial, that an extreme neediness is hiding behind it, located right underneath this unapproachable surface. This neediness can be easily roused, though care should be taken not to dislodge too much all at once. The therapist could ask the patient to make a small gift to someone once a week. It is not advisable to ask him about his financial situation or his savings account early on.

Type 3: The Have-not

The Have-not is tantalized by his archetypal Fear of Privation so much so, that he converts it into a fear of abundance. Anything holding the promise of luxury, generosity and affluence will arouse an aversion and a slight feeling of nausea in him. Inversely, everything that helps avoid this abundance, this opulence, feels pleasant to him. In his lifestyle and attitude he confines himself to the most basic necessities. He abhors everything »too much.«

He feels comfortable in that role of frugal unpretentiousness. And this applies to all areas of life: he doesn't make any great demands, be it on his work or on his relationship, not on his living quarters or on his food. Whatever it is, somehow it's good enough for him. If ever he should suspect for once that there could be something more or better, he immediately talks himself out of it by comparing with people who have much less than even him. And they were coping too, after all.

The Have-not likes everything that comes with the flair of utmost modesty. When someone else makes a demand, he is quick to condemn it as excessive or even immoral. It can be deduced from this attitude that, although the Have-not is racked by feelings of envy and resentment, he doesn't show them openly. They rather reflect in his disparaging remarks about those who want more of life, daring to draw on the abundance more than he does.

He frequently lives at the verge of mere subsistence level, not because he couldn't afford more, but because it gives him a feeling of deep satisfaction. If he has money, it doesn't mean much to him. If he has none and, in an emergency, cannot fall back on a nest egg, forced to sponge off his family or the social community, he tries to block this fact from his mind. He hopes to somehow outwit fate by this cleverly contrived method of always acting modest, so that in return fate agrees not to take more than he's got -- that being little enough as it is.

So a Have-not trusts on the generosity of life or the divine powers as a recompense for claiming so little all his life. But he does hope for rich reward in kingdom come at the latest. He can also be seemingly generous in that he likes to give of everything abundant, which is what he is afraid of. If a Have-not should unexpectedly come into money, he will soon distribute it among those he feels need it more than he. If he inherits a cottage, he'll offer room to so many people, that in the end there's hardly any left for him. Should somebody give him a present he can't possibly refuse, he'll sooner or later pass it on to someone else.

Features

An aura of paucity surrounds the Have-not. His clothes, his furnishings, his books, his dishes and his food all have something strangely old-fashioned, an out-of-datedness about them. He likes to wear hand-me-down clothes or outwear his own until they are faded, completely shrunk, or have become totally unfashionable. At the same time, he is mindful that everything should be quite practical and equally suitable for different purposes and opportunities. His flat is small and looks as if furnished with junk recovered from a curbside collection. Oftentimes he has inherited and taken over objects from relatives. It's just that old-fashionness and usedness which he likes about it.

His food consists preferably of dishes he loved eating as a child, when mother didn't have much housekeeping money left or otherwise had few means at her disposal: French toast, milk soup, mashed food, packaged soups and instant blancmange. He generally has an enhanced appetite for childlike sweetish things and pastry.

A Have-not can often be met at flea markets, both as a buyer and vendor. He likes to collect cast-offs and useless items from other people, for example at house clearances or recycling depots.

There is, however, also a Have-not type of considerable means who, similar to the Miser, is unable to maintain a joyful relation with his fortune. The life he leads not only doesn't correspond to his means, but is in contradiction of it. Among them, one often finds so-called dropouts and people who are proud to figure out potential money-savings at every occasion. Also rucksack travelers, considering it their mission to show others how to travel the world on a dollar a day, or people settling just fine on welfare aid by exploiting all opportunities available, yet remaining poor. At the same time, they like to display their eminently frugal lifestyle, carrying it around like a billboard saying: »I don't need anything. I am not like the others.«

Typical physical features of a Have-not are dry facial skin, thin lips, eyes squinted a little, and big hands he often hides behind his back. If he wears dentures, they frequently look as if they were not really fitted for him, wobbling and rattling a little, or exposing several clasps as if patch-worked. The glasses are old-fashioned, perhaps inherited too.

In a conversation, the Have-not will soon mention that there wasn't much one could expect of him, that he himself was really dependent on the generosity of his fellow people. It may also happen that he tries to bargain for special conditions, price-cuts or some other favor from the therapist. He frequently talks about how he finds things far too sophisticated or too expensive or too fastidious. A certain vanity is discernible when he talks about his own modest needs.

The Have-not is frequently vegetarian. He or she has great sympathy for the poor and feeble of this world, people stricken by hunger and drought, for starving children in war-zones and maltreated animals. It's in those that they see themselves reflected, and all the sympathy they deny themselves is revealed there. The Have-not strongly identifies with everyone suffering existential lack, because it's on them that he can sincerely wish all the abundance he doesn't claim for himself, even though he could.

Typical Complaints

Some eating disorders can be observed with the Have-not, especially the habit of eating irregularly and often also inferior food. This is neither due to an addiction structure nor refusal of food. It should rather be investigated what he eats and when, and the motives enticing him to take up too many sweets and high-carbohydrate – filling, childlike foods that burn up so fast that he is nevertheless always ravenous, always staying skinny.

Occasionally, an early onset of old-age diabetes (diabetes type II), but also youth diabetes, can be observed. Stomach cramps and diarrhea can be brought to heal when it is revealed and explained to the patient that these symptoms are related to foodstuffs which were a bit off already and not thrown away, out of thriftiness.

Psychiatrically conspicuous is the frequent fear to be robbed. The Have-not is afraid that his last shirt might get stolen off his back; that he'll end up under a bridge or at least in the poorhouse, totally destitute. Also recorded have been delusions of impoverishment in different stages, accompanied by manic-agitated states. He is often haunted by the idea that his relatives, the tax office or the bank are all out to cheat him of his last pennies and possessions. He doesn't trust financial institutions and keeps his few personal belongings or money stashed away in the house somewhere, then forgetting exactly where, which drives him into a profound despair. Or he is parted from his cash by con artists taking hold of the hoarded fortune.

Indications for Treatment

The first thing the therapist should do is enter into a pact with the Have-not. A clear agreement must be reached on whether the patient or client feels himself worthy of enjoying this treatment, and whether he is also prepared to pay the usual fee for it. It will, of course, rarely happen that a Have-not consults a therapist solely for his ascetic renunciation attitude. His ostensible reasons will initially be typical problems such as sleeplessness, partner conflicts or indigestion. The case history then will soon reveal that there is a deeper correlation, and that the asceticism attitude he somewhat vainly touts is what actually leads to the root of the other complaints.

The therapist is well advised to subdivide the sessions into blocks or units, even when covered by the health insurance, and to reach a new agreement or obtain a renewed promise for each of them respectively. The problem here is that the patient, out of a feeling that he isn't worthy to afford himself this therapy, develops a projection on the therapist not being worthy of consultation.

When it has been positively established that this is a patient with the basic fear of the ascetic Have-not type of Greed – whether male or female – the usual therapy method should be enriched by sweets. To start with, a bowl with inexpensive sweets, i.e. licorice allsorts, jelly babies or candy should be placed on the table within the client's reach. Typically, the patient won't dare take any at first. Then the therapist can encourage him to help himself, almost forcing it on him, and keep him company by picking out something for him- or herself, too. This scheme should be little by little stepped up. At one point, chocolates can be offered, next a piece of pastry or even cream pie. Quite imperceptibly, the patient will get used to correlating the therapeutic sessions with sweetness and affluence. Should the patient raise the issue and remark that this wasn't really common practice, the therapist can, in the interest of the therapeutic objective, claim that he usually has an appetite for something sweet around this time of day himself and needed to boost his blood sugar a little, or something along those lines.

Whenever the patient shows up at the session with a less worn out garment, or giving the impression of having indulged in or treated himself to something, it should be commented on and complimented. As the therapy progresses, a request can be made that at each session, the patient report of at least one incident where he has »made a demand« or has »treated himself« to something.

Any whims of »I don't need any of that!« or of exaggerated reservation, including taking a comfortable seating position or taking up the space that is due him, should be drawn attention to and discussed in the treatment. Although the actual primal Fear of Privation and the stinginess, envy and greed feelings connected with it should best be indirectly addressed or disguised, as long as the therapeutic relationship isn't firmly established yet. Once it is, the therapist may start to show sympathy for his or her early childhood deprivation which brought about this fear of abundance. Because when it comes down to it, a Have-not too longs for abundance. He is just so terribly afraid it could be taken away from him again, that, at least initially, he feels safer owning nothing at all.

Universal Energy 6

Arrogance – Fear of Vulnerability

General

Fear is a phenomenon of the material, worldly sphere. Fear in the way humans experience it doesn't exist in the astral dimension of being. Most important, however, is that fear refers to all phenomena and problems arising from the physical state and the body's will to survive. Hence physicalness, material compactness and the violability of the body are essential aspects of existence which cause fear.

Based on the »priestly« fear vibration of the universal energy 6, a person with Arrogance can remember, better than people with any other primal fear, the invulnerability, the translucent non-physical state of his soul on the astral plane. Due to this specific worldly fear vibration, he has primarily one desire: either return to the fear-free astral plane of non-physicality, or to experience a similarly invulnerable condition here on earth, the way he remembers from his original bodiless state in his astral home. This knowledge is the premise to understanding why to an arrogant person, any intellectual, emotional or even sensory insult feels like a bodily injury or a physically inflicted wound. While his intellect knows that his body is unharmed, the pain is just as burning, as threatening and life endangering as if he had been physically attacked. People who aren't dealing with Arrogance in this life, but with one of the other seven archetypal fears, will find it hard to understand how overwhelming the suffering of an arrogant person is. Once they do, however, they will meet him with more sympathy and react with more serenity to his intense defense mechanisms.

The arrogant person feels himself to be »living on trial«. He escapes into the comforting fantasy that, due to this bond he has inwardly upheld to the astral plane, he could return there any time, should the injuries get so bad as to require such an act. This sort of online connection to the astral world also serves to explain his superiority complex, his feeling of being a step above his fellow men, be it with respect to intelligence, sensibility, or his ability to reason and comprehend. Only someone perceiving himself as a soul being who has accidentally gotten lost here on earth, someone unconsciously comparing himself to angelic purity and innocence, can rise above others in a way that makes them feel small and ugly simply because of their human fallibility.

It is understandable that this archangelic self-image, though hidden from the arrogant person's consciousness, separates him from the mass of »sinners« and »insensitive people.« Based on his self-image, yet without wanting to or realizing it, the arrogant person stylizes himself as a being of a different category. At the same time he has that infinite yearning for what he defines as normalcy, which, to his amazement, other people seem to represent, notably to be able to cope with injuries and insults, to simply ignore things or just not feel and suffer at them. His contempt for this ability and longing for such normalcy condition balance each other.

There are openly arrogant and almost unprepossessing arrogant people. Those classified as openly arrogant are ultimately less afraid to show themselves than those anxiously concealing their sensitivity and vulnerability, fearing to perish of it. The openly condescending individual faces the hostile army like a hero. The timidly vulnerable prefers to hole up in the orderly room or the sick-bay, believing it the only way to survive unharmed the war of energies.

This oversized – and for others often incomprehensible – vulnerability is not only coupled with a heightened, often fearful, intuition. The arrogant person is also inclined to apply this rather cold empathy for defense purposes, or to use his knowledge about his fellow men's Achilles' heel as a weapon of counterattack. They usually have a highly sensitive telepathic scanning ability they develop early in life, helping them circumvent any potential injuries already far in advance. They use their intuition to fearfully sense out people and situations in order to dodge them. Given an inner readiness, however, they are also able to forgive, converting the totally self-absorbed touchiness into a warm-hearted empathy for others, and to sense out and understand situations or circumstances not just fearfully, but openly and uncensored by pride. The distressing over-sensibility can be transformed into a finely tuned sensitivity, to be used and applied constructively.

The Poles of Fear of Vulnerability

– Vain	⟷	Proud +

A healthy pride out of love for the self is a sign of positive self esteem. The positive pole of the Arrogance however refers to a fearful, segregating pride, a pseudo-virtue providing the arrogant person with a means of rescue and refuge by entrenching himself in his castle, which serves two-fold: to punish the ones who hurt him with his cold retreat, and to withdraw behind the walls of pride to hide there. This pride marked by fear pretends to be a virtue and is often mistaken for dignity. The arrogant person falls back on it whenever he's at a loss for other resources or feels unable to maintain a satisfactory contact or communication with the person who hurt him. »I've got my pride too«, he says, considering the relationship to have come to an end once and for all. His primal

Fear of Vulnerability makes him believe that such wounds cannot heal. The option to back down is closed to him as well, believing his pride forbids it. Or he is convinced that it's the »damned duty« of the person whom he painfully feels to be his enemy now to make the first step. If the »guilty« party then does so, he relishes in brusquely rejecting him or her, because it gives him an opportunity to once more fatten his pride on punishing the one eating humble pie by refusing his offer of reconciliation.

This kind of pride has nothing constructive or positive. Yet the arrogant person believes this proud attitude to be his only rescue from fatal injuries: »I don't ever want to have anything to do with this person again!« He is unaware of the injury he is inflicting upon himself by his hardened pride. It separates him from pardon, sympathy and the readiness to talk about his hurt. In his fear, he is unable to recognize that he has added a grave self-insult to the initial slight. He believes that unless he retreats behind the wall of rejection, he would be forced to hold out the other cheek, inevitably collecting still more blows. That there are other possibilities of contact after an insult, he rarely realizes. But these can only be investigated if he overcomes his proud stance in humility and shows his wounds. Such an act is linked with a signal to the supposed aggressor – who is perhaps genuinely unaware of his offense – that a careful rapprochement is desired which would make a conversation, a gentle touch, a forgiving gesture possible again.

His fellow men can often only suspect why he has distanced from them in hurt pride, not calling any more, changing to the other side of the street with a stony face or breaking off contact in some other way. Occasionally, this can be merely an inner or energetic distance. It happens between parents and children, between lovers and also in business life between colleagues who, although they have no choice but to continue seeing or being physically close to each other, completely interrupt the genuine flow of contact. Married couples can live side by side this way and sleep in the same bed for years and decades, while in truth one of them has retired behind the wall of his pride long ago. They are unable to find a way to open up again, abandoning themselves to the other and show their love. Behind his wall of pride, the arrogant person torments himself in his pain and longs for someone to finally pry the walls of his prison open.

The negative pole of this archetypal fear describes a condition of vanity permitting him to always feel in the right whenever any conflict between him and his fellow people develops. The vain arrogant person sees only his own point of view, his interests, his concerns, unsuspecting that his vanity is only a sign of his apprehensive helplessness. It keeps him from including his fellow men with their feelings and sensitivities in his perception. He believes that only he is sensitive, only he would know what was going on and who was in the right, and that of course, is always him.

The complacent individual only revolves around himself. He contemplates his ego in his conceited delicateness and nurtures his vulnerability and actually suffered injuries alike. He keeps coming back to the incident again and again, enjoying himself in the role of not wanting to forgive, even taking pride in his loneliness. This vanity also refers to capabilities and talents. The vain person always compares with others to his advantage. Or he shuns comparison altogether, because it is beyond his imagination that others might possibly have more or even better things to offer than he does.

The vain arrogant person is just as aloof as the proud one, the difference being that it's less difficult to approach him emotionally once the mask of vanity has been removed with some effort from his essential nature. Although that's something which can't be accomplished by his fellow men; only fate or the craving for true love and real closeness, having developed behind this mask, can achieve this. And only the vain person himself will be able to peek from behind his mask and show his true self, which in turn can only

happen when he meets someone who sincerely and wholeheartedly wants to see his true face.

His complacency and pride make fellow beings out to be stupid
and insensitive. The vanity inherent in this attitude – just like the
pride of the positive pole – leads to segregation. Segregation is the
keyword the arrogant person should put his focus on once he feels
ready to work on and curb the anxiety lurking behind his assumed
superiority or vanity. The annoyance his attitude causes and the
resulting unpleasant feedback the arrogant person must deal with
may be motivation for him to change something.

The Released Potential

Arrogance as a fear characteristic of the »priestly« energy 6 is predisposed to transgressing limits and maintaining a strong bond to
the transcendental sphere. An arrogant person willing to get closer
to his fellow humans again must learn, in a first step, to actually
feel his fear, then carefully and gradually reducing it to surmount
his limits. He will then make a wonderful discovery: The greater
his forgiving love and closeness to his fellow humans is, the finer
his perception becomes to the spheres lying beyond the human
condition and emphatic humanness in general. His sensitivity, his
intuition, his ability to let himself be inspired by the divine and
transcendental supra-humanness will increase by the day.

Bound in arrogance is a high permeability which, in the released
state, has not only that painful, detrimental effect, but can also be
applied to the benefit of the respective individual and moreover of
his or her fellow men. A mediumistic susceptibility will automatically develop when the arrogant person leaves the barriers and
walls raised around him by pride and complacency behind. Yet he
can't simply shatter or break through them. He must actively step
out from behind them and reach out for life, for the people around

him, for his next neighbor. If he does that, he will simultaneously feel how the vulnerability previously tormenting him will change into a high, vibrating sensitivity. It will enable him to let the Divine's infinite readiness to forgivingly accept all human beings also shower down on himself. Then, the arrogant person too will be able to forgive and absolve, without thereby infringing on his natural pride and loving affection for the self.

Three Types of Fear of Vunerability

1. The **Snob** lets his fellow men know at each opportunity that he is above them and that they may, at best, approach him on their knees. He instills a feeling of inferiority in them they don't otherwise have, flashing his superior qualities and skills at them whenever he can to make them feel small and keep them in their place.

2. The **Avenger Angel** harbors his injured feelings until he has detected a weak spot in his enemy. Even if it takes years, he hopes for the day on which he can restore the balance of his energies again by inflicting an equally hurtful insult or some act of revenge.

3. The **Mimosa** is characterized specifically by a certain vanity, founded on the fact that this arrogant type senses everything much more acutely, delicately and precisely than most other people. The Mimosa is proud to be so oversensitive and capitalizes on it. It conveys to its environment that one must treat it with infinite care. At the least occasion threatening to damage this sensitivity, it immediately retreats into its cotton wool wrapping.

Type 1: The Snob

This arrogant fear type thinks himself better than everyone around him on all accounts. In his eyes, they are miserable and inferior, neither sensitive nor smart enough to meet his standards. »Better« in his understanding is everything he considers valuable in himself. This might be his knowledge, experience, talents, his insight and logical skills, and furthermore a lot of things not of his own power, such as physical merits, intelligence or social origin. Although endowed with it from birth, he uses these faculties as if they were wholly attributable to his personal efforts.

The Snob lets others feel that they can't compete with him. They simply aren't a patch on him and shouldn't even try. This works out fine till such time when the Snob realizes that he has put off, one after the other, all the people he deems important, and that he's standing all alone now. Because when there's nobody up to par with him, then soon no one will want to play with him either, thereby offering some gesture of communication or contact. Initially, the resulting solitude is a natural consequence the Snob is ready to accept, because he is in some way aware that his self-image resembles that of a nobleman or princess. By their high birth, they naturally stand above others and mustn't expect to enjoy closeness or the affection of the mob.

But as time goes by, usually toward the end of young adulthood, the Snob realizes that solitude contains just as painful an injury as to be underestimated by his fellow men, something the Snob believes to be subjected to all the time. No one seems to properly recognize his personal qualities, his wonderful skills and competence, his high ethical standards and his extreme sensitivity. And hardly anyone seems to show consideration for it either; he must spell it all out himself, rubbing it into their faces. So in a huff, he retires into the high tower of his hurt pride. With age, however, he cannot fail to notice, if grudgingly, that other people too have their merits, possessing positive or even high-value qualities. And, as he is now trying to reach out for them, painfully bumps into the glass barrier of solitude he has uprighted between himself and others.

As the years go by, the Snob notices that his relations and ties with his fellow men didn't quite develop as successfully as he had imagined. Lovers, feeling rebuffed, leave after some time. Friends have to muster a lot of energy to digest the insults the Snob has inflicted upon them. The condescending and arrogant person notices that he is getting lonelier all the time. He increasingly realizes that the people whom he deems attractive or lovable do not turn away from him because they are too stupid to recognize his qualities, but that he has caused them suffering. He's got to face the fact that his fellow men's reactions have something to do with him, with his own primal fear of closeness and the potential injuries inherent therein.

This is the time when it's up to those who – despite various rejections – flattened their noses on the glass pane to see where the Snob has retreated to, and fetch a glass cutter. They can cut a small hole into this glass wall, just big enough to extend a hand through, which the Snob can seize. Should someone have the only seemingly helpful idea of completely shattering this glass barrier, a new and much thicker, bullet-proof glass plate would rise again within seconds.

So caution is advisable in dealing with the Snob. Circumspection may also require that a partner ready to accept, love and free the Snob from his prison of solitude must exaggerate a little, the same way the Snob does in the embellishment of his self-image. For a little while then, a lover may exaggerate a bit in asserting to the Snob his true or putative qualities, boost his grandness, praise the fantastic wealth of knowledge and admire his or her supernatural beauty. Though it mustn't be with tongue-in-cheek; rather in such a way that the Snob himself can't help but smile to himself a little, feeling: »well, this is really a bit out of my league! I am, after all, not SO indescribably wonderful, audacious or brilliant as the person aspiring to love me makes me out to be.«

Communicating with a Snob isn't easy. In a conversation it will inadvertently happen that they make some arrogant, hurtful remark or express criticism meant to be constructive but having a destructive effect. The Snob simply can't keep his opinions to himself for long. It takes him only seconds to note everything which in his view is imperfect and needing improvement, in fact, must be improved, by his hand of course. He radiates the message: »I'd handle it all quite differently, you really aren't up to it!« Though he will seldom express it in words, it nevertheless comes across as a condescending energy.

In unknown surroundings, among people he is unfamiliar with, the Snob withdraws energetically. While he is intellectually very present, physically he is mysteriously non-existent, as if covered by a camouflage coating, except for his hyperactive, critical brain. He unconsciously acts as if he was, temporarily, returning to the astral plane, which he regards as his true home and sanctuary.

The Snob is surrounded by a circle of acquaintances who, in a distant way, admire him; but he has very few or no close friends. Only seldom does he cultivate close relationships that might protect, comfort and carry him, delivering him from his inner solitude. He also keeps at a careful distance people wishing to share his life with him, signalling: »Don't get too close to me; I'm afraid you might hurt me. I'd like to let you come closer, but I just don't see how it could work. I wouldn't survive any deep insult.« He frequently concludes a kind of non-aggression pact with the people sharing his life, unconsciously threatening them with total retreat or definite separation, should they hurt or not sufficiently admire him. So, whoever loves a Snob needs much equanimity and patience.

Features

The face of a Snob is and remains strangely motionless, even with stronger emotions. He's wearing a mask which seems to say: »None of this really bothers me.« The snootiness is also expressed in a slightly thrown back head. The Snob is often the leptosome type, long-limbed and of slim silhouette. The corners of the mouth are slightly drooping, with pronounced nasal wings which quiver when excited, and often relatively large, diaphanous auricles.

He or she tries to keep the high sensitivity in check by various devices. One often finds strong smokers among them, or people permitting themselves little sleep, drinking lots of coffee or harming themselves with alcohol and drugs. It allows them to flee into a dream world where no one can hurt them. They have discovered that these agents make them less sensitive. They desensitize and numb themselves in many ways, so they don't need to remain watchful of injuries all the time. As a compensatory protection against being inundated by their fears of »feeling too much«, snobs often react insensitively towards the sensitivities of others.

A Snob usually values aesthetics in all things. He considers himself a connoisseur of art and literature, of exquisite foods and outstanding wines; it differentiates his sophisticated taste from the insensibility of others. By surrounding himself with noble and rare things, he can see himself mirrored at least in those. It boosts his self-esteem.

It's not by chance that his nose plays an important role in this context. It is often a prominent physiognomic feature, serving the Snob first off to smell already from afar any danger looming. Secondly, this organ helps him ferret out how and when defense must be deployed, and thirdly, he likes to wrinkle it at anything he disapproves of or considers inadequate.

Snobs eyeball their opposites disparagingly, making them feel as if somehow inappropriately dressed, badly coiffed or overweight.

He himself is often a little overdressed for the occasion. His outfit is in any case carefully groomed and styled for hours, sometimes also a bit dandy-like. One can feel that he has spent some time thinking – also fearfully – about his public effect. A perfect outer appearance makes him believe to be less vulnerable.

Typical complaints

The Snob is characterized by a general thin-skinnedness and neurasthenia, his frail nervous system susceptible to overload. He is not resilient, apt to break down even at smallest conflicts and falling ill in difficult situations. Above all, he is prone to auto-immune diseases.

He is so over-sensitive and in need of protection that he sees the potential of getting injured by people or situations everywhere, even if generally considered harmless. And not only emotionally, but also physically, e.g. by some accident, bacteria or loud noises. As a consequence, he retreats so much from the outer world as to reducing any contact to bare necessities, or cutting it altogether.

In contrast to the Mimosa, the Snob veils his self-isolation with allegedly required studies, the conception of a big-time artistic scoop or a serious illness. These pretenses serve him to justify himself and his need for seclusion. The isolation might go as far as hardly leaving the house anymore, having food and other conveniences delivered to the doorstep. The windows don't get opened for fear of a draught; he completely holes up inside his four walls – in short, a mild form of agoraphobia. Panic attacks are also part of the syndromes of an overly self-isolating Snob. Although his fear of potential panic attacks which might occur if he abandons the sheltering cocoon of his home is greater than the actual frequency of such incidents.

Psychosomatic skin problems can be observed, particularly psoriasis, first developing or aggravating in adulthood. These irritations usually show on his hands and face, contributing to his desire not to show himself in public any more. Also manifesting may be an increasing addiction to computer games, substituting for live human contact.

Indications for treatment

At the beginning of a therapy, the therapist should be prepared to assure the Snob of his growing and unrestrained admiration. He or she should bring up whatever seems in the least admirable or commendable in the Snob. It's the only way that the distrust and snooty reservation of the person seeking help can be disarmed. It is crucial, especially at the beginning of the therapeutic relation, that the Snob not develop the feeling that the »inferior« and »insensitive« therapist was underestimating him in his grandness, in his abilities and talents. It would lead to a baleful downhill gradient in their relations. The patient would soon adopt the therapist's role, also knowing and feeling capable of doing everything better. What's more, the patient would disclose the essential facts only in homoeopathic doses, merely opening up at the surface.

When it has been established that the therapist fully appreciates and recognizes the patient's qualities, it is possible to cut one or the other small opening out of the glass wall. Through this little hole, the patient – who has come to seek assistance because he feels sad and lonely – can whisper his need, or seize a helping hand and find some human warmth. Oftentimes, a knowing look or a gentle, unobtrusive touch can help more than so many words.

The Snob would love to withdraw entirely behind his outstanding intellectual skills or his talents. He doesn't know any differently than that people respond to his mental offers. This situation, however, requires a sensitive understanding, signaling beyond words and reasoning: »I sympathize with you. I think highly of you. I'll be there for you even if you hurt me.« Because that is something the Snob will invariably try to do sooner or later: subconsciously test the therapist. He wants to find out how he reacts to his insults or vexation tactics and whether he really stands by him, even when the Snob openly reveals his condescending feelings and comments.

Type 2: The Avenger Angel

This type of arrogant person has – based on his experience and bolstered by his emotional structure – turned the injuries suffered in the course of his life into rage and anger. The hurt has been channeled into aggression. He is generally known as someone not easy to deal with.

His usual reaction to insults is as follows: When he sees no chance for revenge in the present situation, he will abruptly retreat, completely breaking off contact, while waiting like a spider until the fly gets caught in its net. With opponents still capable of delivering him a broadside, either now or in future, he'll exercise patience, even act harmless, until his revenge is fulfilled. This revenge can be extremely subtle or, especially at a younger soul age, clearly targeted to severely damage his adversary's health, life, property or self-worth.

The Avenger Angel is convinced that his need to establish a balance of injuries is quite understandable and justified. He proceeds according to the Old Testament's commandment of »an eye for an eye, a tooth for a tooth.« He imagines himself in the function of a divine authority who, by an act of revenge, establishes a new harmony and justice again on earth. At least that is how he sincerely feels and believes. This again reflects the »priestly« energy 6 of this fear characteristic. Once he has taken revenge – no matter how –

he feels an inner peace at last, which failed to manifest before the act had been accomplished: »revenge is sweet!«

The Avenger Angel realizes only seldom or too late that the injury originally inflicted on him was actually very minor in nature compared to his massive act of revenge. While he acutely feels the pain of his own hurt, wanting to cause his adversary an injury which is at least as painful, he is unaware that, due to his great vulnerability, he has largely misjudged the cause at the root of this dispute, making a mountain out of a molehill. So he wants to inflict an equally mountainous pain to his enemy, who, for his part, failing to understand the intricacies behind it, feels this revenge coming like a blow out of the blue.

The problem for the Avenger Angel is that often, a long time has passed between his own hurt feelings and his act of vengeance as atonement for the wrong-doing, so that his fellow men can no longer recognize the energetic link. The Avenger Angel in contrast hoards and nurtures his injury like something precious, because his craving for revenge seemingly gives him strength. His maxim is: »Just you wait, I'll pay you back for it one day.«

At the same time, and just like the Snob, he tries to avoid admitting his own oversized vulnerability or the importance of what happened, even to himself. He will seldom discuss it with others, because it doesn't quite match his self-image of a »higher« entity to be so vulnerable, rather than being above other people's meanness, jealousy, pettiness, fallibility or some other imperfection. Like the Snob, he feels himself standing way above the lowly demeanor and reactions of the masses in his self-image. He is absolutely convinced that he himself would never do such a thing as what hurt him so. He is oblivious of the fact that his craving for revenge, harbored for years, or the actual revenge itself, contains the same measure of meanness and places him on the same level of humanness as his fellow men. For him, vengeance is nothing but a needed, just compensation.

The Avenger Angel often has an ardent temperament and fierce look (as represented for example in many of Hollywood actor Clint Eastwood's roles). He carefully registers what happens around him and often feels injured even when the attack was directed at others. It gives him an opportunity to act as the avenger of all the disenfranchised and wounded. He strongly takes sides, generalizing and activating his aggressive traits in a way that can also serve him professionally, for example as a union official or an animal conservationist. The Avenger Angel finds ample opportunities to live out his resentment. Among them, one often finds people seeking atonement for what has been done to their ancestors by war, persecution, deceit or medical malpractice.

The Avenger Angel is frequently a powerful, daring and often courageous person, with a more or less thick layer of self-righteousness when it comes to his own interests. He always feels to be in the right and makes no bones about it. The Snob in contrast will be more restrained; he too is convinced of course that his cause is vindicated, but he doesn't necessarily voice it. An Avenger Angel might be able to forgive, but he can't forget, and one shouldn't be surprised if, even after years, he scratches the scab off an old wound again, presenting it anew as if it had happened yesterday.

The »priestly« quality of his energy can be perceived not only in his need to execute worldly justice in the name of God, but also in a certain openness in general contact with others. The Avenger Angel has no interest in erecting a glass barrier between himself and his fellow beings. He actually keeps in touch, watching his future revenge victim from afar; but he also needs closeness. He needs times of peace or armistice, all the more to better aim his strike. He isn't, of course, aware of all this. But one should always be prepared for the Avenger Angel to rake a stale topic up again in an unguarded moment, to drag out some slight believed to be long forgotten and unexpectedly establish some sort of compensating justice. The structure of an Avenger Angel is vigorous and geared to life. Unlike the Snob or the Mimosa, he doesn't segregate from reality and the world.

Features

As a rule, the Avenger Angel is of powerful vitality and sound health. He may be easily hurt and thus emotionally highly sensitive, but physically he is stable. His senses react fast and vigorously. He feels less threatened by external factors such as noise, odors, the weather, medical side effects, allergies and other reactions than the two other arrogant types. His immune system is intact. At most he suffers from auto-immune reactions, as his defense is excessively active, attacking instead of protecting him in its over-reaction. This can also be understood symbolically, because ultimately, the Avenger Angel does himself a disservice with his craving for revenge, resulting also in self-harm.

He is often the sporty type who greatly benefits from exercise and competition, discipline, rivalry and self-assertion, to divert the pent-up rage. His bearing is straight and taut; the look slightly sinister and determined. The brow is frequently marked by two vertical, so-called anger lines. The Avenger Angel is endowed with great endurance, also physically. He is untiring when activity is called for, often needing only little sleep. When forced into inactivity, i.e. by an accident, illness or some situation that makes him feel locked, he gets disagreeable and sometimes develops a depression with aggressive behavior.

His imagination likes to run wild in general acts of vengeance. He loves those reports in the paper about someone »paying back« another. He can show surprisingly little empathy for victims of criminal acts because, secretly at any rate, he feels that the victims probably somehow deserved what has been done to them as some sort of punishment.

Obviously, most Avenger Angels will never actually execute their acts of revenge construed in their minds, recognizing that the original cause and their desire for revenge are not quite in proportion. But their fantasies of revenge are often intense and suffice to give them a deep satisfaction. Still, should the opportunity arise to adequately retaliate against an insult from long ago, it will be gladly seized.

Typical complaints

As children, Avenger Angels often suffer from ADS (attention deficit syndrome). It's not usually characterized by high motor unrest, the child rather seems to be absorbed in dark thoughts. But whenever one tries to force the child to rest or ask it to behave quietly and demurely, it provokes his or her need to do the opposite and take revenge for the reprimands and restrictions. Instead of concentrating on the activities expected of it, like studying, clearing away the toys or obeying, the child indulges in half-conscious or unconscious vengeance fantasies. It's just bursting to smash everything to pieces because it has been ordered to do something it is unable to or doesn't feel like doing. So as a youngster, the Avenger Angel seems rebellious and somber, often earning him harsh punishment, which only intensifies his cravings for revenge. Teenagers unable to deal constructively with this overpowering desire for revenge may turn criminal. They thrash others for no apparent reason, fast to pull a knife they usually carry on them, or play what they call tricks on people, often ending up in nasty results and a still nastier awakening after the deed.

With advanced adult age, the Avenger Angel tends to develop ulcers or pancreas problems up to early diabetes, even when of lean constitution. It's a response of the metabolism to the constant tension in the upper abdomen, because the solar plexus suffers most from the permanent fantasies of revenge. Whatever seems to produce a superficial relaxation on a mental plane actually compacts like armor in the solar plexus, making it difficult to relax this energy centre.

With some Avenger Angels, the self-righteousness expressed in their need for revenge leads to seemingly unmotivated aggressive acts, even running amok and killing their parents. This is especially true for those who previously never voiced their strong aggressions, having gotten totally lost in their cravings for vengeance instead. Others opt for less destructive methods to defuse their rage, writing crime or horror stories, directing films with vengeance as the motive for murder, or turning to professional occupations as surgeon, forensic pathologist, law-enforcement officer or public prosecutor. The armed forces too are a befitting field of activity, though they should beware of exercising excessive rigor or cruelty.

In psychiatric institutions, the Avenger Angel is found among those who feel possessed by Satan or see themselves as his disciples. The guilt feelings a person develops when he senses his thoughts incessantly revolving around revenge, blood and thunder, may actually turn on himself with severe auto-aggressive acts. Or else he converts them into a projection, namely the delusion to execute the orders of an evil, omnipotent voice, commanding him to think and do what he himself considers bad, sinful or wicked.

Indications for Treatment

When treating an arrogant Avenger Angel, the therapist should be prepared to impartially and without prejudice tolerate the client's revenge fantasies, encourage their verbal expression and to bear the detailed embellishment of these fantasies. Only when the therapist is ready to hear what really goes on in the mind of his patient, without moralizingly commenting on it with words, facial expression or body language, can he actively contribute to unearthing the roots of these destructive needs in the memories of early-child-hood insults, of mockery and abuse. Medical treatment assistance only makes sense once the original pain has been activated, and the bitter tears kept in check by his helpless fantasies of vengeance can flow at last. A good means of support can consist in encouraging the patient to take up some powerful kind of sport, such as hammer-throwing, shot-put or boxing. Particularly martial arts are helpful, also for children, to discharge the bottled-up aggressions.

However, more important than talking about his cravings for revenge, or in an alternating cycle as seems fit, are physical measures, such as the permission to thump on a pillow or thump bag, or treatment of the upper abdomen. The latter can range from a gentle, circling massage, up to an energetic transmission at a distance of 10 centimeters. Relaxation will be promoted with heat packs on the upper abdomen and liver compresses. It is indispensable though to encourage the patient to voice the often dreadful thoughts and fantasies surfacing to the consciousness during this appeasing treatment. At the conclusion of each energetic treatment session, the therapist should firmly hold the patient's feet for a couple of minutes. Otherwise the patient might lose himself again in his revenge ideas instead of anchoring in the reality of his possible relaxation and grounding.

At the outset, the therapist should supportively respond to the idea that the original perpetrator or perpetrators indeed deserve punishment. Later on, he can gently lead the patient to accept that there is no need to execute this punishment himself, but that God or destiny will take care of restoring justice, even if that justice looks different from what the patient loves to imagine. There is nothing more harmful than trying to coax the Avenger Angel into lovingly forgive where he can't forgive, to be lenient and kind when he doesn't feel that way inside. Also, under no circumstances, may one agree when the patient tries to corroborate his aggressive impulses and the memory of early injuries with a theory about karmic bonds. The reason is that the notion of a karmic justification causes nothing but a dangerous sublimation of his revenge thoughts and the associated guilt feelings. It doesn't lead to a true liberation from the burden of his revenge feelings, but merely absolves from responsibility.

Type 3: The Mimosa

The extreme sensitivity, permeability, delicateness and vulnerability of this type of arrogant person are discernible from afar. This aura of fragility is applied like a protective spell, designed to prevent injuries and conflicts or grievous and gruff dealings with others to happen at all. The over-sensitivity is transmuted into an inaudible message: »Do treat me gently, I'm really too delicate for this harsh world.« The Mimosa generally represents what has become known as »HSP« i.e., highly sensitive person, in pertinent literature.

While the two other types of Arrogance will hide their sensitivity in one way or another, the Mimosa actually uses this quality, deliberately and specifically with the purpose to achieve a certain degree of invulnerability in life: »Touch me not!« The sensitivity is frequently applied as a personal disaster control tool. Another possibility is total retreat, so that the individual seems to be residing in a kind of permanent inner bunker, into which hardly anyone may penetrate. Contacts are mostly avoided, because a simple sneeze or a little cough will suffice to unpleasantly affect the sensitivity of this type of extremely vulnerable, haughty person.

The issue here isn't primarily injuries or insults, but fearful thin-skinnedness. It's a special form of Arrogance which does create a connection to the personal environment, insofar as the Mimosa always demands from others maximum considerateness, quiet and gentleness. They are also required to either negate or put their own needs last or, at least – I beg you, please! – to act them out in some other place. So, in a subtle way, the Mimosa puts the people around it under permanent pressure to pull themselves together and avoid anything which might affect or disturb its high sensitivity, frequently manifest in somatic disorders such as neuropathic conditions, allergies or a high irritability of all senses.

The Mimosa is endowed with an exceptionally finely tuned sensorial system. A construct of telepathic aerials is extended towards the outside world to pick up in advance any signals – or even just the potentiality – of whatever hazard. The Mimosa anxiously strobes possible sources of danger or threats to retreat into its cotton wool wrap or snail's shell in a flash, should these menaces actually take shape. The Mimosa feels virtually attacked by everything and everybody.

Options to toughen up against this over-anxiety are rarely made use of, since in the self-concept and sense of self-worth of a Mimosa, specifically this oversensitivity is rated as a high-value commodity that may by no means be diminished. The truth is, though, that a person of the Mimosa type will get even more sensitive, the more he protects himself and wraps up in cotton wool, instead of exposing himself to the mostly harmless temperatures of shared humanity.

Besides, the tender aura of a Mimosa is so vulnerable in itself, hardly anyone would intentionally insult or hurt it. Everyone respects the bone-china-like, fragile constitution as represented in a Mimosa. It would actually require quite an emotional rawness to treat this particular kind of arrogant person carelessly or brutally. But such roughnecks will not often be found around the Mimosa, of that it makes sure. When such a delicate individual emerges from his protective cover, gradually shedding his fear of being hurt, he has a high capacity of responding to the sensitivities and vulnerabilities of his fellow men. He feels what they feel. He can empathize with and comfort them like a priest in a prison camp talking to his fellow prisoners, helping them find new strength.

The Mimosa frequently has a history as an energetic outsider, because parents, class-mates or colleagues prepared to be considerate and cut back their own manifestations of life all the time so as not to intrude on the Mimosa are hard to find. Whether it's been bullying at work or made the laughing stock and thrashed in school, or whether it was stigmatized as the black sheep of the family is interchangeable now. The hypersensitive arrogant person needs a boosting of his easily wounded sense of self. So turning the touchiness into sensitiveness is like spinning straw to gold, and in adult age, the Mimosa will frequently be able to convert its vulnerability into empathy.

Features

Both men and women are of delicate phenotype. The tender-limbed constitution of this individual and his thin-skinnedness give it a fragile expression, independent of his or her actual physique.

The skin is often translucent, making the subtlety of feeling also visually obvious. The skin is not only sensitive with regard to allergies, but also in contact with rough fabrics, metals, and any other kinds of substances. The hearing is frequently highly acute, so that music can take on a special comfort function. The sense of smell is also more keenly pronounced than with most other people. Since the taste buds of a Mimosa are just as sensitive as the rest of the sensory structure, it attaches great importance to pure, unprocessed foods. Gourmets can sometimes be found among them, or wine connoisseurs and professional food tasters. Their delicate palate is a useful faculty to have as a sommelier or top chef. The sensory sophistication of this arrogant person will be reflected in everything he surrounds himself with and enjoys, selecting his garments, food and furnishings by the motto: »Quality over quantity« or »rather have less but only the finest.«

The Mimosa is moreover affected by varying temperatures, changing air pressure, a change of air in general, by sunlight or foods. It will be under the weather and predisposed to illness as long as it doesn't cut back a bit on the sometimes considerable ego gain from its sensitivity. It frequently has mediumistic or clairvoyant capabilities. Its aerials are like satellite dishes receiving hundreds of programs, but can only seldom be decoded to intelligible information.

The Mimosa likes best of all to be alone. It accepts the society of its fellow men rather than seeking or needing it for its own well-being. The home is a shelter zone and often resembles a bunker energetically, supposed to not only offer protection against physical attacks, but also against radiation damages. The Mimosa complains about countless unpleasant, yes, hardly tolerable, interferences by terrestrial radiation, underground water veins, magnetic fields or electro-smog. It perceives sounds hardly anyone else can hear. It suffers from vibrations emanating from places or unpleasant vibes of people. These oversensitive perceptions are, however, not completely imaginary. They often are indeed valid, even if its fellow men can rarely fathom such hypersensitivity.

The Mimosa can be considerably shy of consulting a doctor. It anticipates that no doctor will understand it or appreciate its sensitivities, and that he'll surely treat it improperly with orthodox medicine. Healers working on an energetic level and alternative practitioners will therefore play a major role in the life of a Mimosa, sometimes ending up in dependency relationships. Because these delicate individuals rarely feel understood, they are prone to fall for charlatans who promise them too much.

Typical complaints

Many a Mimosa suffers from hyperacusis, tinnitus and sudden hearing loss. When the subjective feeling of noise becomes tormenting, it can often be attributed to a lack of minerals – particularly magnesia – due to a disorder of the intestines' resorption capacity. Mimosas are afflicted by allergies and food incompatibilities just as often as by chronic bowel diseases. The mucous membranes are as oversensitive as its outer skin. Stomatitis, conjunctivitis, mycoses, sun allergies, strong reactions to chlorine-treated pool water and the like are part of the somatization symptoms. So it's quite understandable that this person tries to protect from all these negative impacts. The drugs generally administered to treat these unpleasant effects often lead to further incompatibilities and unwanted reactions. Autoimmune diseases, such as multiple sclerosis and systemic lupus erythematosus should also be verified as to their origin in connection with this fear type.

Psychiatric syndromes are extreme social phobia, compulsive washing from fear of pathogens and infections, excessive disgust of dirt and smells, and a rejection especially of one's own body and its secretions. Suicidal wishes can be observed to escape the burden of extreme sensitivity and permanent threat by the hostile outside world. In an apparent reversal of the super-sensitivity on all levels, sometimes auto-aggressive behaviors develop, e.g. the need for self-slashing and other self-inflicted injuries. It can evolve as the consequence of a preceding, psychological strategy to eliminate all other intolerable physical sensations and emotions. Further symptoms can be »hysterical« paralyses, loss of eyesight and similar means of the psyche to protect itself from the menacing influences of people and the environment.

Indications for treatment

The Mimosa is more apt to seek help from a similarly ectoplasmically oriented health practitioner or psychotherapist interested in esoterism, rather than turning to classical psychoanalysis or behavior therapy. For a successful therapy it is in any case indispensable that the patient feels at ease and can relax in a positive environment based on trust. At the start of the therapy, the therapist should be particularly considerate of the patient's well-being – even if it requires some extra effort. So the therapist should repeatedly ask the client if he needs anything else, whether he would like to sit somewhere else, if it's warm enough or if there was anything else one could do to ensure that he or she is comfortable. A basic premise is to genuinely assure the patient that his sensitivities are totally accepted and shall not be eliminated by the therapy. The goal is rather to help him or her live better with them and transform them into a state that makes this extreme sensitiveness not only a cause of suffering but also a sensuous joy.

Since the Mimosa suffers particularly from the physical reactions of its sensitivity and permeability, a conversational approach will always have to include the many physical aspects, if necessary in cooperation with holistic or naturopathic practitioners. In this respect it is advisable to adopt measures which hold the prospect of better insulating the great emotional permeability, just as that of the mucous membranes, tissue and vessels, e.g. with appropriate homeopathic substances. Even when his skin, his bowels and blood vessels have become less permeable as a result, the patient will retain enough sensitivity that can be beneficially applied for the patient himself and others. But he will no longer suffer from the everyday loss of energy preventing him to do just that. Given the case, it may be helpful to administer mineral supplements to the patient via infusions and treat possible bowel inflammation. Other alternative methods are also adequate to reduce the general systemic permeability. Mimosas usually don't like acupuncture, but they do react positively to acupressure.

It is important to teach the Mimosa to accept its sensitiveness rather than parrying it with self-hatred and rejection. By the same token, one can show them that it is something really precious and of value, instead of regarding it only as a nuisance and agony. This will assist the Mimosa in developing more love and acceptance of the self. It also helps direct the energy available to a practical implementation of his potential for the most subtle perceptions, also on a mediumistic level, and concentrate less on protection and defense. Avoided should be any kind of mockery, even seemingly well-meant, and any comparison with people who are more »thick-skinned«, supposedly enabling them to better cope with life.

It's very comforting for the Mimosa to symbolically compare itself with some rare and precious object, e.g. a fine object of art that is fragile and delicate, with an exceptionally beautiful plant or an exquisite old wine.

Universal Energy 7

Impatience – Fear of Omission

General

Before starting out on their path of incarnation, souls exist in time-less realms. Thus it is a totally new and confusing experience for them to enter into the earthly sphere of time (and space). Where before there was no duration, existence as an incarnated human being is now limited to a specific time period, and the life which has just begun may be short or long. All souls inhabiting a human body must experience and want to explore the phenomenon of time; they also desire to explore the space in which they exist. But a soul preparing to experience the primal Fear of Omission with the characteristic of Impatience is going to deal in a specific and particularly intense way with the dynamics of time and space.

To an impatient person, dealing with the phenomenon of time rather feels as if time were dealing with him. Time is his lord and master; it influences his actions and emotions. It also determines his way of organizing his every day life and his festive days. The need to benefit as much as possible from the limited time seemingly apportioned to him and to live it as intensely as possible – that's what moulds the impatient person's attitude to his present earthly existence. To him, time is a most precious commodity and he must not waste it. Nothing is more valuable, nothing causes him more worry and more joy than the idea to use time as profitably as is at all practicable.

Hence, the impatient person is very intolerant of people who seem to squander time, do not make proper use of time, do not appreciate time. The notion behind this attitude is that whatever needs doing must be done as quickly as feasible in order to gain time for even more activities.

Energy seven is on the plane of activity, constantly pushing the impatient person to DO things. Even though they may only exist as an idea, a vision, a plan in the back of his mind at the moment, they must nevertheless be dealt with and put into realization equally soon. So, viewed from a perspective outside this specific fear characteristic, the impatient person is under the illusion that time can indeed be lost or gained. He believes that he can manipulate the time span apportioned to him or even influence the essentially neutral phenomenon of time itself.

The impatient person subconsciously imagines he could actually change something about time and duration. He hopes to squeeze out more and more time for further activities if he encumbered himself with enough undertakings to be accomplished within the working time or life span assigned to him. The impatient individual's idea of bliss consists in temporizing eighty minutes from one single hour, or to master a job in two to three hours that takes other people a day or two to complete. He is always spurred on by that vague, but enticing, illusion to be able to gain time that way. Yet, he is far from using to his advantage what he has supposedly gained or to have a rest from his efficient bustle. Instead, he moves up what he had originally planned for tomorrow, next month, or for the years following his retirement and presses it into that precious gap, into that extra period captured, aiming to gain in this way even more time. It's the pursuit of an enticing venture that is standing before his inner eyes like a huge lottery jackpot.

Just as he seeks satisfaction in winning time, he worries at the idea of losing time. He doesn't like waiting; stalling makes him very nervous. He feels cut off from his calling when what is supposed to happen doesn't happen right away, forcing him to kill that time so precious to him. Haste is a life elixir to him.

But even to impatient people it happens once in a while that they chance to have time on their hands, unforeseen, beckoning them like a God's gift. For an impatient person, it's an extreme challenge to not reject this gift of God, but to receive it with open arms, lingering for once in that offered, given moment, allowing the phenomenon of »time to spend« to really get close to him as a valuable experience.

Time management is of paramount importance to every impatient individual, no matter which type. He constantly asks himself whether there is enough time and frequently overestimates his measure of time. »Is it much too early, is it far too late? Can I still squeeze some activity into the time frame available? Do I have to bide my time in frenzied impatience or make haste in a frenzied rush?« To an impatient person, such considerations are quite normal. It's only in contrast with people who are not concerned with this fear of omission that he realizes there might be a more leisurely way of living. However, he feels less fascination but rather concern and restlessness in view of this alternative. It doesn't in the least correspond to his idea of a meaningful and efficiently used life. He burns the candle at both ends and likes it just that way.

The impatient individual is usually aware that he can sometimes sink into an apathy or lethargy similar to a depression before some important decision. It is the fear to overlook something important if he acts rashly or opts for an avenue without being sure it's the right one. He is afraid of missing something important and lose the excellent occasion for ever. Overwhelmed by this frightening perspective, he feels as if paralyzed or put out of action for a while. His fear of missing something essential also makes him quite intolerant of himself. When at last he has taken a decision, and time is often on his side, this depressed state falls off, vanishing into nothingness. Occasionally, an impatient individual will be completely exhausted at the end of his week, but on Monday he wakes up fresh as a daisy again. Or he feels like dead for the first week of his vacation, then suddenly gearing up and going for whatever dangerous adventure and stressful sports activity is out there. These depressive states are of temporary nature and should not be confounded with an enduring depression usually requiring pharmacotherapy. If neither audacity nor stepped up intolerance offer him a valve for his inner pressure, the action-oriented structure of this fear mastering strategy can sort of collapse and manifest in intermittent lethargic phases of inactivity.

At such times he feels unable to take decisions or actions of any consequence. Superficially, his condition resembles that of a burn-out without showing clinical symptoms. But it's merely attributable to the paralyzing fear of missing something critically important in his life by a wrong decision in one way or the other. It's a state in which he can't take bold decisions or discharge the pressure to the inside. So he temporarily resembles a coma patient in a glass coffin. But after some days, rarely weeks, the usual mechanisms rev up again. The impatient person will find himself either in a daringly intensive situation or in an even more intolerant efficiency attitude again.

Whoever is inflicted with the fear symptom of Impatience can sink into such lethargy temporarily, not only the type of the ›Apparently Dead‹. It is even advisable to deliberately surrender to this unusual condition, as taking a rest in the grave of indecision will allow him or her to come out of it sooner and refreshed again. His need to make intensity the yardstick of his aliveness has the impatient person rushing boldly into all kinds of ventures, pressing time into space. Everything must happen as quickly as possible, including covering distances or executing movements. That this often means risking life and limb is of little concern to the impatient person.

The intensive feeling of being alive he derives from such daring maneuvers also persists when his bones are broken or an infarct has, just in time, been detected and cured. It's interesting though that, should this happen, he doesn't feel put out of action by this temporary threat, time reduction or shortening of life. Instead, he looks on his health condition and time in bed as a grand opportunity to finally get down to all the things he unfortunately couldn't find a slot for due to all his busyness. Reading, for example, or taking up a correspondence course, dedicating himself to a very efficient diet, finding time to cultivate friendships – at last! There are no limits to the content of how the impatient person thinks he could be using his precious time. There's nothing he abhors more than the idea of having to kill time and feel useless. As a rule, he will try anything to remain active and perky, also mentally, even in what he calls a meditative relaxation. If he does meditate, he strives for immediate results or enlightenment now!

He loves his hectic rush, the turbulence and sharp efficiency his impatience brings about. Although he could be feeling even more intensively and buoyantly alive if he didn't do anything at all for a change, he can't really conceive of such an idea: how can loss of time yield any gain? If, by coincidence, he should have an opportunity to experience the bliss of sweet idleness, he'll feel close to a state of enlightenment. It will suddenly dawn on him what amount of indulgence and pleasure might be gained if he just allowed time to happen.

The Poles of Fear of Omission

– Intolerant	⟷	Audacious +

It goes without saying that a person with the primal fear of Impatience is not particularly patient with himself or his fellow men. This intolerance, which manifests like an imperious inner claim to do everything better, faster and more efficiently, affects both him and his fellow beings with relentless rigor as an unbridled demand. He isn't going to let anyone – and that includes himself – get away with anything. He makes the highest demands on job performance, on moral values, on the honesty and sincerity of his fellow men. He is like a humming-bird looking down on a snail.

He is also rather proud of his courage, his willingness to take risks, his audacity and ability to confront dangerous challenges. He likes to be admired for his readiness, seemingly without batting an eyelid, to subject to life-threatening situations, even seeking them, without the least bit of fear. At least that's how it seems to him as well as to the people around him. Actually, his audacity is a »false virtue« as it is nourished by his fear of omission.

So it is all the more difficult for this individual to comprehend his occasionally extreme foolhardiness as a covert result of his fundamental conflict: the longing for death and the horror of dying, conditioned by his Impatience. He is constantly afraid to miss his life and the sense of being alive. Therefore he lives under constant time pressure. In some unconscious corner of his mind, though, the impatient person longs for peace, for pressure to end, for the end of his life. Death would put a stop to that tormenting time pressure weighing on him. On the other hand, this death longing is coupled with a fear of dying, resulting from his concern to charge not enough intensity into his life span and that way miss something essential, thereby being condemned to a life of dreariness and senselessness because not enough is happening.

So by applying his audacity to actions and ideas, the impatient person tries to kill two birds with one stone. Ventures requiring a lot of courage and holding manifold risks satisfy the subliminal death wish, as they might end his life any time. Simultaneously, dangerous situations provide so much intensity – they are so wonderfully exciting! When he is involved in actions which would terrify other people, he has no time to think about wasting, losing or killing time. This grants him relief for a short while.

Hence the positive pole of the feature Impatience – the false virtue of audacity – is an approach sourced by fear, making believe that his life-feeling is based on a meaningful structure. The audacity can extend to all areas of human existence. The impatient person finds ample opportunity for exciting risks to experience this mixture of death longing and fear – be it deep sea diving or on the stock exchange floor. It's not easy for him to bid farewell to his audacity. To him, it's a high-value commodity and outstanding quality, earning him much admiration for the various dangers he exposes himself to. Only when the essential becomes visible behind the surface can he gradually disengage from the pseudo-satisfaction of taking audacious risks. As he gets older, he can find true satisfaction in an intense savoring of life, instead of always extorting the maximum of existential pressure and danger from it. Another chance for the revelation that the ultimate meaning of life cannot consist in putting it at stake is when audacity gets pushed to the limit and the impatient person is driven to the verge of his emotional capacity. This might be in high mountain climbing, in racing sports, trekking through rough terrain or by reckless business dealings. Or it can be a high-risk private venture like a secret love affair with the boss' spouse or a double life as housewife and prostitute.

When the fear of an impatient individual is so conditioned that, for particular reasons, he doesn't like to risk his health and life nor dare to continually live on the brink, the action impulse otherwise vented in bold activities may turn inwardly. Intolerance represents the negative pole of Impatience. Yet intolerance will hardly be admired or considered positive in anyone, on the contrary, the intolerant person reaps rejection for it. His charisma of high intensity is often felt as a threat by his peers. This perpetual rush, haste and rigor coupled with over-efficiency tend to arouse intense fears of failure in others. He puts himself and others under pressure. He becomes intolerant of those not taking quick decisions, who don't work, think or understand fast enough; who, in his view, don't really make something out of their lives or don't see in advance what action is required. He reaps no praise for the negative pole of this fear characteristic, i.e., his overbearing intolerance, but rather unadorned criticism. But such painful criticism gives him a chance to look judiciously at his intolerant ways and eventually restrain himself a little.

The intolerant person demands best performance of himself and also makes great demands on the people around him, primarily referring to time management. He frequently admonishes himself and others for not being fast or efficient enough, and he suffers considerably from the threat of his lessening capabilities as he grows older. Intolerance also extends to social and political conditions and to issues which, according to general criteria, can't be changed, such as legal situations or economic sluggishness.

The intolerant individual can usually discharge much of his inner tension by his habit of getting thoroughly annoyed about varied and sundry situations. He is irritated at the behavior of people, situations and authorities. He gets upset about all kinds of mistakes he is sure could be easily and speedily rectified by just a little more efficiency. He gets in a lather over the unreasonableness and irresponsibility of those in charge who »can't get their butt into gear.« If only they'd let him, he would do everything quite differently, and pretty damn quick at that. He would definitely take hold of the reins in his usual efficient manner without hesitation and take the necessary risks. The fact that he is rarely given that chance makes him still more intolerant. As his fear increases, he turns into a difficult contemporary seldom content with life as it is. Someone who doesn't obey, dawdles or doesn't do everything as quickly as is called for in the mind of the intolerant person, will be eliminated from his surroundings without delay; an intolerant individual just can't put up with it since it activates his primal fear.

To attain a wholesome balance between mortal danger and the relentless intolerance of life with its own rhythm, this individual must learn to let more clemency and understanding prevail, both towards his own impetuous impulses and the behaviour of his fellow men.

The Released Potential

The primal fear of Impatience represents an aspect of the »royal« energy 7. When an impatient character manages to observe, define and evaluate the extreme spikes of his action pressure, thereby learning – in moderation – to master them, he may acquire quite an impressive royal charisma. This charisma combines a marked ability to take decisions and efficiently turn them into realization, to remedy grievances or problems and lead an intensive, pleasurable life with royal serenity. The haste, the bustle, the efficiency pressure he puts himself and his fellow men under ease to a degree that is beneficial to the whole instead of obstructing it. His audacity will be confined to situations or adventures which truly hold the prospect of a high profit. He will no longer give in so much to his fear pressure and longing for intensity in mortal danger. Fear of death and death desire abate. The fundamental fear of missing life and never having enough time lessens.

A sovereign attitude towards life and its requirements takes increasingly more room. This sovereignty – also in his attitude towards time – reflects in the impatient person increasingly finding the leisure to experience the quality of the moment. He will learn to appreciate also inactivity, inner quietness and repose, instead of constantly focusing on what hasn't yet been accomplished, on tomorrow and the day after tomorrow, or moaning under the burden of his chores. His fellow men will begin to appreciate him for the tempered rigor of his demands. They no longer feel like serfs lashed on by a slave-driver but as human beings, willing to apply all of their energy for a greater goal under his aegis.

The released potential of an impatient personality is the ability to patiently wait until time is ripe. He desists from trying to manage or strive for things not yet ready to happen. Instead of trying to outwit time, he considers it more and more his ally, as a factor of existence to craft life for and with him, rather than an obstacle in his path of mastering his days. The often dangerous and harmful boldness turns into a »nothing ventured, nothing gained« attitude towards life; but the stakes will be commensurate with the potential profit.

Intolerance gives way to an appreciation of the richness of all living phenomena and their validity. Even an impatient person forced to acknowledge the extremes of his fear knows of the right time, the kairós, and the opportunities that release the potential bound in his fear, allowing him to blossom to a »royal« serenity and sovereign perspective of life.

Three Types of Fear of Omission

1. The **Fidgeter** is restless, nervous, fickle. He is constantly in motion; he can't sit still, always working and pottering about. It doesn't matter so much whether this activity actually produces results; he is content when he can dash around, keeping his unrest and impatience in check that way. The Fidgeter can't let others take a rest either, infecting everyone around him with his twitchiness.
2. The **Racing Driver** is always in a hurry. Things never work fast enough and he compulsively pays heed to precision and efficiency. He mustn't slip up. Everything has to happen at utmost but controlled speed. He is the master of his time management. He actually strives to gain an advance of seconds and gets furious when someone delays him.
3. The **Apparently Dead** is exhausted, defeated by the finiteness

of his lifetime. The tasks he has taken upon himself over-burden him. So he often pulls a blanket over his head, feeling as if paralyzed or dead in the face of a mountain of chores he believes will overtax and crush him. His syndrome is the result of having given up the fight against the seven-headed dragon of seemingly unfulfillable requirements. He cannot kill time and therefore plays dead, i.e. »kills« himself instead.

Type 1: The Fidgeter

The Fidgeter is chronically hectic. His unrest manifests in body and mind, because not only is he always on the hop, strained and hyperactive, but also mentally quite distant from the present moment. Erratically, he hurries back and forth between the many assignments, requirements, duties and fantasies. He skips and runs and jumps in squares without being able to keep at a single task methodically for any extended time. His hectic rush makes him want to accomplish too much at a time. But the many balls he tries to juggle soon slip from his hands. He acts like a waiter carrying not only fully loaded trays in both hands, but also balancing a high stack of plates on his head and pushing a trolley with his feet to economize time.

The fact that oftentimes everything crashes in the act can't stop him from trying again and again. If, by chance, things turn out alright, it will make him feel like a great speed artist. And should everything actually arrive in the kitchen in one piece, he might find the time to do all the things he has long planned to do, notably to clean the grease behind the stove and the cupboards at last. Reality, however, usually sees many dishes break and someone else having to remove the greasy dirt in the end.

Such a Fidgeter creates unrest all around him. In his presence or under his energetic thumb, people hardly get the chance for a break. He goads everyone on to join in his hectic daily routine, constantly conveying the impression that nothing is happening at all unless in double-quick time.

The Fidgeter quickly gets bored. The needs of his quieter fellow people make this hectic person nervous and testy. He prefers to storm out of the room then, rather than taking a little nap on the sofa. The best way to calm his sensorimotor buzzing are sporting activities like tennis or jogging, even in the middle of the night if necessary. Fidgeters get told at least three times a day: »Can't you sit down and keep quiet for once? Can't you stop that for a minute? Please do calm down. Put this away and keep your hands still, will you?« Startled, they will look uncomprehendingly at whoever is admonishing them, feeling misunderstood in their innermost nature.

A Fidgeter observes the snail's pace of others with a wry smile and a more or less outspoken intolerant contempt for all those who take more time, who are less bustling and alert, and in his view don't manage to »get the pie in the oven«. That his own pie is often burned he doesn't in the least care about. It's not as if he wanted to eat it; he just wants to get it done and place it on the shelf as quickly as possible.

Typical features

The Fidgeter is characterized by his erratic movements and restless eyes. It's as if he were sitting on a live wire. He often perches on the chair's edge – that is, should he ever get to sitting down rather than saying »no thank you, I prefer standing up«. He fidgets with his feet or jiggles his knees, drums his fingers or hectically organizes his documents on the table. Every other minute he reaches for his glass of water, even when already empty. He likes to play with his hair, scratches behind his ears, fingers his nose or bites his lips – all this to give the appearance of being patient, albeit without success. Others feel the restlessness infecting them like a virus and soon get wriggly themselves.

In restaurants or when invited to a meal at someone's home, the Fidgeter has the subjective impression of having to wait »forever« for his dinner. When it's finally on the table, he finishes it faster than everyone else and starts fidgeting again, rolling his eyes at the sight of his table companions cutting up their food so infinitely slowly, pushing it around on the plate and forking up one bite at a time. But what really heightens his torment is when someone puts down his cutlery just to say something!

His motor restlessness makes it almost impossible for him to sit down for any period of time. Only when sleeping can he blissfully relax. He usually falls asleep instantly and wakes up again after a short, almost dreamless, uninterrupted rest. During this nightly break he gathers the strength to cheerfully jump out of bed, complete his morning toilet at enormous speed, if somewhat superficially, and have a strong cup of coffee on the go. He is ready to face the day now. Coffee addiction is not his problem. He needs just this one cup in the morning to be jumpy all day.

Typical complaints

The Fidgeter frequently suffers from arrhythmia and tachycardia. His metabolism is accelerated, so he is usually very thin, but sometimes also corpulent because he eats too much in a hurry and does not like to sit down for his meal. Mostly however, the Fidgeter is affected by problems of the musculoskeletal system, since he tends to hurt himself in his often uncontrolled motor function and his tendency to take on too much too soon. He will not only report of diverse fractures but also that he suffers from lumbago, sprains, wrist fractures and bruises. He plays it down as nothing serious, nothing that won't cure fast enough and, should he be obliged to wear a cast, he'll use it for his notes.

He often has problems with hiccups and heartburn because he doesn't take enough time for his meals. He frequents coffee shops and snack bars, where they don't make him wait so »dreadfully long« to fill his order. The result can be peptic or duodenal ulcers. If this impatient person is of delicate constitution, also autoimmune diseases such as colitis ulcerosa may develop.

Mostly, however, the Fidgeter suffers from neural disorders, e.g. chronic neuritis or recurring shingles, up to Parkinson's disease and similar neural impairments. These can be partly explained by the short nights, which only seemingly offer the Fidgeter complete regeneration to be ready for new hyperactivity early in the morning. But his autonomic nervous system doesn't sufficiently recover to provide for a deep relaxation of the whole system.

Typical for the Fidgeter is also a stroke at an uncommonly early age – thirty or forty years – or a heart attack out of the blue. People around him shake their heads in amazement: »How could this happen? He was never ill before, always active, doing sports and never complaining of any health problems – fancy finding himself in an intensive care unit now!« In most cases, the Fidgeter will be able to recover from these vascular injuries, in fact taking them as a pretext to opt for a more quiet and contemplative life style. But that doesn't come easy.

Characteristic of Fidgeter type psychiatric disorders is an extreme motor unrest or displacement impulse. Patients will walk the floor back and forth for twenty hours a day, flailing about, erratically stroking their faces, shaking their heads or trying in some other way to defuse their extreme inner tension by repetitive motion sequences. This tension continues to build up specifically because they are condemned to idleness and waiting while in the clinic. The administration of psychotropic drugs which lead to involuntary movements as a side effect amplifies their torment, because the convulsions don't serve to relieve the tension; they rather increase the fear. Chemical »sedation«, having replaced the straitjacket with such restless patients, doesn't improve things, although it is often successful with other patient types. The condition of a Fidgeter will only get worse the less he can move. Mental disorders are moreover associated with considerable sleeplessness. So the remedial effect of sleep as an option for emotional and physical recovery is significantly reduced.

Indications for Treatment

A Fidgeter should be encouraged to figure out himself adequate ways which, following a strenuous physical activity, award him the simple physical need for some rest. His favourite sports are usually squash, tennis, football (soccer), basketball or other sports requiring fast and vigorous movements. But more beneficial for him would be sustained, long-distance cycling, hiking or swimming, because the regularity of uniform, persistent movements helps to attain that need for relaxation that doesn't feel like agony but like bliss.

A child diagnosed with attention deficit syndrome (ADS, ADHD) is frequently simply a Fidgeter fearing to miss life. This girl or boy wants to do as much as possible simultaneously, and ends up getting nothing done at all. All the time the fidgety child gets told to calm down or sit quietly. The adequate therapy for this condition can be found in sustained physical movement. This applies, of course, only to ADS – triggered by Impatience as the primal fear symptom.

Also for institutional patients, an exerting work therapy outdoors in fresh air is more beneficial – if more inconvenient for the staff – than using tranquilizers or sedatives, or immobilizing the patient during »long« conversational therapy sessions. But the

Fidgeter does respond well to massages and sauna visits, provided he consents to it; the application of temperature stimuli eases his unrest. With respect to gastrointestinal complaints, it is recommended that the patient primarily be trained to chew and insalivate his food and to restructure his eating habits. Serving this purpose, for instance, would be joint meals in a generously measured time frame, whereas a lunch break of only twenty minutes would aggravate the complaints. It is also important that he observe a low histamine diet.

If a Fidgeter is given to frequent finger drumming or knee jiggling, learning a classic breathing technique will be helpful. Deep and calm breathing will quieten his system, circulation and nerves to a more composed state, balancing his usual way of »panting« through life. At times of high nervous stress, conscious breathing for just five minutes will often suffice to bring about a positive effect. Implemented twice a day, it represents an essential step in calming the nervous system and digestive functions.

Type 2: The Racing Driver

The Racing Driver is always under pressure to organize his time to a maximum of usefulness and efficiency. He feels the need to function like a precision chronometer. Punctuality is of utmost importance to him, and woe if his fellow men don't live up to his notion of correct timing or fail to take precision seriously. The Racing Driver whips himself through the day. A fourteen-hour working day to him seems just long enough to manage at least the most pressing of his assignments.

Sleep is a necessary evil. He confines his rest to a few hours and wakes up before the alarm clock goes off, since he can hardly wait for this annoying, inactive, unwanted – yet somehow deemed necessary – nightly break to be over at last.

He feels compelled to chart out every hour of the day for a specific activity. He keeps a strict agenda and in meetings gets up unblinkingly at the scheduled conclusion, turning to new issues, no matter if his discussion partners still have things they need to clarify. They'll just have to schedule a new appointment. The Racing Driver depends on his fellow men to function properly and submit to his idea of an efficient daily routine. They don't qualify to work with him or share his daily routine unless they are prepared to abide by these precisely encapsulated time units. If the time unit is called »lunch break«, the Racing Driver is quite willing to have lunch. If a twenty-minute nap is included in his plans, he has no problem using this time to nap. It's just that one mustn't interrupt or upset his agenda when he has planned to accomplish one thing or another during that specific time slot.

The Racing Driver is always set on reaching his target. When, by nightfall, he hasn't achieved what he resolved to do in the morning, he gets ferocious, determined to work through the night if necessary. He never fails to find the strength and energy for it, until the day when he suffers a stroke or an embolism out of the blue. The Racing Driver is under pressure and does the same to others. One must hand it to him though: he is of utmost efficiency in everything he endeavors to tackle. Preparing for an examination, he is done six weeks before the actual date, leaving time to collect additional information which he can then use to excel before the board of examiners. When he plans a holiday, everything is elaborately organized up to the minutest detail. No unpleasant surprises to get in his way. If there were, they'd be as alarming to him as a rock on a racetrack.

The Racing Driver always has his foot on the gas while simultaneously focusing his attention on the brake pedal. The control the Racing Driver exerts over his life and the people around him is less an emotional dominance than the governance over time. He doesn't usually tolerate nonsense and dislikes anything superfluous. He is down-to-earth and fills up any time gap which might crop up by chance with something sensible.

Features

The Racing Driver can't stand it when there is chaos in his life. That's why he is usually very accurate in his expression. His manner of speech is precise and purposeful. He is carefully dressed, with a fine haircut, and he always has his documents ready at hand. He talks fast, interrupting his discussion partners when he feels they are straying from the topic, or some digression or minor issue start dominating the conversation.

The extreme tension of the Racing Driver also reflects in his physical demeanor. He gives the impression of a leopard ready to pounce, every detail taken in, fixed on his target and with only one thing on his mind at that specific moment: to get where his inner drive mechanism directs him. Others will inevitably feel a little intimidated by so much precision, efficiency and target-orientation; they are unable to keep pace with this Racing Driver and his tuned up life machine. They also probably feel that they'd prefer not to board such a dangerous racing car.

Typical complaints

The constant pressure takes its toll on the Racing Driver's vessel system. He has no time to see a doctor. Although he schedules a regular medical check-up, he mostly misses the appointment because something more important has come up at the last minute. So he has little awareness of his medical condition, ignoring also clear signals such as heartache, high blood pressure, racing pulse or breathlessness. What does worry him though is when he's no longer able to remember the multitude of things on his agenda, because it means losing control over his minutely worked out course of life. That this failing ability to memorize things is less a symptom of old age but rather a distress signal from his system to stop overloading himself with too many responsibilities, duties and urgent to-dos next week or next month, should be made clear to him in no uncertain terms. He absolutely needs a break from the continual pre-scheduling of his daily routine.

Many Racing Drivers suffer from diabetes; the permanent strain afflicts their pancreas gland. The Racing Driver also tends to eat too late and too fast, and, with his system always up and running, has an habitually high release of adrenalin. Since he allows himself little rest, and doesn't feel the need for it, his autonomic nervous system frequently gets overtaxed for extended periods of time. As a result, he often falls ill just when he's on holiday or during some other break, because his system is dependent on the permanent hormonal supply and doesn't function when unavailable. The Racing Driver is – to extend the metaphor – addicted to an efficient, racing and intense life-feeling. He only feels really well when he's got his foot on the gas, totally oblivious of the amount of fear he must cope with at such an audacious speed of life.

Be it manager or housewife, the Racing Driver will sooner or later have to deal with the consequences of a burnout syndrome, which is quite humiliating and therefore hard to admit for this type of impatient person. Unfortunately, road accidents triggered by microsleep or inattentiveness during apparently harmless situations are quite common. Such a situation might be when he is crossing the street on a zebra crossing for example, that is, when his habitual control slackens for a moment. Other frequent incidents are tripping and fractures from a fall, which occur when the Racing Driver is emotionally affected by some event diverting his attention.

A Racing Driver, male or female, is thrown into the greatest despair and depression when his life plans are foiled by people pursuing their own practical interests or the Development Goals of their soul. The death of a child, a spouse leaving or some other event that they have no power to influence or prevent in any way, can lead to a collapse of a Racing Driver, requiring long-term treatment. Such incidents put all his goals and life plans seriously into question.

Indications for treatment

The Racing Driver will seldom consult a psychotherapist, doctor or even physiotherapist. When he really does feel bad for once, it means he's seriously in bad shape and usually needs a longer stay in a clinic. This immobilization offers him the chance to gradually reduce his addiction to stress hormones. He is unlikely to fully renounce what he considers the only meaningful way to live his life. But this excess, this exaggeration of control and efficiency, of audacity and perfectionism can be checked by various means. After a few weeks in hospital he will no longer be flooded by his hyper-efficiency or tempted by accident-prone traps like driving at racing speed despite the hazard of aquaplaning. It does, however, require a fairly long period; this can't be accomplished during a two-week's hospitalization. The autonomic nervous system of the Racing Driver, requiring Driver must be reprogrammed. The high cortisol release and also the insulin overproduction need a long-term adjustment to be reduced to a wholesome level.

For the first two or three weeks in the clinic, the Racing Driver, requiring Driver will get worked up about everything which in his opinion doesn't function the way it should. He'll get upset about all kinds of inadequacies, since there isn't much else he can rant about. Then, slowly, he'll begin to feel at ease and start relaxing, sleeping an extra hour and, in contact and comparison with other patients, begin to look at his life with a little more distance. The therapist can provide advice on alternative options and in particular coax the Racing Driver, requiring Driver into talking about his major life complaint, the lack of time and the fear of missing good opportunities. The time factor is what the therapist's efforts should be focused on, the craving for life intensity concealed behind all the audacious efficiency, designed to mask his Fear of Omission.

The therapeutic conversation should always lead back to the fundamental question of what it is that could be missed or needs to be avoided. Whether, with all the controlled planning and efficiency mode of operation, the patient didn't in fact miss the essential, like being close to his family, time to spend with friends, joy of living or health. The Racing Driver, requiring Driver speeds through life, looking neither left nor right nor in the rear-view mirror, but he doesn't really know what his destination is. He just wants to somehow put his life behind him, as fast as possible. This type of impatient individual banks on getting out of his racing car unscathed, even following a multiple somersault at maximum speed. His audacity makes him believe in the dream of immortality. Concealed behind this belief is the need to challenge existence and put his life at stake. In a strange reversal process, existence itself is assigned the burden of proof that it is worth living. So a therapy will only be successful or lead to a meaningful change of his outlook on life when these aspects are taken into account. Caution and particularly patience must be exercised until these issues can be directly addressed, because they have to do with a mental taboo.

The Racing Driver, requiring Driver responds well to tranquilizers and soporifics. Their administration can make sense over a limited time period to afford his organism the opportunity to experience how a little more sleep and quiet can actually be beneficial instead of contemptible, for his nervous system to gradually adapt itself. A difficult phase in the treatment will set in when the Racing Driver, requiring Driver discovers that neither his business nor his family or team of staff have collapsed, despite his prolonged absence of three or four weeks. For this impatient type, the realization of his dispensability is just as painful as is the insight for a real racing driver that his racing career has come to an end and that, after a short while, only few people will remember him as the former winner of the Grand Prix.

Type 3: The Apparently Dead

When, in a current Soul Pattern, the fear symptom of Impatience is matched with MATRIX elements which call for more prudence and contemplation, this will lead to a conflict of energies. Typically, after having succumbed to the frantic zest for action and inner pressure, forced to taking many decisions, coping with – but also accomplishing – a lot of feats, this impatient person suddenly lapses into a seemingly anabiotic state. Out of the blue, this previously hectic and efficient individual feels completely overtaxed, no longer able to meet any challenge or carry out the simplest activities. He is unable to plan anything, nor has he the will to want anything. His condition is apathetic. On the one hand, he will experience this phase as extremely threatening, while on the other also strangely restful. His lifelong inner conflict situation results from the fact that Impatience with its primal Fear of Omission is paired, for example, with the Development Goal of Delay or Standstill. Or it may be due to the need for quiet, stillness and contemplation which is typical for the Soul Role of Priest or simply Old Souls, to provide inner space for inspiration. Such a condition will be a lifelong challenge, imposing compulsive breaks time and again. Naturally, also a Racing Driver or Fidgeter will now and then feel forced or compelled to take a break, even to flag temporarily, spread-eagled. But the impatient type described here falls to pieces all of a sudden and then hardly responds to anything at all.

This apparently dead state may become chronic, because to the impatient person, this inactivity feels life-threatening and humiliating. Condemned to actually watch himself unable to get anything done is so cruelly shattering, that an understandable despair over this much needed idleness may soon issue in disdainful intolerance of himself. This in turn causes self-hatred. The forced break can't serve for the recovery of his organism but leads to a permanent depressive state, to lethargy and apathetic hopelessness for weeks and months on end. Only when the impatient individual is aware of the special dynamics of his fear structure, can he or she deal with the overwhelming panic in the face of prolonged lethargy. This panic would misguide impatient persons of this type to fall into exactly that abyss opening up before them of which they are so afraid. Because to an impatient person, a day can basically feel like a year, and a three-day-long inability to perform whatever activity seems to destroy all perspective of a renewed period of activity.

Features

The Apparently Dead laments: »I'm at the end of my tether, I just can't go on. I'm dreaming of sleeping for weeks on end. Time seems to escape me; I feel inefficient. I can't sleep any more I'm so infinitely tired.« He looks pallid, stressed out and overtaxed. He despairs at even the smallest tasks; everyday chores seem to him like a mountain range he has to vanquish painstakingly on his knees. Faced with this challenge, he prefers to sit down and cry at the foot of the mountain, rather than undertake a renewed effort. »I just can't make it any more. I'm burned out, completely exhausted« he'll protest, either resignedly or overly excited. It is particularly noteworthy that the Apparently Dead is mortally afraid of taking the wrong decision in situations requiring resolution. Instead, he keeps a low profile and remains completely passive.

His grief, his conflict and agony are based on his belief that the only way he should or must continue is to work relentlessly like a machine that can't be turned off. Whereas others rest when they are tired, this type treats himself like a donkey that must be goaded on with cane strokes when baulking. Whenever someone with this fear structure spurs himself on beyond his limits, his body will abruptly lapse into this state of suspended animation to prevent a total collapse. This seizure serves as a kind of overheating protection and is only temporary; it doesn't actually mean the goals he has set himself have to be given up completely.

Typical complaints

When the Apparently Dead feels overtaxed, his impatience and need for efficacy and speed will at first seduce him to keep on working and performing even harder, since weakness in making decisions, neglect of duty and incapacity to work are things he can't reconcile with his self-image. Eventually, however, he will fall into an absolute dead-end, apathetic state. He can hardly get out of bed or the armchair; everything is too much for him. He gets irritable and extremely sensitive to noise. Even a walk seems like an almost insurmountable challenge. He suddenly feels so restricted and crushed by his daily chores and responsibilities that his system switches to total refusal. Sleep is no longer a source of regeneration as he suffers from problems to fall asleep, or he wakes up after only a couple of hours, feeling completely exhausted.

His insomnia is the result of being overwrought. This person is so tired, he or she can't float over that threshold into sleep any more. But the yearning to take that dip at last and deeply submerge into a kind of eternal sleep for recovery may easily lead to drug abuse. This in turn threatens to prolong and solidify the anabiotic condition, as the Apparently Dead can't shed the residual tiredness the next day as easily as a healthy and active person given to exercise can. He usually has no physical complaints in this state; he has no infection, fever or pains. He just feels like dead, his mind numbed to complete blankness. He doesn't want to eat.

Now this is nothing else but a deep mental and physical exhaustion as a reaction to too much hectic rush. It's not a physical illness as such. Even children will show this apparently inexplicable behavior. The consequences are insomnia, nightly unrest and hollow eyes, drop in scores and soon also skipping school.

Indications for treatment

Once he has fallen into this lethargic state, the impatient person can no longer imagine that it could ever end. Pharmacotherapy may therefore be indicated to treat this condition, especially when the anabiotic phase extends beyond what is beneficial for the convalescence of the patient. Recommended are mood-lifting anti-depressants of adequate dose and, after a while, also therapeutic exercise. The Apparently Dead needs something to help him take courage to face life again. This can be successful even when he is moved only passively, i.e., when he is put on his feet, taken by the arm and walked around the flat. Manual treatment with physiotherapy will improve circulation and mobilizes the excretion of metabolic products which have deposited during the apathetic state. The individual should be administered a lot of liquid, if necessary with infusions.

Initially, however, time and room should be allowed for the patient's need to be »like dead«. The affected person wants to be left completely alone and not be kissed awake prematurely from his glass coffin. Only after an indispensable, basic inner relaxation or system reorganization has set in, the mobilization and mood-lifting medication may begin. It's very important to really listen for and respect the person's need for silence and quiet, which he often indicates with no more than a small gesture. Therapeutic staff or family members near to him should desist from giving in to their own anxieties by imposing activism in an effort to see the patient »healthy and normal again« as quickly as possible. One should also refrain from encouraging the Apparently Dead to eat when he or she is lacking appetite.

The premise to our perspective of reality and existence as transmitted by the »Source« is the basic understanding that All That Is evolves from **Seven Cosmic and Universal Energies** *and their combinations with each other. This principle cannot be further corroborated nor proved. It can however, be validated in its ramifications – at least to a certain degree – within the realm of our observable reality. These cosmic energies are also the premise for the emergence of the seven archetypal* **Primal Fears***. They only exist in the physical dimension of space and time and are, therefore, of great interest to souls during the delimited time period while exploring the earthly sphere. Being the shadow aspects of the cosmic energies, they are indispensable for human learning and evolution on earth.*

Thus the »fear inventory« of souls incarnated as human beings basically consists of seven primal fears. In duality, learning happens in a space-temporal sequence. Therefore a human being doesn't constantly have to deal with all seven primal fears simultaneously, but with a specific selection of two combined primal fears in each individual life. We have termed this selection, which is made by the soul before each new incarnation, the **Basic Fear.** *It consists of a combination of two of the seven primal fears described above.*

Since this Basic Fear represents the invisible root of the large fear tree and can't be readily perceived, for communication purposes we depend on giving a specific name to the surface of each of the seven primal fears. These are the **Symptoms of Fear***, the Primary Symptom and the Secondary Symptom. A self-sacrificing behavior, for example, can be easily recognized in a fellow man; it may even be considered valuable. At the root of it, however, there is often a deep fear of worthlessness of which the individual is usually unaware. It is the symptom of this fear we call Martyrdom. This symptom can be allied and combined with any one of the other primal fears, e. g. Stubbornness, Impatience, Greed etc. as a Secondary Symptom.*

These two symptoms of fear create a dynamic balance with each other and they may be more or less pronounced. One variation could be a weak Primary Symptom with a strong Secondary Symptom of Fear, or vice versa. Or they can be about equally manifest. The respective stronger fear will often be perceived as the Primary Symptom, even though it may actually be the Secondary Symptom of Fear.

The Secondary Symptom of Fear is mostly effective in the private sphere, that is, in personal relationships. It regulates the feelings of intimacy in partnership, friendship, and family. The Primary Symptom is mostly effective at the work place and in those many life situations which don't usually require an intimate exchange with other people. It covers about seventy per cent of a person's manifestations of life.

It was only in the course of our work with the »Source« that we began to understand that, although one can isolate the two fears from each other for the purpose of theoretical analysis, they actually form a characteristic amalgam in human beings. From this understanding arose our desire to learn more about the different combinations and to put this knowledge to practical use in understanding individual characters. From the combination of two primal fears with their typical behavioral and reaction patterns, indications can be derived which serve to moderate the entire fear structure by cognition as well as specific treatment advice.

The combinations are moreover identified by their Energy numbers. The first number describes the Primary Symptom followed by the Secondary Symptom of Fear. Martyrdom for example has the Energy number 3. This number has no mathematical value but symbolizes a fundamental quality, in this case a warrior-like, belligerent energy. It is discernible by the fact that the typical Martyr tends to sacrifice himself as on a battlefield and almost aggressively imposes his selflessness on others as a way to cope with his own fear tension. If complemented by the Secondary Symptom of Stubbornness, the behavior is moreover characterized by a certain grimness and inalterability. With a Secondary Symptom Impatience, the exertion of pressure on others and the desire for efficiency would get stronger, whereas Self-deprecation as a Secondary Symptom increases the willingness for self-sacrifice bordering on self-effacement and so on. Thus, the composite number of the two Energies already gives a basic indication of the energetic quality of this combination. A more detailed description of the seven Universal Base Energies and their qualities is provided in the appendix.

For better comprehensibility, here is a pictographic description of the basic scheme:

> *Seven Cosmic Energies*

create

> *Seven Archetypal Primal Fears*

as part of a more comprehensive system of Archetypes of the Soul of seven times seven Archetypes of the Soul (see appendix), from which two primal fears are selected. These two jointly constitute the

> *Basic Fear*

in the respective incarnation.

These deep archetypal fears are hard to identify on an outer level. For the purpose of better comprehension we are designating them by their easily observable forms of expression or Symptoms, calling them the

> *Primary Symptoms and the Secondary Symptom of Fear*

Following is an overview of the 42 possible variations of interaction between two primal fears, complemented by suggestions to help reduce the individual, basic fear.

All Combinations of the Primary and Secondary Symptoms of Fear (42 Basic Fears)

1. Self-deprecation with all Secondary Fear Symptoms

Energies 1 plus 2: Self-deprecation and Self-sabotage

The Primary Symptom Self-deprecation complemented by the Secondary Symptom Self-sabotage is intended to prevent that an individual be in touch and interrelate with himself, his existence and growth process in freedom and confidence. Self-deprecation wants to act modestly in the background, while Self-sabotage aims to avoid both joy and love of life. So when the two join forces they meter out the metaphorical nourishment of vitality, of joy and self-love to an individual as if through a thin straw, rather than let him drink to the fullest from the cup of life. The combination of Self-deprecation with Self-sabotage keep warning: »Don't step too far out on the stage. Don't expose yourself to full view. Stay carefully behind the scenes or at least close to the curtain. That way you can always make yourself invisible or inconspicuous, retreat and protect from any challenges if necessary.«

This special combination of self-restraint is like a crop vermin, snapping off an otherwise well grown, strong stalk by a hardly visible bite right at its bottom. It would have to be a strong insecticide, to ensure that the sapling of healthy self-confidence, wishing to blossom and bear rich fruit, to prosper and propagate doesn't die prematurely. It therefore requires strength and a particularly great amount of self-respect and self-attentiveness to confront this combination of fear symptoms.

People with a combination of these Primary and Secondary Symptom as their basic fear should purposefully apply those special virtues as their sustainable protective substance and soul armor. It's important not to miss out on the weekly prophylactic spraying of self-love, as the old bug is quick to infest again. It's not easy to extinguish, but the exercise of due attentiveness and the idea that the precious plant of the self needs this lasting protection will be helpful in this effort. It doesn't in any way violate the ecological laws of the Worlds of the Soul when someone finally refrains from living his existence in an overly modest, assiduous and moreover joyless way. Self-attentiveness means to be on guard incessantly, watching out scrupulously for the harmful bug to re-emerge. This will be instrumental in helping the delicate plantlet of life grow up to be a big strong plant.

Energies 1 plus 3: Self-deprecation and Martyrdom

The combination of Self-deprecation and Martyrdom can easily entice an individual to feel almost too good for this world, capitulating before it, while at the same time trying to muster all strength and all diligence to stand up to its shortcomings. It can't be denied that this combination of Primary and Secondary Symptom represents a special challenge to the self-image. Someone experiencing every single day that he is perceived, both by himself and by his fellow men, as an extremely friendly, good-natured, approachable and kind-hearted individual, furthermore untiringly diligent and always at the disposal of others, won't have an easy time discerning even the shadow of a shadow in his character. In this seemingly so simple and noble combination of fear-driven qualities, however, one should hypothetically assume that a good thirty percent of this over-overly goodness, and thirty to fifty percent of this over-over-exceeding assiduity, is attributable to an all-dominating fear of being otherwise unappreciated and unloved.

Self-deprecation and Martyrdom form an unholy alliance of inappropriate modesty and an almost sickening selflessness, both stemming from primal fears. There is no room for healthy egotism or justified demands. The individual concerned can hardly feel himself. He only feels the tugging needs of the others and an irresistible impulse to please and help. But these forms of selflessness and modesty are preventing the self from unfolding into full bloom. Someone who denies his authentic self, untiringly offering himself as the sacrificial lamb in the name of high-mindedness, shouldn't be surprised when his fellow men don't even recognize this true self, and consequently don't particularly appreciate it either. Only when the person with this basic fear learns to deliberately renounce of too much generosity, too much hard work and too much willingness to make sacrifices, can the self in its natural and radiant worth be brought to shine and flourish. Every day he should repeat to himself like a mantra: »It is no good if I lose myself to gain others.«

Energies 1 plus 4: Self-deprecation and Stubbornness

Self-deprecation fancies itself in the idea of being incompetent in some mysterious and incomprehensibly innate way. The Secondary Symptom called Stubbornness associated with it insists that this poor self-image must not change. The combination of those two fears breeds an assiduous and hard-working, decent, honest and modest personality, who, with grim dedication, accomplishes the greatest deeds in private life as in business, without making a big deal out of it or insisting that the achievements be acknowledged or appreciated.

The Self-deprecator feels embarrassed when his skills are openly revealed. He subsequently applies Stubbornness to keep the treasure of his competences and their results well locked in a chest. Ultimately though, he can't prevent his fellow men from recognizing and seeing which important and crucial, even admirable achievements he or she has accomplished. But every Self-deprecator works diligently at hiding this truth from himself, obstinately insisting that all of this is nothing special and in no way corresponds to the ambitions of his equally exalted and extremely damaged self-image.

The demands a stubborn Self-deprecator places on himself are generally characterized by a high, compulsive perfection where his work or private life is concerned. Nothing is ever good enough; in his eyes, it all remains makeshift or inferior. The coercive marriage between Self-deprecation and Stubbornness can only be severed by one of the two partners moving out of the shared inner flat. Whether Self-deprecation finally comes to terms with the fact that its perfection efforts are futile, or Stubbornness stops insisting on its grim self-abasement, one of them must give in. Then relief can set in.

Energies 1 plus 5: Self-deprecation and Greed

Self-deprecation in combination with Greed results in an unpretentiousness that is tantamount to a starveling existence. This condition of starvation may concern all areas of life. The individual actually enjoys renunciation, confirming the self-image of being unable to fashion one's life with enough joy. Desire becomes dangerous, pleasure a sin. Modesty is by far not modest enough; asceticism is considered a high virtue.

The renunciation of important, essential things from fear of appearing too demanding or coming across as dissatisfied and pretentious, leads to an aura marked by paleness, scarcity, meagerness and poverty. Yet, these Symptoms are often accompanied by fantasies and dreams of affluence and abundance, wanting to have it all and being satisfied with nothing.

The tension arising out of this contrast renders the greedy Self-deprecator restless, as if he had not eaten or drunk anything for a while and now gets delayed or prevented from regaling himself, from feasting, savoring and relaxing. It makes him look like someone who has gone on a hunger-strike without knowing what he is protesting against, all the while eyeing richly spread tables as if through a window. He's got the feeling that all of this isn't meant for him, but he is so terribly hungry. Once this calamitous attitude of renunciation and ideologically exalted, fearful asceticism has been recognized as such, the greedy Self-Deprecator will be able – in keeping with the image – to open the door of the restaurant, enter and seat himself at the table. What's more, he is no longer afraid of having to spend a prohibitive amount for an inordinate meal he can't even properly digest. The dish of life and pleasurable worldly wisdom can be served him in small and nicely decorated portions. But as long as he doesn't take that step over the threshold, he won't be able to do more than look at the appetizing dishes as if in a gourmet magazine.

Energies 1 plus 6: Self-deprecation and Arrogance

Self-deprecation likes to feel insignificant. Arrogance nurtures an exaggerated notion of its own importance. Self-deprecation feels incompetent. Arrogance portrays its abilities in an excessively favorable light. This creates a kind of pendulum effect inside the person in question, feeling alternatingly stupid and brilliant, inferior and important, ignorant and omniscient, ugly and beautiful.

This contrast bath of feelings and self-images causes insecurity.

It prevents the correct or appropriate assessment of one's own capabilities and possibilities. The Self-deprecator with the Secondary Symptom of Arrogance suffers from an impalpable feeling of: »I don't really know who I am, what impression I give, what I know and what I'm capable of. So best if I hide under a magic cap; I couldn't go on living if it should turn out that I'm completely incompetent. Should it turn out, on the other hand, that I'm actually an unrecognized genius, I wouldn't know how to fulfill the expectations that would be raised by that.«

This combination of fear Symptoms produces a kind of invisibility effort, paired with a panic-stricken fear to be exposed in either way. Someone with this coalition of fears therefore prefers not to budge from the spot. He is often highly qualified, but holds a position far below his abilities. He has talents and hobbies no one is supposed to know about because, while he secretly likes to bask in his knowledge and skills on the one hand, on the other he doesn't really like to reveal them for fear of criticism. But probably even worse would be applause that turns out just a little less enthusiastic than he had dreamed of. That, to him, would feel like a death sentence.

This combination of fears is ruled by two fantasies: smallness and grandiosity. And that is exactly the latch point at which the locked chest of hidden treasures can be pried open. It is important to understand that whatever other people may say, the Self-deprecator with Arrogance isn't going to believe them when they criticize, praise, admire or flatter him or her. So fellow people and friends can't be of much help. This individual must take the crowbar into his own hands in the realization that he has only lost the key to the treasure chest, but that all those riches inside belong to him and he is entitled to benefit from them and enjoy their glamour.

Energies 1 plus 7: Self-deprecation and Impatience

An individual with Self-deprecation and Impatience as a Secondary Symptom tends to turn all intolerance, everything testy, the time pressure and striving for efficiency contained in Impatience, on and against himself. It makes him unrelenting towards himself, letting not a single fault pass. He is always critical of and dissatisfied with his performance, no matter how perfect it may be. Such an attitude is often interpreted as a high virtue, even spiritual, since looking for fault in oneself first is considered a form of inner reflection and intellectual discipline. In truth, however, Impatience is used here to intensify Self-deprecation. The result is self-intolerance.

It is a fact that, even when a fearfully modest character doesn't voice his criticism of his fellow men and their achievements, he nonetheless wastes a lot of mental energy on chalking up and substantiating their mistakes. He'll signal to them, if only energetically, how imperfect they are as humans and performers. The intolerance of Impatience is applied to maximize the compulsive self-improvement of a Self-deprecator. An individual with this fear combination who doesn't understand what he's doing to himself will, over time, become more and more dissatisfied with his own performance. The modesty of Self-deprecation gradually changes into an attitude that constantly debases the self, picking to pieces any and all of one's actions or manifestations of character.

As a first step, therefore, the Self-deprecator with Impatience as secondary fear should be encouraged to verbalize his nitpicking of others, if not directly, at least in the presence of a third party, to articulate or find some other expression for it. Otherwise he'll lacerate and vilify himself and will be ultimately hard to tolerate also by his fellow men, since his self-image has turned negative through and through. So, when someone with this fear combination is ready to take a step towards inner liberation, a good start is to not mistake self-criticism for modesty, and not to espouse fearful perfectionism with the efficiency efforts of Impatience. He or she should understand that both arise from the fear of being unable to stand up to life and its challenges and not having enough life-time to reach perfection.

Impatience tends to take action blindly, Self-deprecation prefers inner retreat. Yet both approaches can be wholesomely and actively combined when a person with this fear structure is prepared to renounce at least part of his know-all, know-better and eager-to-do-better attitude. He must leave some room for the existence and actions of his fellow men, which actually serve well enough the demands of the majority of people.

An individual with Self-deprecation and Impatience endeavors to stylize himself to some exceptional figure who, driven by a secret ambition, is going to accomplish something infinitely great one day – if only he is sufficiently strict and drives himself relentlessly enough. This tyranny leads to no good. Someone striving for true inner growth will realize that and unfetter from the straitjacket of his drive for perfection.

2. Self-sabotage with all Secondary Fear Symptoms

Energies 2 plus 1: Self-sabotage and Self-deprecation

A self-saboteur with the Secondary Fear Symptom of Self-deprecation hopes that, by utmost modesty and unpretentiousness, he can snatch a mite of life's happiness which, it seems, has been refused him until now. He is under the illusion that he can pawn an increased attitude of renunciation as a pledge for happiness or a claim to love.

Self-sabotage is afraid of vigorous, joyful life energy. The effect in combination with Self-deprecation is that such vital energy is nipped in the bud; it can't develop and so needs not to be avoided either. Someone making few demands on life, cutting himself off from the joy of being, will find it hard to indulge in a happy, care-free infatuation, in prosperity or the blessings it can offer. As this individual grows older, the notion hardens in his mind that it isn't appropriate or ethical to savor the small and great joys of life. This also dips all positive things, which could actually be his for the taking, in a grey, morose light.

But Self-sabotage also has the tendency to spoil the fun for others. In alliance with Self-deprecation it makes for a somewhat complacent air, insisting that others too be undemanding and ex-tremely modest. When people are happy or having fun, this indi-vidual feels a kind of envy, begrudging their insouciant fun and spreading his sour perspective of life by liberally dropping remarks like: »He that sings on Friday shall weep on Sunday«, or »Don't get your hopes up too early«.

It's only when this unsavory connection has at last produced an intolerable lack of joy of life that a reversal is possible. When this individual is tired of his listlessness, when he feels no more joy in his joylessness, the time has come to recognize that both manifes-tations of fear – the discontentment in his own existence and the undemanding attitude with regard to his fellow men – are targeted at his basic vitality and health. From there it will be amazingly easy to let go of this form of self-damage. Once the person has cottoned on to the fact that life can actually be fun and that his comrades are often more than willing to freely give their support, affection and care – happy to be asked for it at last – the tide can turn. A thoroughly positive attitude to life can indeed evolve from this fear constellation.

All it requires for someone with these fear Symptoms is to learn to ask for things – and to enjoy. Asking for something is what builds the bridge to his fellow men. The enjoyment should be fo-cused on his own possibilities and opportunities. It's no secret that a person able to enjoy his life, at least in moderation, gets more attention and appreciation from others, simply because it's fun to be with him.

Energies 2 plus 3: Self-sabotage and Martyrdom

An individual assailed by Self-sabotage with Martyrdom will become all the more unhappy and joyless, the more he tries to please others, do noble deeds or act selflessly. Everything Martyrdom commands – to sacrifice oneself for a project, for one's fellow men, for the Third World or whatever else draws heavily on inner resources – turns in some strange way against the person, entailing a discrimination that seems completely illogical. The less egotistic this individual tries to be, all the more selfish the others will get. If he lends money to someone, he or she will turn around and betray him. He takes care of an elder person for years and then someone else inherits everything. He renunciates things important to him for the benefit of a third person and gets ridiculed in return.

This combination of fear Symptoms is particularly painful as long as the individual concerned doesn't understand that it's his harmful efforts at over-generosity which render him a terrible disservice. He believes to be doing a good deed, but doesn't recognize that it happens out of fear to be otherwise rejected or unloved. The proverb: »Nothing is as hard as man's ingratitude« applies in special measure to this fear combination. Self-sabotage as a means to reduce or even prevent the joy and lust of life makes use of Martyrdom as its instrument.

Among these people one finds persons who slave away all their life, toiling till they drop with hardly any recompense. In working life they are underpaid or don't get promoted. In private life no one thanks them for what they do for the family, friends or neighbors. So gradually in their adult years, they will become increasingly embittered and disappointed contemporaries. They are often ill and go on early retirement. Then, to top things up, the pension fund miscalculates the benefits due them so that, without noticing, they get less than what they are entitled to.

The key to change is to sever the Gordian Knot which has tightened up from the hope for zest of life on the one side, and self-sacrifice for others at the expense of one's own life energy on the other. There is only one way: the individual concerned must stop volunteering his services to others when they haven't even asked for it. He must stop defining himself as a particularly noble-minded being and strictly refrain from actions which come under this category. Only then will he or she achieve the desired result. Zest for life and happiness grow – if just for the simple reason that the individual with these fear features has much more time now to enjoy himself or take a rest. Self-sabotage subsides when it is stripped of the instrument of Martyrdom.

Energies 2 plus 4: Self-sabotage and Stubbornness

The combination of Self-sabotage with Stubbornness as secondary fear creates a philosophically disguised life attitude which insists that life is by definition nothing but a bitter and difficult matter, ill-designed by existence from the start. Everything about existence appears to be wrong.

To someone with this combination of fear Symptoms, the living days feel like being thrown, without rhyme or reason, into a condition he cannot conceive as positive. From this, he derives his life philosophy that it would have been better not to be born at all, and that the same is in fact also true for his fellow men. So it's all the more difficult for this individual to understand that others see their life in a brighter and kinder light. When reading the paper, he only spots the negative reports and catastrophes, feeling confirmed in his thinking. Looking at the people around him, he only sees unhappiness and disease, not the joyful events and genial pleasure they can take in each other. He insists that his perspective is the only right one, that others are simply kidding themselves and just don't understand what they've gotten into on this earth. His spiritual ideas correspond to his conception of the world: God is dead and Kingdom Come a yawning chasm.

This notion of existence can be changed when a person with a combination of Self-sabotage and Stubbornness gets closely or intimately acquainted with someone who embraces a diametrically opposed life philosophy. Through closeness and the living example experienced day by day, the stubborn Self-saboteur will understand that he has created an earthen ogre of human life, which can be easily destroyed again with just a few kicks. What surprises him most is that he can suddenly look at the fragments of his idol with an undreamt-of satisfaction, the reason for it being that hidden inside the ogre of clay was the golden figurine of a dancer which he now discovers as his potential for joy and adaptability to the great gifts of life. So it is occasionally desirable that someone imprisoned in his combination of Self-sabotage and Stubbornness gets dragged from his dungeon with loving, well-intentioned violence, and the idols he has adored be shattered. He can, of course, help this process by kicking the walls from the inside if he feels too constrained in them. He can free himself from the casing and develop a philosophy of life which at least calls into question that everything is indeed as grey and unalterably negative as he has imagined.

Energies 2 plus 5: Self-sabotage and Greed

The effect of Self-sabotage as Primary Symptom combined with Greed as the Secondary Symptom on the life story of an individual is that he keeps reaching out with both hands – and always comes away empty-handed. That he tries to take as much as possible from life – but finds himself on the wanting end again and again. That he is financially well-endowed to start with – yet loses everything. That he is successful and later goes bankrupt. That he is loved dearly yet hurts his partner so badly that he or she takes to their heels. Whenever there is abundance and pleasure, wherever the prospect of bounty and expansion is looming, Self-sabotage sets in and purposefully works at destroying what has been achieved, turning anything too much into not enough. So Self-sabotage with Greed produces strong fluctuations on a material and on an emotional plane.

The »negative« imaginativeness characterizing Self-sabotage has the curious objective of portraying or interpreting flops, financial collapses and the failure of relationships as something that is actually positive – known as the »sour grape syndrome.« For the individual who, due to the workings of his fears, is left empty-handed, it's a way of creating a vicarious satisfaction, because he is able to make himself believe that he is better off now than before.

When this Self-saboteur wants to work his way out of his trap, and moreover make sure it doesn't snap shut once again, it's important to focus on the Greed aspect and reduce the desire for excessiveness. Instead of alternately being a shareholder millionaire one day and the next day reduced to chewing bare bread in a bedsitter again, the option is to strive for less and retain the fruits of his achievements. What it takes is that the Self-saboteur with Greed consult with his fellow men, entrusting himself to them and seriously consider their advice, instead of reaching for the stars in the dark all alone. Otherwise he'll experience over and over that he is left with nothing to show for in the end, or that his pleasure is only short-lived. But if he communicates and joins forces with others – who may not always be cleverer but have a different combination of Fear Symptoms to prevent them from walking into the same trap – he will succeed in holding on to the luck, which, as it is, he sees primarily in material things. And he will refrain from embellishing his losses.

Energies 2 plus 6: Self-sabotage and Arrogance

The combination of Self-sabotage and Arrogance leads to a person who increasingly protects himself, retiring more frequently behind the retaining walls of his existence than is necessary or beneficial for him. He erects these protective walls everywhere: in his professional as well as in private life, to be shielded even from his own view, and of course the eyes of those who desire to get close to him in love and affection. He cannot allow having breaches or gates opening up somewhere in this retaining wall, because an angel named »Joy of life« might enter and spread the light of happiness and bliss. And this is something the energy of Self-sabotage must try to prevent. Complemented by Arrogance, Self-sabotage develops an attitude adjudging that zest for life is a cheap, somewhat shabby enjoyment for naive contemporaries.

Due to the Secondary Symptom of Arrogance, this person is often quite conscious of his actions and thoughts. He is well aware of his inclination to self-isolation. While feeling safe behind his walls, he also knows of his solitude. But the idea that a bright, healing, warm light might shine through the open gates or the breaches knocked from the inside out, just feels a little eerie to him. And the visit of an angel would certainly confuse him; someone with this combination of fear symptoms is likely to comprehend such an appearance as a phantasmagoria or a ghost, better to be scared away again. But his longing for deliverance from his solitude and sadness gets stronger with age. His desire to tear down the walls and step out of the ruins increases by the day, because the vulnerable joylessness accompanying this fear combination leads to segregation from what this individual values most: from the inner light of recognition.

So Self-sabotage plus Arrogance can be knocked down a peg, without leaving the scene completely, because this fear combination makes the individual particularly sensitive. So he must be able to withdraw into the ruins of his fear structure from time to time and hide there for a while. But ruins can no longer be shut off completely. They virtually invite visitors to come and admire the architecture of this dilapidated edifice, marveling: »In the past, you were much more reserved, quite inapproachable; now you show yourself, I can get close to you and recognize your true nature.«

Energies 2 plus 7: Self-sabotage and Impatience

Self-sabotage intends to avoid vivacity and joy as best possible. Impatience is troubled by the notion of having not enough life-time available. So how, under these circumstances, can a man still find reason for having fun, for enjoyment? When these two forms of fear combine, they often produce an ebullient, almost extreme greed for life and a breathless impulse to squeeze as much zest, experience and intensity as possible into a short lifespan. Due to the permanent stress of this excited intensity, the beauty and relaxing qualities of joy of life cannot possibly find room to unfurl.

Self-sabotage and Impatience have a common goal: exerting a maximum of time pressure and to not let any joy develop in one's achievements or aspirations. Self-sabotage suggests to the individual concerned that his most efficient efforts will never suffice and that joie de vivre while there's so much work to do is really a trifle immoral. In view of all the things that still need to be done or achieved in this short life, one has no right to enjoy the moment, maybe later.

As a consequence, the person with the Primary Symptom Self-sabotage and Impatience as Secondary Symptom tries to postpone enjoying his life to some time in the future, for example retirement age, consoling himself with the proverb: »Business before pleasure.« What remains, however, is that constant feeling of having missed out on something. This feeling makes him so sad, so utterly distraught and puts him in such a state that he actually longs to fall ill, thus awarding him the chance to get some rest, at least for a short time. Some slight disease, an accident, a handicap seem to suddenly turn into sources for joy of life, as strange as this may sound.

Yet Self-sabotage also knows what control is. Setting his mind to it, he can apply this capacity for control positively and keep the tormenting Impatience in check. That way, self-control may be converted from a fearful quality to a conscious self-taming. It shuts the self-damage – which lies in ambush in this combination like a wild beast – into a cage and, while still feeding and caring for this »animal«, not let it run free anymore.

3. Martyrdom with all Secondary Fear Symptoms

Energies 3 plus 1: Martyrdom and Self-deprecation

Martyrdom overexerts itself in hard work and achievement, while Self-deprecation endeavors to prevent that this be noticed, attract attention or – heaven forbid – be complimented. So this combination of Fear Symptoms induces the individual to hide behind his commitment and diligence, maneuvering himself ever deeper into a situation in which he reaps neither gratitude nor recognition for his work, while concurrently practicing humble self-devaluation. It all boils down to this: whatever he does or doesn't do, he won't get any appreciation from his fellow men because – so he or she is convinced – there is actually nothing to be appreciated.

The self-disownment of Martyrdom, in the sense of a fearful undervaluation of the self, and the oversized modesty of Self-deprecation, already blushing at the mere thought of praise and fending off any potential positive feed-back or reaction, form a joint defensive attitude. It effectively prevents that any natural appreciation, admiration or grateful reverence from the people around him penetrate into his consciousness. The selfless diligence, even if motivated by fear, nonetheless meets with resonance from his fellow men, be it respect or contempt. But the self-denying Martyr refuses to let any of this enter into his perception radius, since it would call for a reaction from him one way or the other: either joy or else getting furious. This he tries to avoid, lest he wake up from his strange illusion of virtuous modesty and invisibility.

Once the self-deprecating Martyr realizes the game he's playing with himself, and that it's he himself turning a blind eye, deaf ears and a locked heart against his fellow men's appreciation, he'll want to put a stop to it. Because it's a game that can lead to severe injuries and lasting damage. Slowly it will dawn on him that making himself so small and ugly is utterly undesirable. Ultimately, the notion that someone is loved more if he doesn't stand out, incriminates, if he devalues or showers himself with reproaches, can't be satisfactory to anyone. So it's appropriate to opt for a different course and check out whether that love and appreciation, respect and affection he so wistfully craves for won't increase by the measure that his self-devaluation and self-humiliating modesty attitude decrease.

Energies 3 plus 2: Martyrdom and Self-sabotage

An individual with the Primary Symptom of Martyrdom doesn't think much of himself. Paradoxically, he hopes that others think all the more of him the less he appreciates himself and respects his own dignity. With Self-sabotage as the Secondary Symptom sacrificing primarily life energy, vitality, health and happiness, enjoying existence or partaking in life's blessings is forbidden. So this person maneuvers himself into a situation which ensures that he doesn't feel the least bit of joy in his outstanding performance, his noble behavior and self-sacrificing selflessness. Rather, he gets increasingly sad and depressed.

Occasionally – if nothing else works – this combination may even lead the self-sabotaging Martyr to attain what he desires by some obvious self-damage, or at least revel in the fantasy of hurting himself. By falling seriously ill, having an accident or by developing a depression, he hopes to finally get the attention and appreciation, affection and tenderness which has been denied him in a healthier state – only to discover to his great dismay that people find this manner even more tiresome or annoying. On the contrary, it earns him nothing but reproaches because his effectiveness dries up and he gets blamed into the bargain for the problems and costs resulting from his accident or illness. Even if not explicitly verbalized, the diseased or sad self-sabotaging Martyr acutely and painfully senses every indirect accusation.

This moment of suffering will make him want to stop his joyless self-devaluation. The first step towards a solution consists in dissociating himself – inwardly or even physically – from the people around him which occupy a firm position in his old fear system. As a rule, a change to more joy of life and increased self-esteem can only occur when sustained by the beneficial support of loving, caring fellow humans. The hitch is, of course, that the self-sabotaging Martyr has mostly surrounded himself with friends and partners who need his particular fear system to act out their own anxieties. So if they aren't willing to co-operate or able to adjust, a clear distancing is called for. It doesn't necessarily mean separation, but certainly a distinctive switch in awareness, so as not to offer the old schemes to his surroundings any longer. Once he recognizes that he can increase his zest for life, thereby automatically reducing the pleasure at culpable suffering, he will soon acquire a taste for it and successfully fight against debasement and energy vampirism.

Energies 3 plus 4: Martyrdom and Stubbornness

A human being with the Primary Symptom of Martyrdom suffers silently and is generally used to vague or strong guilt feelings like to his own face. In the combination with Stubbornness which is characterized by the unwillingness to change, this individual will initially see no reason to make any effort at improving his situation. He feels quite safe and content in the fear system he has ensconced himself in. In his own perception, the things he does or desists from doing are absolutely normal. His suffering is representative for the suffering of the world, and his lack of desire for change is quite understandable as it feels like an expression of his deep empathy with the lot of humanity. And anyway, who would want to jeopardize a fairly tolerable situation when, after all, others were much worse off? Change is undesirable.

The Martyr with the Secondary Symptom of Stubbornness believes that by sheer inner resistance he can put an adequate stop to his extreme self-devaluation. He adheres to the motto: »Never change a winning team.« As for the rest, he is quite confident that by his unrelenting, virtually grim efforts and drudgery, circumstances will soon change – as if by a miracle and quite by themselves.

He emphatically insists on his idiosyncratic perception of his personal worth, whereas in reality his fellow men quite obviously keep humiliating and demeaning him. In his opinion, though, this has nothing at all to do with his behavior; it's their misguided attitude! A person with this fear combination often endures such damaging, humiliating and debasing situations for far too long, stubbornly hoping for a wondrous change and recognition at last.

One day, however, even the stubborn Martyr feels he's had enough of such indignities. He can't keep up the incessant, high-minded efforts at trying to change his fellow people any longer, and finally gives up. The day this happens usually comes only late in life, because his deep fear of being deserted by those he wants to love him, concealed behind the symptom of Stubbornness, requires great pressure to surface into consciousness. Then the stubborn Martyr begins to investigate what he himself contributed to the situation he wishes to leave behind. And it requires a fair degree of honesty towards himself and his motives.

In this fear alliance, self-debasement seems always justified by the whimpering fear of loneliness and abandonment. The individual accepts all kinds of humiliations, even up to blows, to avert being lost and lonely. It's only when this fear penetrates into his awareness and he or she is able to recognize it as either factually unjustified or ultimately tolerable, that the knot finally becomes undone. Instead of embellishing his fear of abandonment with devoted selflessness, it is now openly revealed, and this unveiling is immensely wholesome.

When this stubborn Martyr, male or female, is ready to be happily alone with himself, he will be able to see and understand his intrinsic, existential worth – not just theoretically or defiantly insisting upon it, but deeply felt. He can save himself from feeling helplessly deserted by consciously cherishing his own valued company. This is the premise for a relaxed and contented life.

Energies 3 plus 5: Martyrdom and Greed

Based on his own negative assessment of his worth, the individual with the Primary Symptom of Martyrdom is given to victimhood, feeling disadvantaged by life. Yet because of his Secondary Symptom of Greed, he would always like to have more than he needs or is possible. Martyrdom in combination with Greed results in a disappointed and resigned, dissatisfied life attitude. The greedy person is never quite sated by what he has and is, while the Martyr in his imagined situation of scarcity develops his own proof that he doesn't really deserve more. Just now and then a feeling will creep up in him: »But this can't have been it. It can't be true that life holds so little beauty and happiness, so little bounty in store for me«, triggering anew the effort to reach out greedily for more and more satisfaction.

But a Martyr seldom dares ask for anything. A greedy person in contrast likes to stake his claims. As long as a Martyr with this fear combination isn't trying to reach for something unattainable, making excessive demands on existence itself and his fellow people, he can basically rely on getting more than he dreamed of. That's why it's important that someone with this combination of Primary and Secondary Symptoms of Fear should occasionally examine whether he doesn't even settle for too little. But he tends to always vacillate between two extremes: Wanting too much and, as a result, getting too little.

The fears of this individual are two-faceted. One can be described as the fear of ensuing guilt feelings, if he should dare demand for something at all (»I'm far too fastidious«). The other is fear of punishment and rejection, or a bitter disappointment when, having actually asked for something, it isn't granted to him right away or downright refused.

But the attitude »I prefer not to ask so no one can refuse it to me« is no solution here. It is rather advisable to practice how to make requests and demands sincerely; it's the key to a change in attitude towards his fellow men.

Previously, the greedy Martyr would more or less openly signal: »I actually don't need much and I don't make any demands. But you must guess what I want and then give me as much as I'm worth to you.« From a change of consciousness evolves a more open attitude which gives others a real chance to say Yes or No to the Martyr's request, providing some room for generosity and capacity for love at their own discretion, without coercion. When the greedy Martyr overcomes his fear of blame, his shame of asking for or claiming something, and his anxiety to be punished for his desires, he's got a life of plenty and gratification ahead of him, sustained by a healthy sense of self-worth.

Energies 3 plus 6: Martyrdom and Arrogance

Martyrdom has an evident problem of self-worth, but Arrogance doesn't like to admit that this might be so, because is too humiliating. Arrogance likes and needs to feel that it is »something better«, while Martyrdom keeps belying this very feeling. Martyrdom debases and humiliates the self; Arrogance exalts the self and puts it above others. The supposed benefit lies in the enormous effort of both fears jointly acting more generously, selflessly and lovingly than anyone else around.

The person in question may feel lofty and exalted, while forgetting that this gigantic effort to constantly and unassailably think, feel and act nobly – i.e., to be of incontestable »high worth« – is merely due to his fear of the deathblow of an irreversible loss of worth. It's not surprising then that a person with this fear combination works with great zeal at his self-image, and appears rather strained in the effort.

He or she mustn't show any weakness. Should such weakness be uncovered by someone or by circumstances, it will take a long time before the wounds of shame can heal and a new run-up be taken to reassert the self-esteem. Only this time around, he will be less insisting on being always the best, most clever, noble and sensitive of all. Ultimately, it's because someone has scratched at his façade, set up with so much difficulty and spruced with so many layers of paint, that the precious fresco of authenticity hidden underneath the coatings of false nobility and superiority becomes visible. The person with the fear combination of Martyrdom with Arrogance suddenly becomes aware of his wonderful innermost nature, may-be for the very first time.

He can even play with the idea of other interested parties coming to ask permission to remove still more of the whitewashed façade, to see what other precious, rare and highly delicate paintings might be concealed underneath it. This scratching will help him learn to appreciate himself more. Most of all, it will help him interact differently with his fellow humans. He will acquiesce to being appreciated and honored – not for his slick, shining pseudo-noble surface but for the most beautiful thing he has to offer: his authentic, colorful nature.

Energies 3 plus 7: Martyrdom and Impatience

A Martyr wants to prove by exaggerated, blind activity that his existence is worthy and indispensable. The impatient person is equally geared towards action, though this action is about fighting the panic of not getting by on the time and lifespan apportioned to him by destiny. When these two fears unite as Primary and Secondary Symptoms of Fear, they produce an enormous, agitated compulsion, hardly granting the individual any rest for a night's sleep. Taking things easy for a day or two is equaled with idleness and makes this person quite nervous.

The sharply calculating efficiency of an impatient person who is always busy and makes plans for every minute of his life, including the times for rest and leisure, meets the martyr-like attitude of not deserving relaxation and holidays until everyone in his environment has been provisioned with boundless energy and selfless sacrifice. That there won't be much strength left is quite obvious, of course. It would require a long period of recovery to get the impatient Martyr to recognize his selfless bustle and free himself from the hamster wheel of his high-minded endeavors.

Yet the impatient part of him doesn't like to abide the time required to regenerate, because idle relaxation feels like boredom to him after a very short while. Whereas the martyr-side of him in turn develops guilt feelings: »Other people, too, fulfill their duty. I'll sleep when I'm dead.« So the hectic rush and lack of tolerance for his own need of rest leads to a double activity pressure in this combination of fears which, unless he finally surrenders, is likely to drive him to the verge or fully into an emotional and nervous exhaustion.

No one can prove nor increase his existential worth by however much activity and efficiency he invests. Viewed in the cold light of day, this is really a most inefficient application of one's energy. The Martyr rarely gives others a chance to appreciate or praise him, and it's not much different with the impatient person. He always wants everything off the table at once, better even yesterday. He gets irritable or testy when jobs he has planned to complete don't get done.

He pressurizes other people incessantly. Since the impatient Martyr toils like a slave for others and slogs away in prospect of some future respite, only to be granted when everything has been accomplished, the activity spiral using up his time reaches into infinity and is lost from view. So there is only one solution: The spiral must be capped by an act of consciousness as if by large wire shears. There is no other possibility than to ask oneself: »What am I actually doing here? Why do I do this? For whom and for what? What stops me from finding some rest?« These questions are very wholesome. They'll rein in this harassed hustle and bustle which used to feel so utterly philanthropical and timesaving to him but was not.

When all the time a person believes to have saved is squandered with acts of selflessness, and all worth enhancement he believes he must work for and conquer, falls by the wayside from rigorous performance of duties, life will indeed seem much too short, because there is no time left to enjoy the moment. So the impatient Martyr needs a health cure, a cure of awareness so to speak. Every time a kind of blind activity tornado starts hurling him around, he should stop his robot machinery and remember that this engine has long since run idle and doesn't produce the desired result: gratitude, admiration and appreciation. Then at last, time is available like sand by the sea, and his feeling of self-worth increases by the amount of time and affection the impatient Martyr devotes to himself, completely without plans, intention or wanting to accomplish something.

4. Stubbornness with all Secondary Fear Symptoms

Energies 4 plus 1: Stubbornness and Self-deprecation

The fear structure (Basic Fear) of Stubbornness combined with Self-deprecation induces this person to grimly insist that everybody overestimates or assesses him wrongly. He imputes that they simply don't recognize how few competences and abilities he really possesses. He or she becomes obstinately fixated on having to work extra hard, being particularly diligent and demonstrating utterly selfless commitment. And yet that gnawing feeling of somehow deceiving the world never leaves him. Nobody except him seems to notice how little substance there really is behind all his work and efforts and that with a little more dedication, he could actually have achieved even greater success.

Naturally, his own interests range second to those of his fellow men. The self-deprecating stubborn individual is convinced to be quite tough, able to take on all kinds of burdens where others would have given up long ago. Since he can hardly – sometimes not at all – feel his own needs because his torpid stiffness has numbed body and spirit, he involuntarily slips into the emotions and needs of those around him instead: his partner, family or colleagues, Stubbornness acting like blinkers for his own feelings and behavior. He is unaware of what he's doing and doesn't want to be relieved. Consequently, he is often exhausted without being able to stop, finding it hard to let go and relax.

He sticks to the guns when others are taking a break; he musters his last bit of strength to keep on toiling, only realizing how terrible he feels when everyone else has disappeared from view to enjoy themselves.

Self-deprecation is modest and Stubbornness obstinate. What characterizes this Basic Fear combination and distinguishes it from others is the dogged insistence on unpretentiousness, on having no emotional needs, on being able to do everything single-handedly without any help. Or on being insignificant, acting unobtrusively in the background, all the while demonstrating a considerable inflexibility and perseverance in this attitude.

If a so-structured individual wants to change, he must start by recognizing that his (false) autonomy, of which he is so proud, and his ambitious assiduity, which renders him so lonely, are the result of his anxieties. But he can learn to ask for support, for affection and relief, to suddenly find that his world is full of kind helpers. Whereas someone who always signals »I can do it all on my own and do it better!« isn't going to have many friends. It is undeniable though that the Secondary Symptom of Self-deprecation allied with Stubbornness as Primary Symptom, given a little self-awareness, spawns particularly capable, seriously hard-working, reliable and devotedly responsible individuals.

Energies 4 plus 2: Stubbornness and Self-sabotage

An individual combining the Primary Symptom of Stubbornness with Self-sabotage as Secondary Symptom tends to make life quite hard for himself by obstinately nursing harmful habits and getting into the same situations which don't do him any good over and over again. Or he keeps making the same mistake because he fails to see that it was a mistake already in the past to act or react in that particular way.

It's difficult for this man or woman to take things and life in general easy and not burden his days with excessive conflict. Either he doesn't see problems anywhere – or else everywhere! He doesn't like to admit that those taking their daily chores, their relationships and working life in a more fleet-footed manner than he aren't necessarily superficial, irresponsible or careless. Someone with this Basic Fear pattern will react quite astonished to the advice: »Now please, don't take everything so seriously; don't always be so hard on yourself.«

Quite unwittingly, he frequently spreads a morose or heavy atmosphere. He himself considers it a justified attitude in the face of life's fundamental difficulties, because in his opinion, problems are the essential aspect of reality.

He reacts with considerable resistance to changes, especially when his unconscious signals him: »Your life might possibly become easier, happier and better by this change.« To him, it feels as if he were robbed of his stability, as if life was tripping him up and taking from him what he has acquired in terms of security and dependability. He usually remains locked much too long in friendships, employments, relationships or family situations that are evidently to his disadvantage or make him unhappy. Faced with voluntary change, he feels so helpless that all he can think is: »But there really isn't any alternative. What else could I do?«

The individual concerned should ingest the idea that, whether life feels easy or difficult doesn't depend only on fate. Wallowing in homemade problems, the habit of always perceiving the glass as half-empty, preferring to lament difficulties rather than find a solution, all of this can be changed. Because inherent in this Basic Fear composed of a »Scholar's« (4) and an »Artist's« (2) energy are the ability to reason and an added freshness of mind, which can both be released by self-induced changes in one's life perspective. And no one could be more thoroughly pleased at the successful change of his life circumstances. A half-filled glass is no longer an illusion but reason for celebration.

Energies 4 plus 3: Stubbornness and Martyrdom

Stubbornness and Martyrdom produce a Basic Fear which can be described as a grim willingness to make unnecessary sacrifices at all cost or as an especially humble rigidity. Stubbornness and Martyrdom negatively complement each other, although they seemingly neutralize each other, but in reality both sustain the extreme fears of losing one's footing when unable to gain – or afraid to lose – the appreciation of one's fellow beings. A »Scholar's« (4) obstinacy in pursuing a goal and a »Warrior's« (3) apparently noble-minded readiness for self-sacrifice produce a harsh view of the world.

The alliance of Stubbornness and Martyrdom always entices this person to be obstinately kind and indulgent, because the deep panic to be deserted, punished, ignored or belittled is omnipresent, lurking behind every corner and every action. So this stubborn person with the Secondary Symptom of Martyrdom will try to do everything in his power to shield his inner house against the storms of criticism, conflicts or corrections by his fellow men. Windows are barricaded from the inside as if against a permanent tornado, doors sealed up with silicone. From the outside, everything looks normal and unassailable. Inside, however, smolders a deep fear of the collapse of human relations and an ever-imminent, destructive partnership-thunderstorm, from which one cannot escape even by retreating into a panic-room with maximum-security level. Soon the air feels stuffy and suffocating; relationships turn into prisons. What characterizes this Basic Fear is an almost total inability to handle criticism or any unintentional downgrading with some degree of flexibility or humor.

As he gets older, and with the experience of having weathered such storms in the past, the person's ability improves to outwardly behave as if he could handle those situations, to act as if he wasn't a screaming bundle of fear at the erroneous idea that to be admonished automatically leads to desertion. But inside, the helplessness against any utterance that just might be understood as criticism or devaluation remains. It needs nursing as if it had been an almost fatal stab with a knife, requiring a prolonged convalescence. At the root of this is the fear of having no worth and of being discarded as unlovable, with a coherent fear of any unpredictable, loveless reactions by his fellow humans.

All his life the stubborn Martyr has tried everything to be loved, yet he or she never quite believed in the ultimate success of this effort. He stubbornly insists that in the end, he is probably going to be dumped after all. He equally stubbornly insists that others can never love as selflessly as he does, being a Martyr, and people will never understand how lovable he really is. The frantic efforts to do good, loving and noble deeds, and to deposit successful relationships into the account of one's own merits – like federal savings bonds unperturbed by price fluctuations – are extremely exhausting. So people with this Basic Fear are often very tired from the hard work of proving themselves valuable.

When exhaustion from suffering and the fear of loss become intolerable, a change for the good may at last result. The individual must learn to feel trust in the love of others without being able to justify that trust. He can endow relationships with a credit on the capacity for love of his partner. He will get the chance to understand that relationships don't have to be solely sustained by him. The realization will be highly valuable that eternal forgiveness and constant goodness in order to avoid conflicts only seldom contribute to stable relationships. As a result, martyr-like stubborn individuals will be truly unwavering in their relationships, faithful in friendships and ready to make sacrifices when indeed required in the name of love.

Energies 4 plus 5: Stubbornness and Greed

The Basic Fear produced by the two Symptoms of Stubbornness and Greed produces a perspective of life that fiercely sways between the extremes of too much and never enough. The stubborn person with the Secondary Symptom of Greed categorically feels that he's never really getting what he needs and it takes some convincing that the opposite is actually the case. He acts like a person wearing very dark sunglasses in a softly lit room. Since he is in denial of this, he judges the lighting conditions in the room quite differently than people not looking through dark glasses.

This individual sees the world from a permanent perspective of privation. He would like to have more of everything but doesn't quite register when this »more« has been achieved or already been granted him. He maintains that it's the others wanting and taking too much. He projects his view of the world carved by a feeling of paucity onto his fellow men, on those who possess more material means than he does, who cause too much or too little political or social change, or those not meeting his expectations. He is often envious. Only seldom does he recognize that it's his own angle of view that causes his permanent dissatisfaction with conditions in the world and in his own surroundings.

Someone with this combination of fears is either tenaciously stingy, granting himself only the most basic necessities and doing without conveniences that seem totally normal to others, or he takes for granted his personal notion of material contentment that doesn't allow him to lower his expectations or accept any changes in his economic situation, because change severely threatens his feeling of safety. When it comes to material loss, a stubborn person with Greed is very inflexible. He finds it difficult to adapt to the pulsations and fluctuations of his life circumstances. He considers his family, his partner, his inherited and earned wealth as an unshakeable, inalienable possession, as a jealously guarded property on which he has once and for all acquired a title which no human shall take away from him.

Practicing a new habit is what helps here: to adequately give, to donate and offer gifts and tips, even when he thinks he can't really afford it or the beneficiary doesn't quite deserve it. Once he has gotten accustomed to being more generous, even charitable, with his worldly goods, he'll be able to keep it up. He'll gradually become emotionally aware of the neediness or material hardships some of his fellow beings suffer. Then he can permit himself to donate regularly, to share or give without his own interests coming up too short. This also applies to feelings. And to the amazement of the stubbornly greedy person, he will get back more than he has given.

Energies 4 plus 6: Stubbornness and Arrogance

The Symptoms of Stubbornness and Arrogance tend to entrench themselves behind walls of superiority. They make each other believe that retreat, shelter from the world, the delimitation against everything and everybody who might penetrate into this refuge, is a genuine solution and promises a permanent feeling of contentment and emotional security.

The stubbornly arrogant person tries to keep the requirement of coping with anything new down to a minimum and doesn't love surprises. So when confronted with someone new in his life, it will be inevitable that this new individual in his otherness holds some surprise for him every day – often with a manifestation of life or behavior which hurts or threatens to hurt the stubbornly arrogant person. That's why he prefers to maintain as few contacts as possible and only peep out from his emotional fortress when it seems absolutely sure that nothing at all can happen to him.

Stubbornness produces a hard shell, and Arrogance ensures that this shell, while hard, is also fragile, as if made of thin glass. The stubborn arrogant person protects himself behind this glass shell, although he knows quite well that the mere pebble of a fellow man trying to make contact could hit the glass pane any time and unsuspectingly shatter it into a thousand pieces. Then he or she would be defenselessly exposed to love. Yet nothing better could in fact happen to the stubbornly arrogant person. If at first it's a most unpleasant surprise, he will soon realize that he couldn't have emerged of his own power from behind the glass pane, even though it was transparent. But once broken, it can never be put up in the same way again. The air of freedom and the perfume of subtle sensitivity are so exquisite that the individual concerned feels no real desire to retreat once more into the hermitage behind his glass barrier. Or at least, now there will always be windows which can be opened from within. The best advice to him or her is to take every chance of an emotional exchange when offered. Nobody has yet perished from closeness.

Energies 4 plus 7: Stubbornness and Impatience

Stubbornness and Impatience are like brothers who don't get on well. Each would like to outshine or outwit the other. Each wants to be their parent's favorite child. Both demand equally full attention. In this case they demand the attention of the »I« acting out this Basic Fear. Stubbornness wants to persist; Impatience wants to change quickly. Stubbornness needs time; Impatience wants to move on. Stubbornness holds tight; Impatience dissolves. To realize this alliance in one's own system, gendered by the same parents so to speak, represents a great challenge. Both fear siblings must be satisfied, each according to its needs. So a stubborn person with the Secondary Symptom of Impatience should once in a while leave room for change through his Impatience's impulsion; likewise, the impatient part must occasionally make the concession to Stubbornness that things may remain as they are.

Sometimes, these different and contradictory inner needs result in a »torn personality«, often seeming unpredictable in all manifestations of life: today one thing, tomorrow the opposite! Stubbornness closes its mind to imposed change as best it can and doesn't like surprises. Impatience needs the unexpected, the intense excitement of an unpredictable future like it needs air to breathe. Both needs tug at the »I« in a maddening rage.

Sometimes, the anxiety caused by the incalculable ramifications of a decision leads to a strange torpor. However, shelter and independence, safety and openness can be reconciled with each other, both inside and in the outside world or in relationships. Impatience steers the life-boat to new shores, then Stubbornness with its need for quiet, order and stability amongst the unknown makes itself at home there. This combination is sure to produce some difficulties and inner conflicts; on the other hand it can occasionally be quite exhilarating.

Because Impatience will never let it happen that Stubbornness gets as forceful as in many other stubborn combinations of fear symptoms, and Stubbornness will never grant Impatience so much compulsive change that its obstinate will to persist no longer plays a role. So as mature grown-ups the once inimical brothers mutually influence each other by correcting and moderating their sibling, and that is their advantage. Impatient stubborn people are flexible when they have to be. They adapt if that's what life requires. They are lively and full of spirit, persistent in essential things and stormy on the surface.

5. Greed with all Secondary Fear Symptoms

Energy 5 plus 1: Greed and Self-deprecation

The Primary Symptom of Fear Greed in combination with the Secondary Symptom Self-deprecation produces a forcedly modest person, someone always pulling himself together so as not to appear expecting or demanding too much. He will seldom claim anything for himself. This person acts modestly and unpretentiously, because he is already embarrassed at the mere idea that his Greed might be conspicuous in some way or that he could be criticized for it. So this combination of Fear Symptoms tends to cultivate a fearful self-denial in a maximum number of areas of life. He must keep his wishes and desires under control to prevent that these become obvious, both to the individual himself or to others.

The self-deprecating greedy person makes himself small rather than big. He doesn't extend his hands towards the blessings of life but hides them behind his back. He smugly enjoys a renunciation attitude instead of nurturing the idea that the opportunities life offers are actually meant for him and his well-being. What he feels most embarrassed about is keeping any material possessions for himself. He gives away and lends things so that, from an objective perspective, the others always have a bit more than he has, although thanks to him.

This also applies to affection and attention. The person with Greed and Self-deprecation is content with little, in fact too little, while he, in contrast, virtually wastes his energy on others. He promotes and admires them, and bestows on them all the things he himself would secretly or unconsciously like to have. And he is rather proud of his unpretentiousness, a clear sign that it's the testimony of his fear and doesn't originate from casual modesty.

But there is a chance to somewhat loosen this correlation and shift to a wholesome middle both the excessive modesty and excessive must-have, resolved in Greed and controlled by modesty. It lies in becoming alert to the moment this secret pride in the renunciation attitude begins to swell. The right decision then is to seize or accept nonetheless, or to refrain from making a generous gift, instead of heeding the insinuations of fear that only he is a good person who gives all and takes nothing. That is, the attention should be focused on the complacency which begins to spread every time one hasn't asked for what one is actually entitled to, or parts with something one really needs. Once complacency has been identified as a yardstick of fear, the fear can be shed. Accordingly, the individual concerned needs to turn his attention only on one single factor, and that doesn't lie outside but inside of him!

Energy 5 plus 2: Greed and Self-sabotage

A human being with the Primary Fear Symptom Greed and Self-sabotage as the Secondary Symptom has, in fact, access to abundance and profusion, to luxury and the blessings of existence. He can recognize abundance also where others hardly see it. He could enjoy it to the fullest if he weren't destroying it the very moment when pleasure and relaxation are within reach. He acts like a man who can afford to buy a large, expensive bone china vase, then proceeds to the florist's to buy a wonderful bunch of flowers and carries both home. He arranges the flowers in the precious new vase and places it on a small table of which he knows – and has known for years – that it's a bit wobbly and the legs need fixing. He steps back to admire his arrangement, at which moment the inevitable happens: The little table caves in under the weight of the vase with the magnificent flowers, and all the splendor is gone in one second. The greedy person with the Secondary Fear Symptom of Self-sabotage witnesses this course of events in manifold variations time and again and is disconcerted; he can't understand how it's possible that just when things could be at their best, something goes wrong and he is denied the fruits of his efforts.

A new behavior is possible only when the individual turns his gaze backwards to that brief moment when his instinct or intuition had given him a warning and of which he can afterwards say with full consciousness: »I really knew it beforehand somehow. There was that moment when I should have taken a different decision or backed out.« It helps when this person fully acknowledges that he actually has this intuition, and that this intuition keeps trying almost desperately to catch his attention, just before Self-sabotage gets ready to spoil the savoring of the fruit of Greed.

Greed will be reduced the moment the individual understands that wanting to have the cake and eat it too triggers his Self-sabotage and suppresses the intuitive red flag. A minimal reduction of his needy wanting everything at once by only about ten to fifteen per cent would already suffice to offset this mechanism. The issue here is not the preciousness or the cost of the vase, but that the filled vase was a little too big for the small table. We certainly wouldn't recommend to someone with this fear combination to completely restrain him- or herself. But cutting back his want by just a fraction will open up opportunities of more long-lasting enjoyment to him, also satisfying his Greed.

Energy 5 plus 3: Greed and Martyrdom

The combination of Greed and Martyrdom has primarily one goal: »I want to please, I want to please, I want to please more than anyone else!« This is not so much about being loved and respected than about a queer sort of vanity that basks in being a particularly selfless, good and helpful human being. It rarely becomes obvious that this desire first and foremost serves the objective of self-adulation and self-satisfaction. His fellow humans frequently notice it much earlier because they start feeling a nauseating cloyingness at the good deeds the martyr-like greedy person presses on them, almost trying to force it down their throat against their will. They neither want to accept nor take as much, and eye with distrust and sullenness what they have been given, instead of enjoying it.

The greedy person with Martyrdom as the Secondary Fear Symptom always does and wants too much of a good thing. It's striking, however, that he prevents others to bestow such goodness on him in like measure. He fends off their endeavors and usurps the whole space of generosity and readiness to be at the service of others for himself. This often creates a tacit annoyance in his surroundings. Eventually though, his family and friends simply submit. This soon results in so much work and so many obligations and so little time for himself, that he starts complaining about the inconsiderateness of others. But instead of withdrawing in frustration, he will perform a still more selfless deed, intended to serve as a shining example to those who allegedly behaved so pettily. The issue here is always self-esteem, felt to be so poor by this individual that it needs incessant gilding and polishing.

Someone with this basic fear combination has stylized himself to such an idol of kindliness, that – if he is really serious about wanting to progress and curb his fear – he has no choice but to look with some sincerity at the results of his actions over his first thirty, forty or fifty years of life. Only then will he be able to recognize this idol of goodness he wants to pass for in its stark reality and – if not immediately shattering it completely – relegate it to the closet or the basement. It saves him to look at and polish it all the time, or showing it off to others as the most precious piece of the collection. Perhaps he'll be able to see then that this idol isn't really made of solid gold, but that the gilding has been applied very thinly on cheapest metal. He will recognize that he can hold his own before himself and his fellow men without this overly shiny self-image.

Energy 5 plus 4: Greed and Stubbornness

The focus of the combination of Greed with the Secondary Fear Symptom Stubbornness isn't so much on coveting, wishing or desiring, but on wanting to keep. Collecting, hoarding, stacking and building up stocks is the objective of the person with this combination of Fear Symptoms. This doesn't only apply to everyday objects but also to physical matter, for example excretory products or metabolic deposits, body fat or toxic substances. It's something the greedy person with the Secondary Fear Symptom Stubbornness finds difficult to shed or part with and which is generally not subjected to his will. His body reflects, as is usual with Stubbornness, that barely conscious longing to not let go what has once been absorbed or taken into possession.

The endeavors of this individual to accumulate and hoard often show in his home, cluttered with flea market items and souvenirs of times long gone. It shows in his bank account, which is seldom overdrawn but in general enjoys a considerable financial padding, just like his body, which is often stout, firm and compact, because it tries to store whatever is storable. The persistence with which he or she expects an emergency to occur sometime somehow someplace, some dangerous situation in which they would badly need what they have collected and saved, makes this general stock piling seem like the most sensible thing in the world to them. They can justify it any time and cite sufficient examples of how their reserves have helped them in the past.

The greedy man or woman with the Secondary Fear Symptom of Stubbornness isn't stingy. He can give if someone else is really in need. He is actually quite content then, because need is something he understands perfectly well. Yet, while he shares with the needy, he considers generosity on principle as unreasonable. And when he owns things two- and three-fold, something inside of him calms down. This can even make itself felt as a definite sensation of satiety. The individual with this basic fear combination loves to host dinners and invite guests because it makes him feel good to show that his barns are full and his larder is well stocked.

When this person feels ready to make a small step out of the compulsion of his fearful hoarding, a specific exercise of consciousness will be helpful. This requires his objectively and physically verifying what he has accumulated in the course of his life. This exercise doesn't necessarily mean to let go of it all but to take stock, make an inventory so to speak of the inner and outer provisions, designed to get a clear picture and realize: maybe one doesn't need it all, maybe it's OK now and then to part with one or the other item when the moment feels right. It should, however, be left completely up to the individual concerned because when someone else suggests that he should give away something, he will react obstinately and unruly.

Separation feels unpleasant to the stubborn person; to the greedy it's a horror. But a voluntary separation can bring tranquility, a relief as if easing a backpack full of rocks by a few kilos. The burden need not be thrown off completely. But letting go of some boulder stones makes a great difference, providing more lightness, which also applies to superfluous pounds or accumulated toxins. People with the features of Greed and Stubbornness are well advised to take a body cleansing and detoxification cure from time to time.

Energy 5 plus 6: Greed and Arrogance

A greedy person with the Secondary Fear Symptom Arrogance nurses on two seemingly contradictory illusions. The first one is: »Only the best, in fact the very best, is just good enough for me, because I am of such superior worth that this worth must be reflected in all its aspects at each moment of my life.« This first variety primarily strives for exclusiveness, not abundance, i.e., for the choicest of the best: not many diamonds, but one big one, not many clothes, but only the finest silk and cashmere pieces. Much time is devoted to image cultivation and styling and grooming the outer appearance. The greedy, nothing-is-good-enough-for-me personality needs admirers. So he mingles with the elegant or true nobility crowd if possible, even if he is not from the same background. The rich and beautiful are his audience. Only when he feels the admiration and appreciation of this exclusive circle will his fear system be reassured and calm down.

The second type of this fear combination thrives on the illusion that one doesn't need anything at all but finds satisfaction in a self-imposed frugality. With everyone needing all kinds of things and he nothing, he becomes something special and spiritually particularly valuable into the bargain. Since Arrogance is a »priestly« energy, this second attitude can go so far as to entering a religious order disclaiming all possessions or subscribing to a life-form of asceticism: as a troglodyte in the woods, living in a garden shed with no running water or heating, or as a globetrotter existing on one dollar a day. That this is a specific form of greedy Arrogance can be spotted when the individual enjoys dwelling in great detail on his needlessness, looking down condescendingly on those who

need »all those material goods«. Whereas he, often for ideologically well justified reasons, rejects all that – until the time his fellow
men withdraw from him because they feel degraded in their harmless needs and ridiculed for their bourgeois desire of a good and
comfortable life. An arrogantly greedy person radiates a certain
kind of unrest, because he cannot truly dissociate from his inner
drive to get something. It is merely converted into an attitude of
not wanting anything.

This alliance of Fear Symptoms can be countered with a good
dose of humor and self-irony. By looking at things neither through
the gilded mirror of the rich nor the dark pond of needlessness,
but in the clear well of honest self-observation, the enormous tension will be revealed that the person with Greed and Arrogance
is under. It's a high voltage emanating from great insecurity and
a considerable self-dissatisfaction. When this individual understands that being normal is something really special, that it actually reflects his exquisite character when he moves unobtrusively in
the middle between his illusions and his self-aggrandizing wishes,
he'll be able to assume a new stance towards the self. Usually, however, this will only occur in his mid-years, when the proud greedy
person has learned to see through the hollowness of his striving for
the very best or else for renunciation. Instead of residing in a castle
or dwelling with matted hair in a hermitage, he can now move
into a metaphysical, four-bedroom apartment and spread there in
a way to finally feel his emotional contours, his possibilities and
his limits.

Energy 5 plus 7: Greed and Impatience

A greedy person with the Secondary Fear Symptom Impatience
lives by the motto: »Higher, bigger, faster, further!« He wants
everything achieved or done as soon and as superbly as is human-

ly possible. The goals are set high, the pressure to reach them is immense and the time factor plays a pivotal role in the life of an impatient greedy person. He isn't so much interested in material things, unless it is simultaneously linked with a meteoric rise, a stunning success or a prodigious-child kind of fame. When he sets up a company, it is supposed to be listed on the stock exchange with several million dollar sales within a short time. If he strives for a career, say as an actor, it doesn't mean anything to him unless he gets a call from Hollywood before long. A prospective chef does his utmost to earn three Michelin stars in the shortest time possible; an investment banker targets an international career at dazzling speed. Apart from the ostentatious and fame-yearning conceptions of life, the said also applies to the less spectacular – and from an outer perspective seemingly banal – curricula vitae. It includes the young girl practicing grimly at the ballet barre, or the class nerd learning Chinese on top of his regular school work, while also being a computer hacker or taking first prize in a contest for young pre-university scientists.

Ambition is the distinguishing feature of the combination of Greed with Impatience. It fills this individual with deep sadness, even inducing him to let himself drown in depressions, when he doesn't reach his goals in his youth or at least before his 30th birthday. To him, it means his life is devoid of meaning, virtually botched up, because he hasn't got the patience to wait until the dynamics of his existence finds a resonance in his potential and talents.

But if he can relax and enjoy his existence – frequently possible only thanks to an accident or an illness – there might actually be a chance that he reconsider and re-evaluate the hectic rush and urgency marking his life. So his later years offer the prospect of a high degree of fulfillment, based on the experience that not everything is as urgent as it seems or as important as it has been labeled. If this individual wants to avoid being forcibly brought to a halt, he should take heed of his fellow men's comments about how hectic and stressed out he looks, how little time he has for friend- and partnerships or how seldom he seems relaxed and at ease. Then he can act on it and make the right moves that will help him feel more comfortable on the one hand, while on the other – and there lies the secret that needs to be impressed on him – contribute to promoting his career efforts. Someone who meditates for example, thereby becoming more composed and relaxed, makes a more likeable impression on his fellow men than a hectic person. It also benefits his reputation and the social dimension of his ambitious efforts, because merely doing and wanting things isn't going to fulfill all the objectives he or she strives for. If he acquires a less breathless but rather a level-headed, serene demeanor through regular meditative pauses, he'll be able to accomplish a lot more than in his treadmill ways without any personal contact or pleasant exchange with his co-workers.

6. Arrogance with all Secondary Fear Symptoms

Energy 6 plus 1: Arrogance and Self-deprecation

The arrogant person nurtures – if sometimes in complete secrecy – a grandiose self-image. The Self-deprecator in contrast makes himself smaller and feels more incompetent than he or she really is. The combination of these two fear forms creates a double-edged apprehension: to not be noticed on the one hand, and to somehow attract attention on the other. To the individual with this fear structure, either one is similarly disagreeable. As a result, he deploys very long, not to say miles long aerials – both anxieties being situated on the inspiration level – to explore far in advance whether any danger looms for his self-image, for example from people bad-mouthing or making fun of him.

In general, an arrogant person afflicted moreover with Self-deprecation is exceedingly touchy and slighted at the least occasion. He is sensitive in a way his fellow men can hardly fathom, feeling deeply offended by whichever harmless – though insulting to him – events, remarks, jokes or situations. So a major part of his energy is taken up by his efforts to cope with subjectively suffered insults, to cultivate or suppress the memory of any indignities, and to lick and nurse his wounds. The incessant strobing of his surroundings and situations for potential injuries lets the arrogant and self-deprecating person develop a kind of fear-laden mediumship. Long before any danger becomes real, he usually senses whether someone might get too close to him, pityingly sneer at him, treat him condescendingly or in some other way not acknowledge him in his magnificence.

Given a conscious and deliberate reduction of the fear-level, this »negative mediumship« can be transformed into a mediumistic receptivity that will be beneficial both for himself and also for his fellow men. It requires that the individual concerned starts to look at and examine the enormous discrepancy between his own perception of relations and events as compared to the generally acknowledged as valid reality of occurrences. The process of a rapprochement to life and the people around him can begin when he realizes that it's not only flattering to be as highly sensitive as no other, but that his oversensitivity is also self-harming in that it separates him from his fellow men. It distorts his perception of reality, consumes his energy and leaves him weak. But as long as he believes himself emotionally in the right and the others to be insensitive clumsy clots, things will continue to be difficult. With advancing age though, the arrogant person with Self-deprecation as Secondary Fear suffers increasingly at his painful isolation and his proven ability to hear fleas coughing, even when they don't cough. This will help him develop, out of his own volition, the motivation to gradually adopt a different perception of reality, instead of rigidly insisting on his position that he is the only one ever to see things the right way. A treasure of sensitive warmth and empathy lies buried in this combination of Fear Symptoms, waiting to be lifted. And this is something the individual suffering under his solitude and repudiation of affectionate closeness feels quite clearly.

Energy 6 plus 2: Arrogance and Self-sabotage

Arrogance with the Secondary Fear Symptom Self-sabotage has the person adopting a painful and detrimental habit of ruining his life and spoiling his relationships, his success and appreciation by others. We are talking about a habit because a habit can be broken and changed. Though the arrogant person with Self-sabotage considers the things happening to him – caused unconsciously and brought on by himself – as fateful. »Nothing ever works out for me. I'm just an unlucky fellow.« With such remarks he keeps reinforcing his fear structure instead of reducing it.

No one comes into this world as an unlucky bird, not even this individual. But Self-sabotage doesn't like it when things run smoothly and the sun shines any longer than a couple of days. Then fear ensures that dark thunderclouds cover the sky and lightning hits the daily routine of the self-sabotaging arrogant individual. In his »priestly« arrogance of course, he feels authorized to interpret these incidents as acts of force majeure and fateful workings. He conveniently forgets that he failed to fit his house with a lightning protector. It's part of this image that the arrogant person with the Secondary Fear Symptom Self-sabotage feels to be a scapegoat of the Gods. It is his attempt to take an outstanding position amongst humans, even if he feels to be chosen in the negative, and doesn't recognize that it's his self-image causing him all these difficulties.

But as indicated earlier, habits can be shed. The most promising way to go about it is with a great boom instead of piecemeal or furtive efforts. The method can be applied for example when the individual applies himself to support and care for people who are suffering from great, fateful distress, i.e. by wars or natural disasters. This enables him to put his imaginary persecution by higher powers into relation with real calamity. So it is very much advisable to every arrogant person with Self-sabotage as Secondary Fear Symptom to deal hands-on and face to face with people who really are in great need. In doing so, he will meet a number of other people there with a similar personality structure, offering him the opportunity to observe in them the mechanisms driving him into his inner misery. The »priestly« compassion which is bound in Arrogance and inhibited from unfolding by Self-sabotage can then begin to soften the heart and shine out into the world. The more an individual with this combination of Fear Symptoms develops a natural empathy for the misery of the world, all the more his own fears abate. He will stop tripping himself up and offering his oversensitivity as a pledge of his existence. By closeness to others he will come closer to himself.

Energy 6 plus 3: Arrogance and Martyrdom

The combination of Arrogance with the Secondary Fear Symptom Martyrdom fabricates a self-image that enjoys suffering more and also having a greater capacity for suffering than one's fellow men. When it comes to self-injury, Arrogance likes to overtax itself, and Martyrdom's cause is to offer itself as victim when no one else is ready to take on this role. In this specific way, Martyrdom strengthens Arrogance.

The martyr-like arrogant person is torn between the two needs of completely withdrawing from the world, and offering himself time and again as the oaf to be kicked, abused and betrayed. When he emerges from his hermitage because he can't bear the isolation any more, he will immediately – as if arranged by some strange necessity – meet someone who not only recognizes his longing for emotional security, closeness and understanding, but also exploits it. He gives alms freely and soon after lets his purse get stolen unawares. And in this way, the sacrificial, arrogant person sees his fearful prophecy fulfilled that the world is bad and that his fellow humans are up to nothing but evil and insult.

It's difficult for this arrogant type to recognize that his need to help and serve has something haughty about it by presenting himself as being above things and needless at the same time, and by condescension bringing his misfortune about himself. He wants to support others like someone throwing a large bill at the feet of a beggar. And because the beggar isn't all over himself with joy, bowing to him in deepest gratitude, he turns away embittered. He doesn't feel how much arrogance lies in this gesture, nor is he aware of the energy in which he – however he does it – presents his alms to the needy. He wants to feel sublime in his generous magnificence. That this behavior signals a strong double message and therefore doesn't go down very well with his fellow men goes almost without saying; it certainly doesn't generate the sincere gratitude the martyr-like arrogant person secretly expects.

Now how can this individual discard his surplus fear? He will succeed by applying a vice on both ends, Arrogance and Martyrdom, bringing the two fears more closely together. This works by adopting a new attitude to consciously and freely admit to others that one is in need, requiring and desiring help – be it with household chores, the challenges at work or with relationship issues. Before, his or her huffy response always was: »Thank you, I don't need that!«

On the other hand, a person with this fear structure must learn not to nurse his Martyrdom on excessively noble gestures and condescendingly volunteering support. Asking for help for him- or herself and refraining from arrogantly helping others is the right approach to reducing this combination of fears. The process requires the deliberate request for the former and consciously withholding the latter. This way, the less fearful aspects of the two anxiety features can join more and more frequently: the sensitivity of Arrogance and the helpfulness of Martyrdom. When Phoenix rises from the ashes of fear with those two wings, he leaves behind him a secret suffering that has accompanied the person until then. The small pile of suffer-ashes becomes a memory on his path of life, and a readiness for tender closeness develops like sacred smoke from this burnt offering.

Energy 6 plus 4: Arrogance and Stubbornness

Someone uniting Arrogance with Stubbornness as Secondary Fear Symptom believes himself to be a paragon of orderliness, organization or systemization of everyday processes for his fellow men. The notion to be and actually be supposed to act exemplary is promoted by a self-righteousness that manifests itself ever stronger in the course of his life, because the stubborn arrogant person frequently manages indeed to have his life and everything he wants and does under control. Based on his Arrogance he is convinced that: »If everyone handled everything they way I do, by God, there would be a lot fewer problems in this world.«

The stubborn arrogant individual feels called to instruct and teach his fellow men how to do things better, and »better« means doing it his way. The stubborn part in him ensures that the events and feelings determining his life get neatly classified into specific categories, being accompanied, however, not only by self-righteousness but also by self-reproach. Should he make a mistake once or something go wrong, he gives his inner-self a good talking-to, reprimanding it and making quite clear that »this mustn't ever happen again.« The stubbornly arrogant person is an exigent teacher of life, both with himself and others. Depending on the field of activity, this might also extend to a spiritual guardianship which he or she sometimes takes on for individual or a group of scholars. Here too, relentless rigor prevails and anyone proving to be repeatedly fallible either in ambition, discipline or inner control is a failure in the eyes of this adamant teacher.

In his relationships, the arrogant and stubborn person is often secretly jealous and unobtrusively controlling. But he would loath to admit that something could be threatening his self-assurance. Tender words only seldom pass his lips, since he feels naturally entitled to a devotedly faithful partner. And besides, they couldn't really find a better partner than him or her anyway. The insecurity hidden behind such condescending demeanor is easily detectable by the people around him, though it makes it no less contemptuous for it.

When a person with this fear structure is willing to change, thereby moving a little closer to the lovable fallibility of his fellow humans, the insight that rigid perfection is no quality of life nor of divinity will help him succeed in this endeavor. The order of all animated life is always flexible and not without compassion. It is inwrought by threads of unordered chaos and for this very reason remains creative and changeable. The unconscious belief of a stubborn arrogant person that he has to represent superordinate, even superhuman notions of correctness and order gets softened when he stops seeing himself as a priestly representative of heavenly justice. So the best advice to this individual is: »Make an effort to stretch a point now and then, and love your weaknesses. Strengthen them rather than weeding them out, because infallibility – as much as you may cherish it – separates you and builds up barriers between you and the love of your fellow humans.«

Whenever someone with this combination of Fear Symptoms discovers that he has said, done or wanted something that in his eyes isn't impeccable or according to the rules, he should make an effort to not only admit it, criticizingly, to himself, but also forgive himself, true to the priestly energy of his Primary Symptom. Admitting a fault to others, himself broaching the subject that he feels helpless and thinks himself incompetent, or that he's got the impression of being unable to maintain proper control over his life, is very wholesome for him. It makes him lovable. It brings him closer to those who have no problem to cope with such a harmless loss of control. They can comfort him and teach him how to deal with human weaknesses without punishing oneself or fearing divine wrath.

Energy 6 plus 5: Arrogance and Greed

Arrogance in combination with the Secondary Fear Symptom Greed first and foremost makes demands. Yet these demands don't focus primarily on material things – unless at a younger soul age – but preferably on the quality of inter-personal relations. Thus, the arrogant person with the Secondary Symptom of Greed needs an enormous amount of attention, demanding great mindfulness in all dealings with him or her. He wants to take uncontested center stage – for individuals or a group of people – and in his wistful and wishful thinking, this center ought to be a climax. He would like to be someone unforgettable. He wants to be admired, adored and highly respected, dedicating a lot of effort to earning himself this reputation. Those not bowing to the dictate of his adorability but reacting with irony, criticism or reservation, will soon fall from the greedy arrogant person's grace and be pursued with arrows of wrath. Irreconcilable enmities can result from it.

»I am something eminently special, and if you don't appreciate this you had better get lost!« Such harsh words will of course not pass the lips of this greedy arrogant person, but his demeanor speaks volumes. This individual is often surrounded by a devoted circle of followers. He manages indeed to gain the admiration of these devotees by unusual accomplishments of intellectual or other kinds. At heart, however, he doesn't want to be admired for his deeds – his literature, his research results, his patronage. He would rather have an array of cast-iron friendships, faithful pupils and acolytes, praising and worshipping him beyond his death for having been a personality of unusual rank. The dynamics can be described as follows: »Worship me like a demigod, even though I allow you to know me intimately, witnessing and experiencing also my human side.« Like an absolutistic king having his chamber pot delivered to him by his ministers, wishing them to be present at his morning toilet, so the friends of a greedy arrogant person shall also be allowed to openly see his most basic human impulses of jealousy and envy, his biting remarks about »inferior« beings, his ailments, his unhappy affairs and a lot of other character flaws. Such specimen of greedy arrogance remains present in the minds as someone living to the fullest, binding others to him by his readiness to let them see also the negative aspects of his personality.

The covert complacency concealed behind the mask of this basic fear characterizes a yearning, lonely human being who cannot trust on being shown affection simply because of the way he is, which is often quite unusual and flamboyant indeed. He deeply longs to be accepted and live in the company of benevolent fellow humans -- and he is prepared to do anything to accomplish this goal. So in fact, a communicative ineptness leads to the pronounced pattern of his staged indispositions.

When the day comes that the individual concerned has had enough of acting the curt, condescending, standoffish and fallible snob, he must start looking for other friends. He'll find it relieving when someone actually laughs good-humouredly at his affected behavior, intimating that it wasn't necessary to act the unlikable guy to gain sympathies. The opportunity of getting to know other people than the usual crowd of admirers can be arranged when he joins new circles of society or goes on a journey incognito, where he makes an effort to show himself the way he truly feels, i.e. needy, lonely, longing and overstrained. It gives him the chance to learn and practice that he can win people's affection even when he reveals his genuine weaknesses, not only the pretended ones. For someone with this fear structure, his true weaknesses are in reality great strengths, provided that he manages to reduce the claim to his super-human status so far that he may indeed become a truly special person – in that he finds the courage to show his unmasked face, at least occasionally. Then he will be blessed with deep, sincere friendships and a personality able to effortlessly manifest true greatness in his older age.

Energy 6 plus 7: Arrogance and Impatience

The basic fear of Arrogance with Impatience as Secondary Fear Symptom designates someone ambitious, tense, success-oriented and often also pompous. Arrogance in combination with a Secondary Symptom on the action level doesn't only result in intolerance towards those who don't finish their work in double-time and aren't as brilliant and efficient, or prove to be less assiduous and target-oriented. The impatience is also directed against the individual him- or herself, with great intolerance of one's own actions, and in particular with regard to the speediness applied to their completion. His speed efforts make the arrogant person with the Secondary Symptom Impatience a slave-driver for himself and others. Unless he and everyone in his surroundings is under pressure, running as if steam-powered, he feels all work processes as if decelerated and boring.

The combination of these two Fear Symptoms affects, of course, not only the working life but also the private life of this person. He's always got something on the agenda, rarely finding the leisure to rest. He has a hard time being around people who don't want to go out or do sports every night, rather spending their leisure time with idleness instead of working around the house and garden. »Geez, you really aren't up for anything, how boring« is a reproach the impatient arrogant person will commonly utter. And if it should happen that he for once doesn't move at the highest peak of his activity level for a day or a week, he likewise chides himself: »I'm really up for nothing!« He feels threatened as if by a dark power. Should someone actually dare accuse him of being not efficient enough, he will be deeply hurt. To him it means that all his endeavors to lead a meaningful life have been either unsuccessful, or he feels misunderstood in his innermost being. Seldom does he register that he too hurts the people around him just as often by criticizing them for their inability to use their time efficiently. But that's exactly what eventually alienates his friends, partner or employees from him. Having other fear structures, they can't bear the constant time and work pressure for any length of time.

The opportunity of causing a change in the attitude of an impatient arrogant person must necessarily be oriented on the Primary Symptom, because it's the Arrogance insinuating to him that he is a higher-order human being for cheating time from morning till night time, or in any case someone who is entitled to look down on those who are slower. The vanity concealed in this affected behavior and the excessive pride the impatient arrogant individual feels when he has once again accomplished something three times as fast as everyone else are the starting-point for change. With this pride, this vanity, he hurts himself and his fellow men without meaning to. There really isn't any reason to be proud of the effects of one's fear. Yet, if he examines the pseudo-satisfaction characterizing these sensations and the yearning for quite a different dimension concealed behind it, he will be able to recognize that what he's trying to do in reality is to get his life over with as quickly as possible, so as to abbreviate the incarnated condition of constant vulnerability. The imperious time pressure he puts his fellow men under also serves to have them not even think of hurting him; they simply have too much work to do. To everyone not suffering from this fear structure it's obvious that these mechanisms can't work efficiently or be upheld over a long period.

So every time the impatient arrogant type finds he is particularly proud of his achievements again, his ambition seemingly satisfied, he should pause and beware, to examine his motivation with a powerful magnifying glass. Then he should, at least tentatively, turn his focus on the dark hole of »death longing« opening up behind it. In the name of love for the self and of better communication with his fellow people, he should reduce the pressure. This alternative isn't characterized by desperation at time going by, but by the perception that the course of time and what may happen in the context of time cannot be totally governed by Impatience and Arrogance; it has its own dynamics independent of the person's doing. This insight will help the impatient arrogant individual to revise and correct his notions of life. Time is a powerful master, and the acknowledgement of this great power will relieve him from the charge of having to control the course of events solely himself. The outcome will be a state of relaxation hitherto unknown to him, but most of all a deeper trust in whatever happens and the superordinate laws inherent therein.

7. Impatience with all Secondary Fear Symptons

Energy 7 plus 1: Impatience and Self-deprecation

The combination of the Primary Fear Symptom Impatience with the Secondary Symptom Self-deprecation makes the affected individual shower him- or herself with reproaches. He has the highest standards concerning his time management, his efficiency and the perfect and swift handling of his everyday or special tasks. Yet, his Self-deprecation never lets him be quite satisfied with himself and his achievements. He always finds something to niggle about in his performance; perfect is never perfect enough. Rarely can he rest on his laurels. His fellow men in contrast don't find much to disapprove of, not in him or his work results. The only thing bothering them is his dissatisfaction with himself, his annoying habit of reducing his accomplishments; to never judge them really good or fully approve of them; to always believe that they could still have somehow, somewhere, somewhat been improved.

So Impatience and Self-deprecation lead to a paradoxical condition, because Impatience is in the highest degree efficient, whereas Self-deprecation feels itself to be in the highest degree inefficient. This combination of contradictions creates an inner torment preventing the individual from relaxing. He is constantly under steam, and if there's no one to criticize him, he'll do it himself. The criticism doesn't primarily relate to the quality of performance but to the time required for it. And so the person with this combination of Fear Symptoms keeps heaping reproaches on himself, decrying his ability to manage his time optimally. To others it's obvious that these self-reproaches are often driven to absurdity; they can't fathom why it should represent a worth in itself to complete things as fast as possible and under the highest pressure. But a person with this basic fear feels inept and helpless, incompetent and slow when things don't work the way his Impatience dictates to him.

This self-conception ultimately assumes a specific perspective: the fear of being unable to cope with life and its challenges and to fail before the requirements of delimited time. These fears are the reason that the self-denying impatient person generally encumbers himself with much more than would be necessary or that he can actually handle. So he digs his own pit because each activity simply takes its own time. Someone who, with beautiful regularity, does his best to achieve twice or three times than what is actually possible, will create situations for himself in which he obviously has and had to fail. Then his fear is content and all is right with his world again; all fears have been confirmed.

In the habit to encumber himself with more than is humanly possible also lies the key to a potential reduction of the fear level. Only when this individual can see that he expects things inhuman or superhuman of himself, can he step back and have a look at his self-imposed pressure of time and achievement from a distance. The disposition to self-criticism may then be applied to find fault not with time management itself, but with the fact that he creates such crazy pitfalls for himself. Although humor as a loving aspect of self-criticism isn't exactly a strength of this over-efficient, harassed individual, humor can still be encouraged if he is willing to once watch the way he is toiling and somersaulting, jumping in squares and, standing on his head, whipping himself on to top acrobatic feats into the bargain. Not even he can take this approach seriously. He is bound to recognize the comical side of this behavior and begin to chuckle about himself. Laughter about the extreme efforts he undertakes to avoid facing his fear of failure is the remedy for this combination of fears.

Energy 7 plus 2: Impatience and Self-sabotage

The combination of Impatience with the Secondary Fear Symptom Self-sabotage has the effect that this individual behaves like someone driving a fast car without having checked if the brakes are functioning properly. He puts his foot down on the accelerator, pleased with the increasing speed. But as the first obstacle approaches and he tries to brake, the brakes don't work; he loses control and turns over, landing in a ditch by the roadside. Having escaped the accident fairly unscathed, he immediately gets himself another fast car, again forgetting that good brakes are indispensable to reaching his destination unharmed. So the impatient person makes the same mistake over and over again, just to fall flat on his face again. He doesn't realize that a small detail – notably the annoying loss of time by a trip to the garage – could solve his problem. Self-sabotage tries to make him believe that it was normal to have non-functional brakes, and that it was the fault of the manufacturer or the car vendor if he had an accident. He denies his self-responsibility, even though his intuition and power of observation had signaled him already at the first street corner, i.e. long before he reached the motorway, that something was wrong with the brakes. But he doesn't want to listen to this hint. He is in a hurry and wants to get as fast as possible to wherever he is going. This example is intended to demonstrate that pleasure and self-damage aren't good friends, and that fun could definitely be enhanced if he were to abstain from self-damage as much as possible.

The impatient person with the Secondary Fear Symptom of Self-sabotage performs the process described in the example almost daily on a smaller scale, and so he hardly notices how matter-of-factly he takes the frequent minor defeats and setbacks. Wishing to finish his jobs as fast as possible, he hurts himself on a tool, miscalculates his numbers, deletes documents from the PC, gets into a traffic jam and arrives too late for an important appointment. Or, in his usual rush, he fails to take the address along for his rendezvous, whereupon his date loses patience and leaves. The effect is that the self-damaging impatient individual has to permanently justify and excuse himself. His fellow men are gaining the impression that he wants to prove primarily one thing to himself: that he can dance on a tightrope between highrise buildings without safety net. He doesn't feel like using the elevator, walk across the street, then taking another elevator there to get to the forty-seventh floor of the other skyscraper. He prefers to tighten a rope between the two buildings, believing it was faster that way. This is where the audacity of Impatience and the destructive inclination of Self-sabotage join forces. For example, the impatient individual aspires to own a splendid villa although he is still very young. He raises an excessively large mortgage for it and soon after finds himself homeless under a bridge because the bank has taken it all.

It's this craving for status with a lust for risk-taking, extending not only to material things but also to his own person and every-day actions, which provides the starting-point for a kindly-critical self-analysis. The Self-saboteur can learn to question his impulse to want too much all at once too early, and to go after it too fast. He can also learn to heed the warnings of his fellow people instead of throwing caution to the wind. His intuition will be a better adviser to him than the flattering voices of his fear, trying to seduce him. When his intuition lovingly whispers to him »keep away from it!«, he should give in to this voice and really give up his plan or at least modify it. He should in particular become very alert and scrutinize his motivation every time he is about to automatically lay the blame for his mishap, his accidents or his flops on others or on circumstances, as if he had nothing to do with it except being the victim of it all. He can't be spared giving attention to these correlations, and it's definitely worthwhile to analyze these issues not only efficiently but also with imagination. In the final analysis, it is no doubt more pleasant to be successful than to fail time and again. A person with this combination of fears may principally assume that everything which happens too fast leads to adversity. So a careful inspection of the brakes will automatically lead to happiness.

Energy 7 plus 3: Impatience and Martyrdom

The Primary Symptom Impatience with the Secondary Symptom of Martyrdom produces an exceptionally restless and hyperactive individual. The unrest comes from feeling guilty and worthless in some non-specific way when he or she happens to be idle for once.

That is why this individual has developed the seemingly calming habit of working from morning till nighttime, drudging and slaving away. The purpose isn't activity in terms of sports or getting exercise, but an activity that expends energy, renders him tired, and is primarily intended to benefit others.

For himself this person rarely does anything. He always encumbers himself with much more than others around him. He is always ready to come to their aid, his own interests ranging second, and toil till he drops if he sees a chance to make himself popular that way. The strange thing is though that he is far from dropping when others are lying on the ground exhausted. This is attributable to the martyr-like endurance and untiring quality of Impatience, which can really rise above itself with strength and efficiency. Only when he is at the end of his rope, when his heart doesn't play along anymore or he is suddenly befallen by some other affliction due to exhaustion does he become aware that the unsettling and hectic busyness isn't a symptom of healthy diligence and selflessness based on freedom and love. Rather, it's fed by the fear to be an inferior member of the human community if he refrains from the hustle and bustle and the seemingly high-minded sacrifice of his vital force.

Now and then, people's reaction might be: »But we didn't ask you to work so hard. As for us, you could have gladly taken a rest more often. But you always relieved us of everything; we didn't even have a chance to contribute something.« To this, the initial reaction of the martyr-like impatient person is incomprehension and bitterness: didn't he always mean well? He stood in for his fellow workers when they were ill without grumbling or asking for gratitude, let alone some flowers or a bottle of wine. She co-raised the neighbors' children without expecting a word of gratitude. She committed herself to tasks in the community that no one else wanted to take on and felt great and gracious in doing so. And all this shouldn't count for anything now?

In an interruption of the inner and outer hectic rush and the awful tirelessness lies the great, in fact the only chance that the martyr-like impatient individual can even look at his anxious drive for this untiring activity. But as long as he insists that his selfless noble-mindedness and eighteen-hour workday are the characteristics of an exceptional personality, he'll only be proud of his accomplishments -- with a particularly humble pride, of course. He will not otherwise find an opportunity to recognize that about 80 percent of it is motivated by his desire to be praised, liked, feel indispensable and prove to himself that he is lovable and his life worthwhile. Whereas, if he reduces his excessive activity by just ten or twenty percent, as if by magic and quite naturally, everything will become more livable and lovable. His life is going to be worth living, just as he will be lovable to his fellow men when he can admit at last: »I am at the end of my tether. I need time out. I must take care of my health,« or something along those lines.

The path leads from feeling a seemingly unbearable »laziness« towards a relaxation that leaves room for his fellow people to act out their own needs for kind helpfulness. When the martyr-like impatient person finally realizes that his tendency to always be first on the spot and getting everything done ahead of time represents a virtually absurd disenfranchisement of his fellow men. When he understands that the precipitative help he often bestows on people curtails their capacity for self-help just as their own readiness to help, he will begin to restrain himself and learn to pitch in only when asked. As a result, Impatience and Martyrdom will find a beneficial balance instead of getting worn out in constant activity. First though, the individual must recognize that his outer bustle is the result of his inner compulsion before it can be relieved, because the inner compulsion feels unpleasant. He can reduce the compensation possibilities by an act of self-discipline, to the benefit of the martyr-like impatient individual's whole system. The motive which is the drive engine of his selfless hectic rush is a desire for love and recognition. That there are other ways to find it will become apparent with every passing day, and the lovable nature of this individual will really come to the fore when he stops to permanently overstrain himself.

Energy 7 plus 4: Impatience and Stubbornness

The alliance of Impatience with the Secondary Symptom Stubbornness results in a sort of finger wrestling. Each fear unceasingly drags and pulls in the other direction. Impatience is troubled by fear of death and death longing simultaneously, trying to outwit time by too much or too little, too fast or too slow; the means are interchangeable. Stubbornness in contrast wants to persist, under no circumstances giving room to all the impulses and changes Impatience strives for. Stubbornness wants to leave things the way they always were, making sure there are no unpleasant surprises. It's just that surprises are exactly the invigorating elixir Impatience needs to feel comfortable and appeased, whereas it has Stubbornness bucking with fear. So the everyday life of a person with this combination is determined by a certain inner turmoil. Every other hour, Impatience tries to get the upper hand, while Stubbornness raises all strength not to be defeated.

This is so to speak a grand coalition in which both parties deliberately try to disable each other, endeavoring to put the other out of action. In most cases, however, Impatience is going to win the day since life simply is constant motion, every new day bringing some kind of change, so that Stubbornness has no choice but to withdraw into the sulking corner. Now unless this surfaces to the consciousness of the specific individual, it will be accompanied by a considerable amount of inner strain. Occasionally, this high strain tilts over into apathy, because Stubbornness too tries to assert itself, seeking its niche in the system and often knows no other way out than to play dead in order to put Impatience in its place. In this fight, no one can win in the end.

The opponents Impatience and Stubbornness must divorce, because none of them can carry off a long-term victory. When they separate, i.e. when the person suffering from that inner drag and pull of the two contradictory energies, is willing to enforce a separation on the consciousness level, his life will become easier.

A wise way to apply this division is to grant the need for time management, time savings or time gain in some areas of his life, in fact, giving it room. Other areas of life may then be surrendered to the longing for persistence, predictability and invariability, so that it too may be satisfied. Thus, with a bit of lenience, someone with the combination of Fear Symptoms Impatience and Stubbornness can allow free play in both directions. And to his astonishment, he'll discover that when Stubbornness doesn't tug at Impatience and Impatience refrains from dragging Stubbornness along, both fears will gradually abate and be increasingly content with their respective domains. The most sensible partition is to have the Fear of Unpredictability and Change concentrate on the relationship aspect to ensure a certain consistency, quiet and reliability in the family, partnership and friendship domains. That leaves external areas such as work, completion of assignments and coping with challenges in a broader sense for Impatience to focus on. It's a way for both fears to benefit from the positive potential they carry: A person with the gift of performing his business most efficiently finds his point of rest in co-human relationships. This approach helps avert most hazards of the overhasty, dominant and pressure-exerting, overbearing fear of Impatience with regard to matters of love, friendship and comradeship. What remains is a certain rash, irascible jealousy, which may however be kept in check with some self-observation and the willingness to question one's motives.

Energy 7 plus 5: Impatience and Greed

A human being with the Primary Symptom Impatience and the Secondary Fear Symptom of Greed wants to have it all, and, more specifically, not immediately but already yesterday. This »all« is non-specific and can extend to any area of life, material and non-material. Very typical of this person is his great dissatisfaction with himself, his life situation and circumstances and his relationships. He is so little satisfied and satisfiable that he prefers to project his demanding Impatience onto others. He puts them under pressure with verbal and non-verbal reproaches, asking that they must offer him more, have more time for him and look after him better, admire him more and just give him more and more of everything. His fellow men will describe him as a bottomless pit or an energy monger. They sense that they won't ever be able to give enough, and that he or she will never be sated and content, because the time factor tormenting the greedy impatient person plays a dominant, if difficult to grasp role here.

The greedy impatient individual usually needs little sleep and forces others to stay awake and active beyond their limits as well. Time to him is a precious commodity; he considers every minute of sleep as a wasted opportunity to gain as much out of his days as possible. The life of a greedy impatient person is profit-oriented in all respects. He wants to make the maximum out of every hour of his existence. But since he is always in a particularly urgent hurry, he tends to stumble just when he has filled his jug at the well of life and break it.

The feeling to be left empty-handed in relationships or on a material plane is almost unbearable for the greedy impatient person. If his partner leaves him in the morning, by nighttime he'll have met someone else on whom to focus all his needs and hopes. When a business falls apart, he quickly pulls another one out of the hat. He can barely tolerate it when deals don't get wrapped up fast, because the void which might open up – something he rarely ever consciously experiences – represents a profound horror to him. Should he decide to marry, he is likely to continue looking out for other potential, suitable candidates in case the marriage doesn't work out. He will then unrelentingly impose pressure on the wedded partner that he (or she) must satisfy him in all aspects of his existence, until finally the partner leaves out of his own accord, the pressure simply getting unbearable.

The entitlement mentality the greedy impatient individual has towards life is impossible to fulfill. The chance, therefore, to recognize the hidden fear level and potentially reduce it, consists in perceiving these demands as unfulfillable in the first place. The imperious attitude which is derived from the combination of energies 5 and 7 may at times and of necessity meet with response from his fellow humans, but life itself cannot be put under pressure. The individual concerned can help himself when he turns his gaze on the things he has, knows and can do, instead of what he doesn't have, doesn't know and can't do. This is a simple, however very effective change of perspective, if not easy to perform for him or her. The greedy impatient type is bound to let his eyes roam the horizon again, rather than rest on what lies directly in front of him. But it's a matter of practice, and he can always bring himself back to the present. Gradually, a feeling of abundance and contentment will evolve. The time pressure he feels under, demanding that everything must be at hand immediately, only to be wiped off the table as of little interest after all, can fall away. Over the years, someone formerly driven by must-have greed may turn into a person who is – in moderation – content with what he has. He'll be able to look at the affluence of his life with pleasure, without keeping half an eye on returns on investments and dividends all the time. His loved ones and friends will be grateful for it and richly reward him.

Energy 7 plus 6: Impatience and Arrogance

An impatient individual with the Secondary Fear Symptom Arrogance reacts instantly to any potential injury, to disturbances, slights, insults and restrictions of his sphere of influence. He even reacts precipitatively; as if lightning had set him on fire before the thunderstorm actually broke loose. He often feels hurt before any offence has even taken place. But the fast reaction seemingly saves him from more thunder strikes. It serves him as a lightning rod and moreover as a seismograph, detecting the slightest ground motion under his feet and warning him of danger in advance. So in this combination too, the time factor plays a major role. The vulnerability of this impatient individual demands that he immediately retaliate.

He takes offence particularly easily when he is hampered in his drive to accomplish things timely and efficiently or left waiting, when one undermines his organizational efforts or thwarts his hopes of an expedient completion of tasks. Since Arrogance extends primarily to the sphere of human relations, the injury is felt all the more sharper and painful when it's people from his immediate vicinity who hurt and annoy him in such way. It is interesting to note that the impatient person – although quick to react and retaliate in all situations and despite his precipitative »touchiness« response – takes a long time to stomach the insult. The time span the arrogant impatient individual needs to forgive is inversely proportional to the speed of his sharp initial reaction. The combination of a »priestly« energy 6 with a »royal« energy 7 makes the arrogant impatient type withdraw in a huff in no time; so he is used to coping with a considerable amount of isolation and solitude.

A remedy for the individual with this basic combination of fears is to permit himself not only to strike back in his usual hard, quick-as-lightning way, but to let his rage, the hurt and anger about the loss of time or waste of energy also explode verbally. When he really flies off the handle, showing all his agitation and lack of self-control, he'll find an unexpected but considerable relief in this reaction. A blaze of anger that doesn't shun expressing strong emotions entails two things: One, by letting off steam, the individual rids himself of the inner pressure, and really effectively at that, with the added benefit that he can probably laugh about himself. It means that the incident will torment him much less long than if he bottled up his hurt feelings inside.

The second effect of an explosion-like eruption is that his fellow men can directly sense the inappropriateness of his reaction energetically. If they are startled at first, they can soon comprehend that this blaze of rage is a personality-specific outburst which they don't have to blame on themselves in its full force. They will develop understanding for his irascible temper. This helps the impatient arrogant person to forgive and forget much faster, whereas his fellow men, letting this reaction pass by like a fierce thunderstorm, feel after a short time that the air is pure again. The bridge between the two advantages caused by such an emotional outburst is his or her subsequent readiness to give a word of explanation and ask for understanding, even if it's something the arrogant impatient individual won't find easy to do. But it represents the only possibility to make the initial reaction comprehensible and not cause any lasting hail damage.

While the seven Archetypal Fears have been described in systematic order in part I of this book, followed in part II by the 42 variants of Basic Fears, in part III we start to expound this novel perspective of human existence in greater detail through probing questions. For this reason – and because they evolved under most diverse conditions over a number of years – the following texts are less structured and ordered. We have, however, grouped them under specific categories and headings. The answers to our questions deal with each topic from different aspects but are in no way exhaustive.

These answers being messages from the »SOURCE« were either generated at public events, in the context of private sessions or in cooperation with a research group on the subject of »Archetypes of Fear«. Fear plays by nature an essential role in the treatment of people seeking help. Psychiatrists, social education workers and psychotherapists have met with the authors in a prolific cooperation over an extensive period of time to familiarize themselves with the new perspective on the archetypal fears of man. The insights from the book »Archetypes of the Soul« (first published in 1993) with its resource-oriented approach had already been integrated into their respective therapy concepts and their effectiveness put to the test. To the participants of our 10 years of research sessions we owe many important impulses, great support and interesting questions.

We publish the following information out of the desire to complete the basic statements on the Archetypes of Fear; may they stimulate the reader to reflection and verification.

1. The Evolution of the Archetypes of Fear

■ *Does the soul select the Basic Fear (Primary and Secondary Symptoms) prior to incarnation or does this only evolve within the body?*

When the soul plans a future incarnation and choses the MATRIX for a Soul Pattern that will be necessary or useful, the position of the Basic Fear – i.e. the Primary Symptom with the related, collaborating Secondary Symptom – is still vacant in terms of content. The reason is that fear, other than the Soul Role, Goal or Mode for example, constitutes a specific involvement with worldly reality and a reaction to it. While there is already a disposition in the Matrix or Soul Pattern prior to conception and during the first weeks of embryonic development, it cannot be determined in terms of content before a human being starts getting exposed to earthly conditions. That occurs when the evolving body has been permanently ensouled and his MATRIX engages in interaction with various aspects of his environment: with the presence of other souls, terrestrial conditions, but in particular the ubiquitous fear vibrations of the earthly mode of existence. These vibrations inseparable from the physical state are linked both with the feelings of the expectant mother and with the biologically evolving instincts the embryo needs for its survival in the womb.

The previously neutral disposition prepared in the Soul Pattern for the later effectiveness of fear in the body will now lead to different reactions in response to the fear surrounding the evolving fetus. The newly ensouled body is directly related to other bodies in its environment, on the physical and on the astral plane, and the child will find its own reactions depending on the fear structures of mother, father or other persons in its immediate surroundings. Fear is always a response. If, for example, the mother is subjected to blows during pregnancy, or the embryo feels threatened by attempted abortion or even just thoughts of it, if she is exposed to chaos of war or suffers hunger, it will impact which of the Fear Symptoms are going to move onto the hitherto vacant position in the system, as those can't remain unoccupied.

To the evolving human being and his soul it is less important exactly which Primary Symptom in combination with which Secondary Symptom fills the vacant position, rather than that this occupancy by two Archetypes of Fear takes place at all. Once it is completed and the vacant space filled with a specific Basic Fear, the fixation of these archetypal fears begins. Fixation for the duration of a whole life-time is the outcome of feeling and experiencing. The disposition and subsequent occupancy of the blank spot result in a particular attitude to worldly reality, thereby enabling the psyche to develop an orientation towards specific coping strategies with that particular Basic Fear. This serves to fulfill the will of the soul.

Each new experience is scanned and examined for suitability to fixing the assumed orientation towards this Basic Fear. Events and experiences which do not match the fear structure required and desired by the soul, will be assessed as harmless and insignificant. Even their recollection potential is low because the psyche concentrates increasingly on those conditions which are serving it to develop the fear mechanisms. It can be compared to the digestive system needing the exposure to bacteria right after birth to be colonized or warded off to develop an individual immune system. And like the strains of bacteria settling the intestines are neither good nor bad as such but simply needed so that the individual may become viable and resistant, so the »settlement« by more or less threatening events is required to provide the young human being with increasing opportunities to learn to react to these fear-evoking conditions which will inexorably affect him.

So there is, from the start, a position in the Soul Pattern that needs to be filled. Now the Basic Fear taking up this vacancy isn't completely arbitrary either but can – in dependence of archetypal fears elaborated in previous incarnations – provide a restricted, sort of half-open pre-selection of the Seven Archetypes of Fear to be investigated. All this is to say that the soul doesn't totally determine a specific Basic Fear already on the astral plane. It is not predetermined. This isn't possible because the selection of parents, which occurs only later, plays such an essential role in the final filling of the still open fear position. In comparison, the pre-selected disposition of the soul has ultimately less weight than the crucial effects of fear in a specific life situation after ensoulment.

■ *How does the Secondary Symptom of Fear evolve?*
The Primary Symptom constitutes the general answer to the life circumstances of the new incarnation. It colors the view on the whole environment and the correlation of incarnation, whereas the Secondary Symptom of Fear regulates the earliest as well as all later close relationships, and the proximity and distance to any directly associated persons.

The Secondary Symptom of Fear, too, gets firmly established in the womb or within a few days after birth. It provides an additional possibility of getting into contact and coping with interhuman reality. It evolves in response to the personality structures of the respective attachment figures. The nascent human child enters into relation with both the soul patterns of mother and father and with the fear structures of those that shape its development. Next to the parents this may be a grandmother, a midwife or a nanny.

It is unavoidable that during pregnancy, the mother's fear structure already energetically impacts the fear disposition of the unborn child. There is no way to prevent this interaction. Strong fear of the mother also causes strong fear in the newborn child. However, it is not predetermined which of the Seven Archetypes of Fear in the child respond to the mother's Basic Fear. The mother with her own fear system correlates with the fear systems of the people around her, and the Secondary Symptom of Fear will take shape as a reaction to additional fear vibrations in the immediate surroundings of the baby. The lag to the time of formation of the Primary Symptom can be very short or amount to days and weeks.

While it doesn't make sense for the soul to work on the same fear structure for two or three incarnations in succession, the joint effect of a specific Primary Symptom with different Secondary Symptoms (e.g. Stubbornness with Self-deprecation, with Arrogance or with Self-sabotage) each time creates a new perspective on the world. From this perspective, the individual may productively deal with earthly reality with the same Primary Symptom over two or more successive incarnations.

2. Fixation of the Basic Fear and Individuation

■ *How and when do the Archetypal Fears anchor in a human being?*

The fixation of the necessary Symptoms of Fear is a flowing process which can't be mandatorily determined either for an individual or for the development of human evolution in general. Some anchorages take place already during the embryonic stage – by traumatic experiences the unborn being absorbs and cultivates with heightened sensitivity. Then, although the ground has usually been prepared, in exceptional cases some definite fixations take place only in the second year of life, when an intense trauma offers itself for this final fixation.

Only a few or many years may pass until the Primary Symptom manifests clearly and definitely in the character of the child. In general, the development of the essential personality with respect to the Fear Symptoms is completed with majority age; depending on respective societies, that is between age 16 and 25. This is followed by a plateau phase, and only when there is a chance for individuation – and only then! – can the descent from the high plateau of the fixated fear be embarked upon.

As we have said many times before, it is by no means an indispensable requirement of the human condition or any individual incarnation to consciously perform this individuation or even integrate it into one's life plan. If this thought seems inconceivable to you, let us repeat: A life is just as valuable as an experience for the soul when a human being keeps lingering on the plateau of his fears or even climbs the ascending path of his fearful solidification until death, may it occur early or late. If, however, a person has the possibility and the inner impulse in his mid-years, i.e. between age thirty and sixty, to advance to his individual truth and discard a surplus of fear and anxieties, that would be one of many possibilities of emotional development, but certainly not the only one. And each life is equally useful, meaningful and rewarding, even if this kind of individuation does not take place. Otherwise, the unreflecting life of an Infant soul would be in vain. The naivety of Child Souls or the thoughtless striking power of Young Souls -- most of whom never feel the impulse for introspection, of holding communion with the self, to reconsider or examine their life and become aware of their fears – wouldn't have any meaning then. This isn't so; it cannot be.

So the Primary Symptom of Fear is fixated as soon as possible, and more precisely in a way that is meaningful for the individual and his soul in each case. This applies equally to the Secondary Symptom of Fear. Subsequently, this fixation is covered with layer by layer of experiences. The said individual gains the impression that life doesn't hold much else in store than this particular option of understanding all reality through the distorting glasses of the Basic Fear.

One day, however, it may happen that these glasses fall down, shattering to pieces on the ground. Until the new glasses are ready, he or she has to get by without for some time. Suddenly, to their own surprise, they can often see more clearly and precisely without glasses than before, because many people wear glasses that aren't adequate to the actual condition of their eyes. The same is true for the perception through the glasses of the Archetypal Fears. Once the glasses have been broken, which often happens on the occasion of another strong traumatic event, it is easier for an individual with the right disposition – and this we would like to emphasize – to take on a new perspective and really look at what actually caused the glasses to fall down and break. Now a renewed vision of the world can develop.

But many people wear their glasses all their life without any accident and don't even feel them on their nose, and there is no reason at all to blame them for it. Each life has its own dictum. And even a Mature or Old Soul – as we would like to impress on you – has the right and the option of persisting on the high plateau of its fearful fixation. While Mature and Old Souls feel that their physical lives are gradually coming to an end, with the longing for a non-physical existence getting stronger all the time, simultaneously there also grows the knowledge about the relativity of time and space. And while an increasing urgency can be felt at an existential level of consciousness, on another level there is a growing awareness that every soul has enough time to explore all possibilities and develop itself in all spheres the way it really needs to.

But how can added trauma reduce fear?

When an adult in the middle of his life gets into a seriously traumatizing situation, some corresponding experiences from his childhood which, for good reason, were suppressed and forgotten, become »updated«. This resuscitation of memories connected with the Basic Fear, loosens this solidified and eventually matter-of-fact fear system, like screw joints become unfastened by heavy vibrations. Since the new trauma is experienced much more consciously as a grown-up, it can be shared with one's fellow people. And when his or her sorrow finds an attentive and sympathetic audience, when the aggrieved has an opportunity to talk about his agonizing experiences, the early hardening which happened in early childhood can soften a little, too. Tears never cried before can flow now.

Assistance in coping with the new trauma can also be used to heal buried memories of old sufferings. However, this holds true only when the new injury experienced in adulthood concerns the Primary or Secondary Symptoms of Fear in a human being (his Basic Fear), which contributed essentially to the formation of his character and personality. In other words, one cannot presume that every serious traumatization at adult age contributes to the solution of early fears. Only when the new traumatization has the potential to bring about an essential confirmation and reinforcement of the old, early experiences, access may also be found to the repressed fears of childhood. A new trauma thematically not connected with either the Primary or the Secondary Symptom of Fear can't have any potentially liberating effect.

By consciously living through and emotionally processing events that fit the Basic Fear, the structures soften and self-knowledge can deepen, opening up new ways of coping which permit to examine the old solidified, rigid response patterns and change them – at least partly. However, we wish to qualify our statement: not every person may be able to accomplish such loosening or softening of his Basic Fear. It requires an inner readiness to do this, as well as the help of one's fellow men. This doesn't necessarily have to be in the context of psychotherapy. Every other form of human sympathy and loving intimacy can be very effective, too.

Let us round out our explanations by an example: A person is strongly marked by his Secondary Fear Symptom of Stubbornness. From his earliest years he has experienced, or believed to experience, that he is being abandoned time and again, all alone in the world and getting no support in decisive situations. Maybe also a parent or a close family member died early. Especially a stubborn person will, in the years leading up to his adulthood, pursue with great consequence his endeavor not to feel that terrible sensation of being abandoned and alone. He will become a very autonomous, headstrong and capable person who thinks it is wise not to depend or be dependent on anyone. This works out quite well until his spouse suddenly dies in a car accident. Perhaps this person is meanwhile fifty years or older. He has lulled himself into a sense of eternal security. The partner was healthy and true and he had no reason to imagine that he would be finding himself alone in the world again. Now he must learn to deal with this unexpected loss, which in all probability will hit him considerably harder than a person not suffering from Stubbornness as a Fear Symptom.

There are two ways now to cope with the death of his partner. One leads to an added, increasingly evident hardening and bitterness. The other path, i.e., the consciously experienced loss, which includes acknowledging all the old, repressed pain, makes the excessive, panic-like fear of loss visible. The time of mourning, the tears and conversations with friends and family members will help now to deal with this actual situation and also with all those unexpressed fear of being abandoned stemming from the Symptom of Stubbornness that existed since earliest childhood and was compensated by the determination to not ever feel deserted and alone again – at the high cost of not being able to trust and let go.

3. Archetypal Fears and other Fears

■ *What distinguishes other fears from the Seven Archetypal Fears?*
The answer to this question is best provided in a comparison. The distinction is similar to the difference between mortal and venial sins. Eating meat on Fridays instead of fish may be judged in different ways, but it must certainly be judged differently than killing

a human being. Apart from this analogy we would like to say that the Seven Archetypes of Fear with their characteristic symptoms and plus-minus-poles represent an essential interaction with life on this planet as such. Fear is an indispensable factor of existence on the one hand, and of spiritual growth on the other. This does not, however, apply to the »venial fears«. The soul doesn't need them for its evolution. It is important to distinguish between necessary and »redundant« fears.

Now the small fear of a confrontation with a neighbor or the apprehension not to find adequate comfort on a journey is easy to deal with and also easy to treat therapeutically, if at all it torments a person to the degree that he seeks help. In general, nearly everyone copes fairly well with his so-called small fears. He knows them; he understands them as part of his character. Sometimes he even quite likes them because they are closely woven with his sense of identity. He can smile and even joke about them; nor does he take it too badly when someone else makes a remark about it. Maybe he feels a little bit ashamed about them. We do not speak here about pathological phobias. One must clearly distinguish these small fears and anxieties, but also the medium-scale ones, for example of impoverishment, of relationship commitment or ageing, from the Seven Archetypes of Fear and the primal fears concealed behind them. The former are – to choose another image – the free skating part, whereas a person's confrontation with his Basic Fear, as combined from Primary and Secondary Symptom, is part of every incarnation as the compulsory growth program.

The small fears are like spices. The Basic Fears are like a potato field from whose fruit one can produce many different basic dishes. Whether potatoes are seasoned with onions or marjoram, whether they are mashed or prepared as a fasting dish, whether they are served as jacket potatoes or concocted to a fancy French gratin is a question of current necessity and individual need. The respective spices add the distinctive features and moreover a special appeal to the basic dish. If the gratin is dusted with a little cayenne pepper, it gives it a bit of a kick, like the Symptom of Impatience gets a special kick by a somewhat anxious, restless compulsion to travel. The person might even make an interesting job out of it, noticing only later in life that it was in fact Impatience which coined his impelling lifestyle, and not the travel as such with all its anticipated adventures and hazards.

4. The Poles of the Archetypes of Fear

■ *How do the positive and negative poles of a Fear Symptom relate to each other?*

In the context of the teachings about the Archetypes of the Soul we understand the poles of the individual archetypes as the respective boundary points of a given potential. The poles of the Seven Fear Symptoms are different from other Archetypes in the soul Pattern, as they represent a frequency range or an extent of the fear potential between two boundary points of fear, while the other MATRIX variables are boundary points between love and fear. These boundary points are determined individually from one person to another and are dependent on: (1) his or her complete Soul Pattern, (2) the Soul Age, (3) his emphatic capability and (4) the way he is able to explore his fears with consciousness. Individuals cannot expand their possibilities beyond those boundaries.

So the poles of the Archetypes of Fear represent a potential of fear sensation and reaction which, while different from one person to another, nevertheless allows for a describable manifestation for anyone dealing consciously or unconsciously with the Basic Fear in his life. Every arrogant person is aware of the possibility of acting and behaving either proudly (positive pole) or complacently (negative pole) when confronted with people or in a given situation. It is irrelevant in this context whether he is a Young or an Old Soul, or whether he had a difficult childhood or not. He may experience these boundary points of his potential reaction to a fear-evoking situation consciously or unconsciously, but he cannot essentially control his reactions.

It is a fact though that the positive pole represents the stronger manifestation of the fear potential, while the negative pole is the weaker manifestation. This is easy to remember: positive pole here means stronger, added, more forcefully; negative pole means weaker, less, and a more easily manageable fear manifestation. The positive pole describes the stronger fear manifestation and can also be understood by the fact that the excessive, and eventually intolerable, fear must almost inevitably be converted into one of the so-called False Virtues to become tolerable again. As long as a human being dwells in the negative pole of his fear, he can usually handle the implicated states of excitation.

Moreover, the unpleasantness of his fears also affects his fellow men and elicits criticism, so he actually remains in touch with them. In contrast, the manifestation of the positive pole as a False Virtue creates only pseudo-relations. In its result, it really segregates from one's fellow people. The negative pole still allows for blame, controversy, pain, discussion, and a certain degree of closeness. The positive pole in its transformation as a False Virtue rises above others, making itself unassailable.

Within the scope of their Basic Fears and their poles, individuals can also choose to move in a midfield between the boundary points of their fear symptoms. But to have a Primary Symptom of Fear and thereby act out a central aspect of worldly existence doesn't mean being constantly exposed to, feeling or coping with fear. This is where the subjective feeling clearly differs from the actual energetic conditions. Viewed objectively, each human being is required to incessantly deal with his special Basic Fear, and moreover with the negative poles of the other MATRIX variables.

Subjectively, however, he will feel strong fear at one time while, in his own perception, feel devoid of fear at another.

The subtlety and essentiality of mastering fear is a topic of human existence. The possibility of an individual to move between the limit values of his fear polarity is what permits him to be able to deal with this basic condition of human existence in a tolerable way, thereby adding fear (and its opposite, love) as an enriching experience quality to coping with life.

By identifying the Primary and Secondary Symptom of Fear and their interplay in the individual Basic Fear, we reveal a new perspective on life. It allows people to better observe their fears and provide – to a certain extent -- a freedom of choice between feeling and /or acting out their fear, a liberty they didn't have before. Only someone recognizing that he is in the positive pole of his fear archetype, about to convert the overwhelming fear into a False Virtue, also has the choice of refraining from this transformation process. Watching the manifestations of the fear poles, looking at them with a grain of humor and also divulging them to one's fellow men from time to time, is very helpful in reducing both the segregating factors about this fear, and the subjectively sensed feelings of anxiety. Someone who can talk of this fear, having recognized and observed it, is no longer a helpless victim to his fear coping mechanisms.

Dealing with fear as described here reduces the amplitude of the fear potential, the extreme spikes and harmful ramifications on the individual concerned and his surroundings. It reduces the distance between the boundary points of the poles and lets it move from both directions to a more beneficial middle.

▪ *There are another six archetypes in every individual Soul Pattern, each having a love pole (positive) and a fear pole (negative) respectively. How do these differ from the Archetypes of Fear?*
Whenever the fear level of a human being rises due to inner or

outer incidents which activate his archetypal Basic Fear, all other negative poles of his Soul Pattern are affected as well; the whole fear structure begins to vibrate. Fear has a contagious effect and is only too ready and able to infect those spheres of our energy system we describe as the negative poles. A strongly activated Primary or Secondary Symptom of Fear will affect the overall Soul Pattern, at least transitorily. The other way round, however, the effect is seldom observed, i.e. when the negative pole of the Soul Role is affected, it doesn't automatically activate one's Basic Fear potential.

A »Priest« Soul may be quite strict, bigoted and merciless in religious or spiritual matters, thus giving expression to his negative pole. But this character quality need not have any immediate effect on, let's say, the Fear Symptom Stubbornness or Impatience of the respective individual. Or a »Stoic«, considering his life situation, may slip into his negative pole of resignation, but this won't add to his Basic Fear structure, for example Self-sabotage with Greed.

While the high fear vibration affecting the whole Soul Pattern is only temporary and calms down after a certain period of over-excitement, the readiness of the Archetypes of Fear to oscillate between the poles of more or less fear remains active. But as soon as the first agitation has subsided, the positive poles of the other MATRIX variables can be used to appease and calm down the Basic Fear. So the »Priest« from the previous example can apply his abilities to comfort himself and look at his own fears with some compassion to reduce his Impatience or Stubbornness to a tolerable measure. Someone with the Goal of Development »Dominance« can learn to master the manifestations of his fear, while another with the Goal »Acceptance« can lovingly acknowledge them.

But a human being mustn't just be reduced to his fear reactions. The positive poles of the other archetypes of one's Soul Pattern serve – if applied accordingly – in no little measure to cope with fear. This process is based on an increasing life experience, serving to recognize that in difficult, fear-evoking situations one can resort to tried and tested resources made available by one's own soul.

■ *Could we please learn more about the concept of »False Virtue« as a manifestation of the positive pole of a fear archetype?*

Every human being moves between the poles of his Basic Fears with the freedom of discretion, i.e. between more fear and less fear. The positive pole of any fear archetype presents itself as loving, vigorous and positive. In reality, however, it is extremely tense and like a mask covering the fear hidden behind the symptom. This mask is often taken for the nature and personality, for the typical characteristics of a person which, over time, he or she also identifies with: »That's just the way I am!«

Those people hiding behind the mask of their fearful positive pole, the False Virtue, reap certain advantages, because people have adorned it with all kinds of positive projections to be able to deal with the principle and irrefutable fact of archetypal fears on this earth. Consequently, a person can easily bask in his modesty (Self-deprecation), determination (Stubbornness), pride (Arrogance), self-lessness (Martyrdom) or audacity (Impatience) without meeting much social resistance. It requires considerable willingness and ability to question the self and lift the mask of fear from one's naked, defenseless and petrified, true face, at least for some minutes or hours.

But no one will be able to do completely without his fear mask, because all men must wear it in order to function and survive within their respective societies. Wearing the mask of false virtue and shaping the manifestations of the archetypal fears into various phenotypes is actually part of the freedom earthly life offers a human soul within its body, psyche and mind. We would even go so far as to say: Experiencing fear and the possibility of dressing it up with socially or humanly acceptable, pleasant masks is one of the great and fascinating challenges for a soul to incarnate at all.

This is where it can experience something hitherto unknown with a tremendously large spectrum of realization possibilities.

The example of the fear archetype Impatience clearly demonstrates that the activities of a deep-sea diver, hang-glider, high-mountain climber etc. represent strong manifestations of the fearful positive pole of audacity. The often compulsive performance such an individual renders isn't conceivable without a strong positive pole at the boundary point of a high-voltage stress field. Hardly anyone recognizes the fear of death concealed behind it. Since the manifestation of this fear is generally perceived as admirable, even though it represents a False Virtue according to our definition, this person will endeavor to move as often and as close as possible near this positive pole. He will voluntarily stoke up his fear, so as to keep the fire of appreciation and intensity burning.

The mask of virtue conceals the naked fear behind it. The expression of fear via the positive pole leads to a certain stress reduction and therefore feels pleasant, notwithstanding that, due to the great audacity, the fear to be dealt with in the Symptom Impatience is much stronger than the anxiousness of someone acting out of his negative pole. The more clearly the manifestation, the more admiring feedback it generates, the more fear the individual concerned must »heroically« surmount, transform and discharge.

5. Therapy and Archetypal Fears

■ *Can therapy influence or heal the Archetypal Fears?*
Psychotherapy cannot repeal the principle of the necessity of fear. But it can be helpful in reducing surplus fear and encourage both the observation of one's own mechanisms, reactions and conscious handling of the manifestations of fear, as well as promote greater inner freedom. It's comforting to people to feel seen and understood in their archetypal fear and its forms of expression.

It may be justly claimed that most people simply live their Basic Fear without ever thinking about the deeper reasons of their reactions. Some few have the ability – and this is not morally better than the behavior of the majority – of introspection and self-observation. This form of conscious analysis of one's fear manifestations or their forms of expression in others can lead to a reduction of fear. But it is in no way mandatory, since, although the manifestations of fear may be controlled and controllable, they continue to persist in their requisite aspects and can't be influenced towards a more conscious experiencing by whichever great efforts. Even a truly enlightened being able to live and see through his whole existence, actions and reactions with fullest awareness, is still subjected to the laws of his Soul Pattern as long as he breathes. His worldly fear potential and Basic Fear as such isn't going to dematerialize.

It is an indispensable, necessary part of incarnation that fear be lived through and dealt with, though it is not pre-ordained how to deal with it. The modality isn't fateful; it is not subjected to the superordinate rule of the Soul Pattern but can – within the individual's range of freedom – be left up to his or her own fashioning.

As outlined earlier, the poles of the Fear Archetypes differ from the other polarities of the MATRIX in that the positive pole represents a greater fear manifestation than the negative pole. Identifying one's Fear Symptom as a False Virtue when subjectively it is experienced as a true virtue, doesn't make it easy for people to look behind the mechanisms of their fear, to see through the mask and break through or change the behaviors this mask requires. So someone who, unsuspecting that it is the kind mask of fear, insists on showing his fellow men primarily the positive pole and also defining himself by it in character, will ultimately find it difficult to escape from the induration of his fear.

In contrast, the negative pole (or an approximation to the negative pole), which feels unpleasant both to the individual himself and to those around him, being destructive and painful also in its consequences, is actually easier to influence by therapy than the positive pole. The ramifications of the negative pole are more obvious and easier to observe, and can in many cases also be more effortlessly relieved. In fact, someone who mainly arranges himself in the negative poles of the Primary or Secondary Symptoms of his Fears, without being able, of course, to completely avoid contact with the positive pole, is ultimately less afraid to expose himself to the criticism, displeasure of and confrontation with his fellow men. He shows himself more clearly in his fear via the negative pole, even though the reactions out of the negative pole are equally strong defense mechanisms as the mask of False Virtue. But it would hardly occur to people to classify the obvious manifestations of the negative pole as a virtue or admirable.

Necessary fear, notably the share which is indispensable for the growth and development of a human being, cannot be influenced and therefore not reduced by therapy either. Fear is a factor and will remain so. It is essential for the learning process, in an individual life just as in the course of the full incarnation cycle. Surplus fear, however, can be diminished and nearly dissolved by insight, life experience or psychotherapy.

We give you an example: Starting with incarnation and, at the latest at birth of a stubborn person, the vibration sets in between the poles obstinacy (negative pole) and determination (positive pole). Now a whole life can be led with little obstinacy and much determination or with mean values of both, or with great obstinacy and little determination. To select just one or the other is not an option. We know and you know that it is more pleasant to live more determinedly and less obstinately. Both, however, serve the soul and its incarnation goals.

When it becomes manifest that too much obstinacy and too little determination cause the incarnated human being problems, the behavior can be moderated by insight or by appropriate therapy. This doesn't change the Archetype of Stubbornness at all, but it provides a larger bandwidth of experience and more liberty in the implementation and accomplishment of the Soul Pattern of this incarnated stubborn individual. It also promotes his emotional maturation.

Therapy serves the emotional well-being in that it impacts the range of experience and examines the mechanisms. It serves the psyche, but it does not serve the soul, because there simply isn't anything that could be useful to it in this respect. We repeat that the soul also benefits from ninety per cent obstinacy and ten per cent determination or vice versa, or from a lifelong, high fear level. It is an experience like any other experiences. All the soul wants is to make experiences; these do not necessarily have to be pleasant or positive. It's the psyche that benefits, though. Naturally, a more enjoyable experience diminishes fear, thereby serving emotional maturation because the psyche functions in a specific way: the more often it has experienced relaxation and loving vibrations, the more it gets used to it, striving to reduce the other conditions to a minimum. The soul in turn ensures that also the negative pole of fear with its most unpleasant implications occasionally shows up on the radar, to uphold the necessary tension between the two poles as a potential that inures the psyche to the benefit of the soul's overall experience.

Let's take again a person with the Fear Symptom Stubbornness as an example. Depending on a particular event, person, cause, or the way he feels on a particular day, and according to the conditioning and patterning of his psyche, he usually moves on a certain frequency range in the stress field between determination (positive pole) and obstinacy (negative pole). When he realizes that he quite often reacts obstinately, maybe because other people point it out or accuse him of it, or when he physically feels his doggedness, e.g. by gnashing his teeth at night or suffering from painful neck stiffness, it will be easier for him to consciously experience obstinacy. But when his fear gets more violent or really out of hand for some reason (mostly when threatened by abandonment), requiring a firm determination or approach, he is unlikely – in the moment of his panic – to become aware that his determination is a manifestation of his fear. If he has the capability of reflection, he will perhaps realize days, weeks or only years later that his extreme determination and the desire to get a situation under control again was a sign of fear far beyond his habitual obstinacy, and that the resolute reaction and action served to reduce an intolerable fear pressure. It is an essential function of the positive pole of all archetypal fears to sublimate this surplus of fear. Therapy can help the client to identify and observe these mechanisms.

> ▦ *Is raising the archetypal fear to consciousness the crucial factor in positively affecting it?*

Man can experience his fear consciously or fully unconsciously. It doesn't affect the basic tension of his fear field. He can experience a lot of fear consciously or unconsciously, or he can experience very little fear consciously or unconsciously. To most people, awareness isn't an issue anyway in as far as it concerns their Fear Symptoms, the root of the big fear tree. They simply act out what is currently »on the agenda«.

Therapy reaches its limits where the patient's ability to reflect and his conscious awareness are restricted. But when, for example, a beloved one dies, even a person not trained in awareness knows that this is a reason to feel fear; a kind of consciousness links with the event. Someone who learns that he has a tumor will quite naturally connect all his fear symptoms and sensations with this information. But it doesn't mean that they experience their fear in terms of the archetype consciously. Only when an individual knows that he is impatient, stubborn or arrogant, and that this represents the root of his personal fear tree, can he start to patiently observe himself, not only during inner wartimes but also in peacetime. This helps him figure out where his individual trigger points are that bring this fear to manifest.

Psychotherapy gains in depth when superficial fear manifestations are understood to be the fruits of a big fear tree, whereas the invisible, i.e. unconscious, root underground consists of a Fear Archetype. When, for example, mad jealousy or severe control compulsions are identified as Symptoms of Stubbornness, this fear root can be treated without the need to reference any childhood experiences. Access to it is faster and more direct.

An Archetype of Fear as such is predetermined on the soul level. But only incarnation and aliveness create the frequency range between the two poles. This is where correction can start, nevertheless always working on the psyche, which suffers from excessive fear, rather than on the Soul Pattern level. The psyche reacts positively to any facilitation in dealing with the Soul Pattern. But an emotional change isn't going to change the Soul Pattern itself. A highly intolerant, invariably surly person for example represents an open manifestation of the negative pole of his Impatience. An extremely reckless person represents the manifestation of the positive pole of that same Symptom. When an impatient person moves in the middle between both poles, both manifestations will be less obtrusive. He will be generally considered quite impatient with a tendency to intolerance and occasional testiness, and he will continue to seem audacious and daring to others at times. Yet he will no longer permanently risk his life or be hostile and intolerant through and through to anything foreign, e.g. in religious or political affairs.

Therapy cannot spare anyone the necessary conflict with one of the Seven Archetypal Fears, it can only take the edge off, it can clarify and explain. But it is neither possible nor sensible to completely liberate an individual from the most important impulse of his soul's evolvement. The impatient person must deal with the phenomenon of time up to his last breath. A stubborn person will always struggle with life's unpredictability. An averagely impatient person often honks his horn, is quick to lose his temper, ranting loudly and harassing others with his own sense of fleeting time. An averagely stubborn individual is obstinate and hard to influence; he plays deaf or even dead and hates everything unexpected, in particular any unwelcome changes. That's how it is and will remain.

We don't stipulate that an impatient person should teach himself patience. But the experience to temporize and act with patience can occasionally be very instructive to him. It creates a sense of satisfaction that feels much better than just working things off as fast as possible, which merely relieves the fear stress. Relaxation techniques always have a moderating effect on fear; also a glass of red wine can occasionally be helpful. A stubborn person should give room to his need for security; it calms his fear.

The most important thing, however, is that people don't forget love as a fear-abating factor. Love and fear cannot really co-exist. As much as the possibilities of therapy and self-reflection should be held important, love and understanding is still the most effective antidote to deep fear.

■ *Could we hear a specific and practical advice on how to alleviate fear?*

If we give you some suggestions on how to deal with fear and use the healthy, nurturing and helpful parts of the psyche as tools to cope with fear, we can only do so for your immediate cultural area. The reason is that other peoples require measures and techniques which, unusual and weird as they may seem to you, reach their particular psyche directly. There are, of course, also possibilities for people in the western hemisphere to master certain illusory fears – e.g. fear of hell or spirits, or of vengeance for past sins – with suitable conjurations and magical provisions. It helps reassure and calm the individual concerned. When a Sicilian suffers from the evil eye or fears that his life has been jinxed, it can only be dealt with on that same level. So the adequate cure would be, for example, to perform some ritual or give him an amulet and reassure him with great authority and certainty: Now, no one can harm you anymore now.

Generally speaking, one must distinguish between anxieties that are based on the actual fear of solitude, isolation, abandonment or of being an outcast in the broadest sense, and those other fears relating to coping with life. The former can best be treated in group therapy or in a one-to-one session with gentle physical contact methods. An exercise can consist, for example, in asking which part of the body feels most lonely, isolated, split off or expulsed. While the attention of the anxious or anxiety-disordered person wanders there and the fear shifts to this part of the body in his imagination – be it the stomach or his right foot – the therapist should ask permission to touch this part in order to feel why the fear concentrates just there. Following some calibration, the patient or person affected can carry out this exercise himself. The anxiety is sort of gathered and concentrated in one place. While before it seemed to suffuse the whole body from top to toe, infesting every spot, this exercise forms a virtual center now that can be properly treated. The patient can be instructed to place his hand there or perform a mental heat exercise, treating the spot as if he was giving himself a mental chemotherapy which acts just on the fear cells, leaving the rest of the body basically unaffected.

As mentioned, however, there are other forms of fear not primarily connected with loneliness and isolation, but dealing mainly with issues of mastering life. It includes questions like how to cope with the challenges of life or finding just the right person to feel comfortable in life. Many fears exist about somehow not being in the right place or in the wrong job. Such fears can best be handled with imagination exercises, with images focusing on the »maximum possible« this individual believes being able to reach for himself. We'll call this the »boldness exercise«. The idea is to lead someone who is insecure in the face of the abundance of options life holds in store and his anxiety of being unable to make proper use of any of it, to develop a fairytale-like and often seeming completely exaggerated fantasy image of what he wants and would consider as the highest fulfillment and optimum goal of his existence. Exaggeration is the healing principle here. It is recommended to fragment the whole big anxiety into individual segments, so that the person seeking help gets an opportunity to portray his best possible idea of family, of the highest form of love, the most satisfactory job, the optimal financial situation and so on, one by one in large, elaborately adorned images. This will be very difficult at first, since this person's fear consists in just that he or she doesn't dare demand of life what the soul has designed for itself as a potential.

When the highest grade of seeming boldness has been reached, that is, almost a shamelessness in aspirations and self-crafting of opportunities, this 150-percent maximum will lead to boosting the actual, modest state. The more the patient fantasizes uninhibitedly, creating audacious images, the more frequently will he notice that his modest conditions improve a little by the day, his radius getting larger, so that reality gradually catches up with the visualizations. It's important of course not to let this exercise escalate into megalomania, but to always relate back to the latest, small, everyday improvements and affirm them; to stipulate them as if there was hope to reach the 150-percent maximum one day, even if it is a long way to go.

This is a sort of opening-up exercise, initially providing a wide field of possibilities, then bringing the potential of the individual in small steps closer to the large fantasies. As a result, the range of the visualizing individual will automatically expand. His life reality does not, as might logically be expected, stay way behind the envisioned image, leading to disappointment and depression. The knack of this exercise consists in exaggerating so much that the old feelings of powerlessness, contrasted by exaggerated fantasies of omnipotence, which are secretly weaving and wafting in the client anyway, can actually be named.

■ *What is the difference compared to the »miracle question« technique?*

Our »boldness technique« is much more elaborate than the »miracle question« (in which the therapist asks the client what the effect would be if the problem disappeared overnight as if by miracle). The »boldness technique« isn't oriented on the actual possibilities of the individual concerned, but has a fairytale-like, colorful, iridescent quality. It isn't based on an almost realistic expanding of possibilities as stimulated by the »miracle question«, but on a completely cloudy, fabulous, almost supernatural fantasy, potent enough to fulfill all wishes in one big swoop.

6. The Psyche

■ *Please explain to us your understanding of psyche in correlation with fear.*

The psyche of a human being is a non-material organ of the body (cf. Worlds of the Soul, p. 31–45, in German). If we talk about an organ, we use this term to describe an indivisible part of the physicalness of man; in non-physical dimensions, psyche doesn't exist. It evolves and expires with every single incarnation and is completely individual, depending on genetics, environment, moment in history, surrounding collectives etc. Although it's not in the body, it is of the body and pertains to its earthly existence. Its corporeal effects can be significant and lasting. So we continue to speak about a non-material organ, knowing that you understand now that one cannot examine or dissect it like a liver or heart. The location of this non-material, but indeed very functional organ of every human being is in the energy sheath (»kosha« from Sanskrit), which materializes around the body after ensoulment and evolves from there.

You may have heard about an astral body, a mental body and other energy strata, or also about the aura. The psychic identity of a human being is embedded in the so-called emotional body. This is just another name for what we wish to explain to you. The emotional body has different dimensions and can be described as follows: It's an energy sheath which, with a sensitive hand, can be felt at a distance of about ten centimeters above the skin of a relaxed, emotionally and physically fairly healthy person. When a person is physically ill, emotionally unstable or severely threatened by outer circumstances, this emotional body can expand up to several meters in diameter. It is a very flexible energy sheath, the function of which depends on what is required. It is fitted with myriads of emotional receptors or aerials, which are activated as soon as a human being feels any kind of threat.

This non-material organ isn't the only layer enveloping a human being. We just want to intimate that, for example, the ability to recollect former existences and encounters with other souls in earlier lives is stored in another, non-material enveloping body or sheath. It isn't identical with the psyche we are describing to you, although there are some points of contact.

Imagine now that the psyche as an energy sheath and force field were fitted with a switch, providing it with the functionality to record or store events, images, thoughts etc. both in the cortex and in other parts of the human body – but most particular in those nerve cells which are comparable to a second, less cognitive brain in the belly. The psyche transmits every impulse it receives to two vital, material receiver stations. These in turn process them, each in their own way. So when we originally talked about the non-material psyche as a fear-processing organ of the body, we meant that it uses other organs of the body receiving their impulses from the psyche, and transforms them into processes of the metabolism, into electromagnetic and other endogenous processes.

The psyche picks up any kind of threat that might prevent a person to live up to his mission and possibilities and accomplish what his soul has envisioned for the current incarnation. It isn't important for the psyche whether they are imaginary threats, intellectual concepts liable to shake the mental structure of an individual, or threatening memories or real, serious physical threats. Depending on the kind of fear, either a switch to the person's brain is activated, or energy will be sent to the less cognitive areas of other body parts. When we are dealing with anxiety fantasies, imaginary threats, fears going back to traumatic experiences or anxiety from intellectual concepts alien to this person, it's primarily the cortex or brain stem with its different response options that gets switched on. The brain will somehow process what has been picked up and will metabolize, understand, classify and archive it. When, in contrast, there is an immediate physical threat, be it by another creature, by hunger, natural disaster or a collective event like war, the switch activates the second receiver system, notably the fear-processing capacity of the other body organs and all the non-cognitive possibilities of a person of dealing with anxiety. For example, the psyche can send an impulse to the legs, prompting the person to run. Fear impulses can also be transmitted to the bowels, the stomach, the glands or other organs like the kidneys, the bladder or the hormone system, impacting those functions. So when someone confronted with some kind of hazard feels a stomach-ache, this is a sensible body reaction to bring home to the person affected: you are being threatened, you must react. The signal to someone wetting his pants out of fear is that he must act quickly to find something which makes him feel safe, enabling him to find a way out.

The switching-points from the non-material, emotional sheath to the body are highly effective and can activate further connections between the other, emotionally less differentiated areas of the physical body. This includes, for example, developing goose bumps in non-specific fear situations. The skin wires up with the brain, which can subsequently build on highly differentiated cognitive experiences to analyze and observe the unconscious reactions of the rest of the body, understanding and converting them into thoughts, actions, reactions and verbal remarks as a way to channel and control them.

Until now, we have spoken as if the psyche were separable from other aspects of the self, e.g. the spirit or the soul. But it will be easy for you to realize that this separation is only an attempt at explaining our topic and not at all human reality. The human soul in the astral sphere doesn't know fear as such; but as soon as it incarnates in a body, inhabiting it and thereby exposing itself to worldly threats, the soul needs the psyche to be able to clearly articulate itself and develop a meaningful strategy to deal with earthly fears.

Another aspect of psyche, which, while falling into the category of »non-material human organ«, cannot be categorized as »fear-processing«. It is the sum of all conceivable impulses connected with joy. It is via the psyche that an incarnated soul can feel joy and ecstasy. This fact establishes some balance to the continual threats every person is exposed to. It is this other realm of the psyche that gives people the courage and readiness to deliver and abandon themselves to the human condition with all its challenges in the first place.

Once incarnated, the individual eternal soul – via its individual transitory psyche – triggers the essential energies of joy, confidence, courage and hope for a successful outcome of the incarnation and communicates it to the emotional apparatus. In this way, humans benefit from a double influence of the psyche. While they have to deal with the difficulties of worldly existence and all its hazards, they draw the energy required to do this from a different sphere of the psyche, giving strength, hope and courage. This is also the sphere which at all times upholds a more or less unconscious dialog with the individual's soul family and its superordinate purpose. The closer the conscious or unconscious connection of a person to his soul is, the more confidently can he master his life, and the less he will despair of the difficulties it offers. Incidentally, this »positive« aspect of the psychic organ is also the realm of intuition, inspiration and mediumistic receptivity. After all, where else than via the functions of the psyche should these take place, conveying the impulses received to the conscious brain and there transforming them into intellectual recognition?

The emotional body we spoke about isn't identical with the aura. By aura we understand a number of luminous bodies surrounding a person in different densities and levels of brightness. These bodies or sheaths aren't energetically charged in the same way as the psyche. The aura of a human being pulsates differently from the psyche as we have described it. The aura contracts when confronted with fear; the psyche, in contrast, extends. The emotional body is an invisible energy stratum; it cannot even be seen by aura readers. It can only be sensed. And although it can be felt, and not only by those trained to do so, but by all fellow men focusing on it or letting themselves in on perceiving this stratum, it is seldom intellectually perceived.

Just imagine entering a room with a person in it who can only be seen from behind and isn't moving. You will nevertheless be able to sense very soon whether this person is afraid. It will strike you already at the door, assault you even with an uncomfortable feeling, seizing you unpleasantly. Fear virtually infects and directly affects your own psyche, i.e. your own emotional body. You react to the fear of the person in this room with your own fear – two emotional bodies melting together. Now if you transmit this brief, indirect threat to your cognitive system, you will be able to separate the fear of your fellow man in this room from your own. This fear you have identified in a split second, maybe by a queasy feeling in your stomach or an accelerated heartbeat, will enable you to help him articulate his own fear, to recognize and maybe also reduce it. As we said, the energetic sheath of the psyche can pulsate and spread, forming even big fields or clusters. Fear is highly infectious in that it can fuse several or even many emotional bodies into a vibrating, trembling structure, producing mass fear or panic.

Now, a diseased psyche suffers from an overwhelming amount of mental receptors, impairing the metabolism of the brain. Thus, the brain can no longer deflect the fear impulses via the body, resulting in blockades or stases. The cause is primarily memory threats, e.g. as a consequence of long past traumas, or else delusional, imaginary fears, the origin of which cannot be found in the immediate, actual reality. The person thus affected cannot escape anymore from the webbing of his anxiety fantasies by his own efforts. The body in turn reacts to old traumas with a number of clearly visible phenomena like rashes and eczemas or chronic diseases, cramps, ankylosis, aggressive acts and much more. The body also has a great range of seemingly relieving responses, signaling to the individual, his physician and his surroundings in multiple ways: This is nothing unimportant or transitory. It's an emotional condition requiring treatment and comfort; it torments the individual so much that he can't cope with it alone. In contrast, in the case of a basically healthy person with a resilient psyche, time is indeed the great healer.

7. Development of the Psyche and the Soul

■ *How do the development of psyche and soul correlate? How do they differ?*

The information we are sharing with you is meant to help you understand that psyche and soul, psychological development and development of the soul, must be examined separately. It is no longer commensurate with your intellectual cognitive faculties to intermingle or confuse these lines of development of man.

Both the maturation of the soul (which takes millennia) and the psychic maturation (which will usually happen within a lifespan) follow certain laws and necessities. The soul's maturation can neither be prevented nor promoted. It happens exclusively by the simple fact of being alive again and again, collecting earthly experience. As long as a man lives, he cannot influence this development. The soul's growth is inevitable. That is one of the constants of his aliveness, just like breathing or ageing. Its development inexorably follows the 35 steps of evolution during the five cycles of incarnation – from the Infant Soul until the last life as an Old Soul.

The psychic development in contrast follows a much less preordained path. It is subjected to the individual formation of will and awareness, the interaction with others, the person's confrontation with various situations and his readiness to deal with and confront his fears.

The Soul Pattern, i.e. the Matrix with its varying choice of archetypes, is a blueprint for a person's potential, which then evolves more or less during his life. This potential describes the framework, the limits and the incredibly multi-faceted possibilities which a person, based on his or her Soul Pattern, brings into the world. In the incarnated condition, the soul will associate and ally with the psyche. It can manifest itself by an adequate development of the psyche through the exchange and interaction with one's fellow men, and unfold hand in hand with the psyche. The soul can then bloom and bear fruit. But a rose is a rose is a rose. It can only evolve inside given limits. The moment a physical body develops and joins with an individual soul, the person's psyche begins to evolve, too. Every incarnating soul takes the body, psyche and mind of a human being as a means of orientation and uses it in order to gain experience through living exactly that specific life with all its ups and downs.

So the Soul Pattern contains all possibilities. The psyche will in turn orient itself on the soul's necessities and plans and react either in support of this potential or by acting obstructively, depending on circumstances. A person's psyche can be affected in many different ways: by neglect or torture, by encounter and emotional security, by love and therapy. Humans in their practically unlimited ingenuity know how to deal with their own psyche and those of their fellow creatures. They have an inherent knowledge of how psyche and body are indivisibly linked with each other, so that they can manipulate or heal their bodies via the psyche and vice versa.

We would like to emphasize here that a person whose brain is severely handicapped from birth, rendering him unable to use his brain to substantially further his mind's development, nevertheless goes through a maturation process of his soul. In this, he or she is not at all dependent on an insufficiently or undeveloped psyche. Even a profoundly disabled person will definitely reveal his archetypal Soul Pattern or Soul Matrix. This is often misinterpreted as psyche or character. In truth, such a person follows the plan of his soul without many obstacles, in a pure form.

The psychological or emotional development in contrast is more erratic and greatly dependent on the possibilities and opportunities a person finds during a lifetime and is able or willing to use in order to chafe against others and come to an arrangement with them in one way or another. There are, of course, also specific stages and requirements for emotional maturity and its processes, analogous to what every – or almost every – man goes through within his physical development and maturation process. The psyche of a thirty-year-old is undoubtedly further matured than the psyche of a three-year-old or a three months' old baby. In this, too, one can easily discern certain rules and laws. But whether a human being liberates his psyche from haunting anxieties beyond the biological measure, enriching them with love and the ability to deal with conflict, is an additional effort or added potential that isn't available to everyone.

We would like to point out another extreme aspect in the difference between soul development and psychological maturation. When a soul incarnates and then its body dies in infancy, that soul's development is – as strange as this may seem to you – fully accomplished and advanced to the necessities even within this short lifespan, while obviously the maturation of the person's psyche could not make great progress. The soul has a motivation to unfold under any circumstances and in whichever state, while man's psyche often prefers to avoid precisely that which affects it with the challenges of fear. We don't judge that, and neither should you.

Development, evolvement and fulfillment following necessities concern the individual soul on its path through all incarnations and thus naturally also the soul family in its entirety. However, all different forms of soul development always remain related to the individual soul and its soul siblings. Emotional development of the psyche in contrast is primarily and essentially a phenomenon of companionship among fellow men. It is dependent on the interaction between ensouled and embodied human beings, e. g. between the newborn child and its parents, between the small child and its brothers and sisters or playmates, between the adolescent and his pals, between friends, couples and various other groupings. These relationships all contribute to the psyche's development while experiencing tension and relaxation, stimulation and soothing.

When a child or even a grown-up person is artificially or forcibly kept in isolation for a long time, his psyche withers or can develop further only with great difficulty. It cannot unfold in accordance with its needs for exchange and stimulation. However, as we said earlier, even such an unusual isolation could promote and be of use for the evolvement of the soul. For the psyche of a person, this loneliness is never beneficial. What's more, the psyche, which isn't conceivable without the body and its needs, can suffer terribly;

it can become ill, be damaged by painful, disagreeable, tormenting events occurring within human relations, just as it can be fostered by pleasant and loving encounters.

Yet, what may torment and damage the psyche can in turn be quite useful to the soul's intentions and its independent willing. The soul will understand even torture as meaningful in this way and will integrate it within its development, with assistance from the soul family. To your societies, which suffer from a wide-spread sense of meaninglessness, it is of invaluable benefit to search for and find out the laws of the meaningfulness of human existence not in the psyche, be it individual or collective, but in the realm of the soul. That must be clearly distinguished from the feelings of emptiness based on emotional conditions. In other words, someone who increasingly understands his soul as a defining factor of his life, won't find it hard to figure out a meaning in his existence. He will certainly find it hard though, if he relates solely to the perspective of his psyche, which often feels lost, sad or damaged.

The development steps of the soul we described to you in 35 steps (cf. *Wisdom of the Soul*, p. 40–49; *Ways of the Soul*, p. 284 p.) are largely accomplished without any actively pursued psychological maturation. This may at first seem strange and incomprehensible to you because the objectives and tasks are formulated in a way that can be easily mistaken for stages of psychological maturation. However, due to the psyche's physical but non-material location, they are only loosely connected with it. We said that the development of the human psyche is a collective and social, interactional phenomenon. What's more, psychological maturation that goes beyond the biological necessity has a lot to do with intelligence, ability to reason, conflict capability, access to therapy, intellectual deliberations and education. The soul in contrast has no need to be intelligent or to revert to mental capabilities in order to develop. That's why we said that also someone with severe brain-damage who can neither speak nor think, or a baby which hasn't yet learned to express itself or think in the way of adults and dies in infancy, complete a development of their soul that follows totally different needs and principles than what you understand by maturation and maturity.

If you look solely at the psychological and intellectual development, then someone intellectually retarded with a poorly matured or damaged brain could never become a mature person. Your notion of inner growth refers mainly to the ability of the human intellect to be able to look at the self with a certain critical faculty and distance himself from his actions, to the ability to comprehend and reflect, to forgive and to lovingly accept himself and other people. All of that is certainly beneficial to the soul, which is developing in parallel as well, but it doesn't essentially advance it. Learning on the soul level also happens when an individual doesn't understand or forgive, shows no self-criticism and doesn't look at himself and his actions objectively or doesn't love with all his heart. The soul, however, will always ensure that – in accordance with the incarnation cycles and their respective capacities – enough lives be lived in each cycle and on each step of evolvement. The soul will direct just such existential learning as if by a growth hormone.

Wisdom of the soul in this sense pursues its own goals and is not dependent on a well-developed intellect or the psyche evolving logically and healthily with progressive physical ageing. Learning in accordance with the 35 development objectives takes place in tens of thousand different ways. As soon as an individual soul as an embodied, separate human being has reached a certain saturation and point of culmination in the fulfillment of this task, it will turn to new challenges and goals. These will usually take up several lives, too, because they must be dealt with from so many different angles and approaches: with an immature psyche in one life, in the next with a mature one, then again with a well developed or little developed intellect, with a great capacity for love or very little. All this contributes to the soul's accumulation of rich experiences and to learning the lessons from the incarnated condition it needs for its progress.

Beyond the development objectives and tasks, every single life, be it short or long, happy or sad, deals naturally with everything a specific Soul Pattern contains or offers in terms of challenges. The manner in which a person, from infancy to old age, meets and responds to his fellow men, how he develops through them and the conditions of his reality, is fashioned by about fifty percent by the inherent laws of his Soul Pattern, i.e. which Goal of Development, which Mode, which Fear Symptoms, which Soul Age and the corresponding Development Objective in accordance with the interests of his soul family it manifests. The other fifty percent are shaped by how his psyche develops this potential in its incarnated state.

8. Fear and Soul Age

■ *How do fear and fear processing by humans differ in the five different Soul Age Cycles?*

Fear contents and its processing differ from one soul stage to the next, and especially from one soul cycle to the next, to a great extent. In the most general sense we can say: An Infant Soul has no concept of things an Old Soul is afraid of, and the Old Soul will smile at what frightens an Infant Soul. In the following, let us look at these cycles in more detail. We can't elaborate on the individual Development Stages here, but will expound the fundamental need for fear as well as freedom from fear which characterize the individual, major periods of the soul's evolvement.

The Infant Soul primarily fears for its life. This particular fear gets more subtle with each stage and from one cycle to the next. While Old Souls, too, fear for their biological survival, in the understanding and feeling of an Infant Soul, life on the physical and the soul plane is almost identical. The Infant Soul, therefore, dreads anything that might directly affect its survival in the physical body, which it has inhabited only since lately. The objects of dread are primarily forces of nature, fights between the different tribes and ethnic groups which, due to their almost instinctive behavior, usually threaten to butcher the respective »other«. The Infant Soul is also afraid of the immediate hazards threatening its body, such as diseases, hunger and mortality in general.

The fascination that these phenomena simultaneously evoke in Infant Souls causes something seemingly absurd: a specific incarnation behavior that is increasingly foreign to Mature and Old Souls. Notably, Infant Souls incarnate preferably and specifically in regions of your planet which are providing an abundance of just those terrifying events and experiences described before. When we say that the soul seeks the challenge to be able to live, experience, cope with or process the fears adequate to its age cycle, you will understand that a Mature Soul for example – and we will come back to that later – has a lesser need to deal with material and concrete threats. It rather looks for emotional and intellectual problems as a challenge for its fears.

The main goal of the Infant Soul is to find out how to live, how to survive and how to die. These are new factors, unknown in its astral home, and those fears serve the soul to revert to a near-feral instinctive behavior in order to deal with the difficulties of physical existence.

Already the Child Soul develops a highly creative imagination to encounter the equally massive dangers of the environment and the incarnated condition. It propitiates its fears by amulets, various magical practices, body paintings and tattoos. Its favorite fear mastering technique consists in frightening others. It develops menacing gestures like chest-beating and roaring, and seeming to appear bigger than it is. It tries to intimidate and master the enemies, demons or elementary powers in some way, e.g. by shamanic rituals and sacrifices, and by taking life like a game in which the stronger always wins. In this second cycle of incarnations, fear has got a certain allure, prompting the necessity to actively meet it by transferring one's own fear of the mystical on phenomena of nature or objects to be animated. Projection is the common method in this second cycle; it calms the fears.

Just like the Infant Soul, the Child Soul too must deal with numerous adversities threatening its life and limb almost daily. Even though imagination now enters into it and imaginary fears, e.g. of spirits, demons, ghosts, the dead or vindictive deities are playing an increasing role, the primary goal is to always have conjuring practices and sacrificial offerings at hand to fend off disaster. This shows that the Child Soul in some way feels in a position to confront – out of its own power – the fears of life under which the helpless Infant Soul suffers. It is able to process and convert it, and to actively exert influence.

The **Young Soul** feels daring and courageous. It assumes a self-assured, defiant stance towards existence, adopting the notion that it can control life instead of having to submit to it. Increasingly, the playful creativity of the Child Soul turns into a fight against anything frightening. Fight here means wanting to win over whatever terrifies and threatens the Young Soul. The goal is to win over nature, over enemies, over one's weaker self and also over diseases, difficult childhood conditions, handicaps, other people's aggressions and much more. For the Young Soul, fight and victory take center stage.

For the first time during this third cycle, fears are considered to be an active challenge, because the Young Soul discovers that one can deny them, disavow and ignore them, pass over them or in any case pretend to be heroically up to them if tackled with enough courage. Insofar, it seems that in the cycle of the Young Soul, fear is playing the least role. But in truth, fears only seldom reach the consciousness of the individual concerned. While clearly visible to everyone else, he feels threatened and weakened by the emotional or cognitive acknowledgement of his fears. He rather evades any discussion or therapeutical approach, unless it strengthens his martial abilities to deal victoriously with his fears. Part of that is also to instrumentalize the fears of his fellow men for his own goals.

The **Mature Soul** finds a new field of activity in its fears. Instead of denying and covering them up, the Mature Soul looks at its fears with fascination and relish. It wouldn't feel complete if it wasn't plagued by one thing or another, if it couldn't conceive itself as a creature that has the sense and grounds to be a little afraid of everything and everybody. Because for the Mature Soul, the world is beautifully complicated and full of problems. And if there aren't enough problems in one's own life at present, there is ample opportunity to discover them in others, in the environment or in a general social context and chafe at, strengthen and develop by dealing with them. So the Mature Soul wishes for and loves its fears and problems because that's how it can best feel itself.

This stage is particularly interesting because it is the first time that souls like to reflect upon themselves and their anxieties. Mature Souls are curious about what happens inside of them; they are interested in their personal reaction to the problems of the world and to the fear of their fellow man.

The **Old Soul** in a way has the same problems as the Infant Soul, but it handles them completely differently. The Infant Soul fears for its life and its physical violability. The Old Soul has walked the earth numerous times and relies on a great fund of living and dying experiences. Even though these are unconscious or stored only in the primeval memory, they are nevertheless on hand.

If the Old Soul complains about its vulnerability, about restrictions in its state of health, about the strife in the world, within the family or the circle of friends, it feels just as threatened by all that as the Infant Soul does by night and thunder. But it won't feel the need to stab the one who has hurt it or throw the person causing problems out of the window. It rather endeavors to accept the facts and learn that there is no life without fear, yet that the possibilities of coping with fear are as diverse as the individuals suffering from it.

The long and sinuous path from the Infant Soul to an Old Soul is the path to self-realization in the literal meaning. Progressing from self-unawareness to a consciousness of the self, one's innermost nature and being, is a way of mastering and dissolving fear; on the other hand, the challenges of self-discovery are as frightening to Old Souls as to Infant Souls. It's just that they feel this fear differently. The individuals react differently, for example with depression – something unknown to Infant Souls – or with a quest for higher structures of meaning, aspects that play no role prior to the cycle of the Young Soul, or with the desire for increasing self-knowledge and taking responsibility for one's actions and reactions, and much more.

However, the wages of fear at the end of the cycle of the Old Soul isn't a condition of total freedom from fear as many may hope. Rather, the soul is reconciled to the fact that life and fear can't be separated, that angst – as subtle as it may be – represents the most powerful and important engine of the quest for meaning and evolvement in the physical condition of existence. When a soul at the end of its incarnations accepts this fact - not only as a philosophical idea, but actually embracing and feeling it inside, it reaches simultaneously the apex and the finish line of its involvement with life and the phenomenon of fear.

■ *Which grades of maturity can the hardly developed psyche of an Infant Soul achieve?*
It achieves all that can be achieved, although there can be no talk of maturity the way you understand it. If you stick to the analogy of a human baby, you'll find the simplest answer. At age one or at eighteen months, much of the small organism has grown but is by

far not yet fully matured. It means that a state of maturity can only be reached within the bounds of possibility, though it will inevitably be attained.

A human infant can lag behind in its development; an Infant Soul can't. At the end of stage 7 of the Infancy cycle, it will have achieved everything that is possible to achieve. Its soul maturity has then reached the required stage to change over to the cycle of the Child Soul. Viewed from your perspective, this person's emotional maturity is still very modest. A certain innocence is the outer sign that a distance to the self, and with that a responsibility for one's own interests, deeds, desires, instincts and needs, can't yet be managed by the Infant Soul. You in contrast understand by emotional maturity the ability to be true to and take responsibility for the self as well as for others. This, the Infant Soul is incapable of, either on the soul or the emotional plane. It is not able to look at itself from the outside or even be aware of others as human beings whose needs it could emphatically consider out of its free will. Although it can see that others are different and realize that they want different things, it remains puzzled as to why this is so and what good it might be for.

■ *Modern psychology believes to identify definable steps of emotional maturation in an individual. Is it permissible to say that the Infant Soul, even when grown up, goes through the initial stages of a psychological development only and then stops, or is it quite different?*

As you are suspecting, these are the very first encounters of the soul with its individual psyche in the process of development; an initial nuzzling and a progressive familiarization with an intrinsic aspect of humanness that is in permanent exchange with the soul. The psyche will be in equivalence with the maturity of the soul in its progress. More isn't possible. So, to repeat what we said before: The psyche of an Infant Soul, even at human adult age, cannot evolve any further than the psyche of an eighteen months' old child at maximum.

■ *Can a similar rule be established also for the next cycle of the Child Soul?*

The psyche of the Child Soul evolves up to about the level of a 16-year-old at maximum. A span of thirty-five to forty-five or fifty years can be analogously assessed for the Young Soul. Since the physical lifetime of Mature Souls can greatly vary depending on the place of incarnation and social or medical conditions, the analogy can't be perpetuated in the same way. As an example, a person can be fully matured at the end of his life at age sixty-five, if the incarnation goals have been completely achieved. Else he may still struggle for his emotional maturity at eighty, or simply judge the subject totally uninteresting. This can't be determined as precisely as in the early stages. The respective optimum is always attained when the individual dies. This applies to the Mature and to the Old Soul. When a Mature Soul reaches the age of ninety-five, it reaches its optimum. The Old Soul may have reached its optimum at age thirty-five or also at ninety-five years.

■ *I observed that people at Soul Ages Old 4 and Old 5 seem to have a disproportional amount of emotional problems. I deliberately phrase this carefully. What is the reason? Please help me understand, specifically with respect to the relation between psyche and soul.*

Let us explain it to you with an image. A Young Soul has quite a thick skin, covered moreover with a cornea and a protective fur. A Mature Soul gradually ablates the cornea. An Old Soul has an increasingly thinner skin; and the more delicate the skin gets, the more the blood vessels are showing through. This is how you may understand what you observe as the difficulties of souls at stages Old 4 and 5.

It's not as if the younger ones had fewer problems, but they are better concealed. The older a soul gets, the less camouflaging hides it has over what goes on inside of it, and all the more it is forced to reveal these veins, arteries and other vessels under its thin-skinnedness. In other words, one can already see from afar what its psyche is worried about. The earlier armor-plating is almost completely gone. The problems themselves – although they aren't really quantifiable – can't be described as greater or worse than those of all other human beings.

A very Old Soul has an inherent urge to be unconditionally authentic, even if not fully supported or sometimes prevented by its psyche. The drive for authenticity is nevertheless there and shows in the fact that the individual is no longer able to conceal his problems under a mask of good conduct and compliance.

9. Spiritual Development

Development and evolvement are essential concepts in the Source's teachings. We humans meanwhile understand more of the body and its development than in earlier centuries. With the theory of the Archetypes, you have now taught us what soul development in the true sense is. I moreover assume that there is a psychic and an intellectual development. Is there actually also a spiritual development, which so many religious and spiritual traditions believe in? How does this concept fit into your system? Many people are afraid of the hereafter because they feel they didn't do enough for their inner development.

We take up your idea of spiritual development, but will use it as a temporary term for now. Set into relation with the physical, the intellectual, the emotional growth and the evolvement of the soul of a human being, the so-called spiritual development is a sub-category deriving its strength both from the realms of the soul and the psyche. It is, however, complemented by historical and social conditions. Lacking a designation for what we wish to describe in precise and new terms, we will initially use the auxiliary term of »spiritual«, although what we mean has only marginally to do with the dimensions of the spirit (Latin = spiritus). It's rather about rediscovering the divine aspects of one's own nature in each new life and in different ways. A spiritual development in the sense of a mental training can be of help, but it is in no way a mandatory premise for this rediscovery.

We would like to describe this development with the image of a thick and dense ball of colored, short pieces of yarn knotted together, which, when unwound, form a long, multicolored thread. Figuratively speaking, each of these shorter and longer, colored sections represent an incarnation of the individual soul – at different times, places and in different societies – and specifically its manifold dealings with transcendence. Coiled up, this colored ball of yarn looks like a unity. At its un-raveling (development), however, a linear sequence becomes discernible.

In its seeming entity, the ball looks intricate and inscrutable, threads always crossing each other anew, covering up older layers. As you know, there is little one can do with such a ball of yarn before it has been worked into a piece of material. It is just this act of processing, which in your Western association of ideas is called spiritual development. In each respective, new life, the maze of confusing threads will be re-organized and processed to another portable garment, which each of you can don as required. It feels warming and protective to some, but like a constricting and annoying cover to others. So, spiritual development is a process that requires various experiences from many former lives. Nothing can be developed that isn't previously available as a potential.

But if you imagine the string of former lives as a definable sequence on a time scale, it becomes obvious that a Child Soul can revert to a shorter colored strand than a Mature or an Old Soul. The experience from more or fewer physical existences thus defines the possibilities of spiritual development in every single, new incarnation, including the current one. Added to that come historical, local and social factors, as indicated above. So it's not only the amount of earlier explored possibilities to incorporate spiritual experiences in a new life, but also the way in which they can be embedded in a concrete human existence that is the premise to the realization of a given spiritual readiness. Where and when a person is born and in which social or religious context he grows up, therefore, plays a significant role for the respective spiritual development open to him or her. It is not detached from social contingencies and cannot be solely attributed to the soul age of an individual. Also his psyche, which in the course of his physical development normally undergoes a parallel development, plays a role. Each human being is born into the world equipped with a potential of possibilities for his inner development, and it's partly up to him and an adequate environment for the other part, to unfold this potential. And here is where we come to the core of your question and this topic: It's in the nature of humans that a part of their physical existences is invariably dedicated to the rediscovery of divinity in themselves. You are embodied soul creatures. Your godly nature is veiled, covered, even concealed by your incarnation and entry into the realm of matter. And each effort to remember this veiled part, to recognize its reality, to feel and animate it is a perpetual and necessary, inevitable and essential task for incarnated souls. For a soul, humanness doesn't only mean to navigate in the world of matter, finding its bearings in the body and experiencing itself in time. With the inrush of all things new to it, the challenge consists particularly in integrating its true origin from the worlds of the soul and the Divinity under-, over- and lying beyond it into the mundane, instead of forgetting it.

It seems like your current understanding of spiritual development and evolvement is rather reduced to the topics of religiousness and self-experience, worldly wisdom and life teachings. These topics can certainly not be excluded from what characterizes spiritual development as a whole. But also irreligious people or those hostile to the religion they grew up in undergo a spiritual development, specifically by behaving or taking a stance the way they do. Someone with no motivation to become aware of and explore the self, to concern himself with psychology, western philosophy or unfamiliar mental worlds, meditation and eastern religions, nonetheless develops his spirituality in this indifference just like someone intensively and occasionally almost desperately endeavoring to pursue a so-called spiritual path.

Understandably, this is a perspective of knowledge which we as a bodiless entity can take more easily than you, since you can only hear and understand us just because you have consciously and purposefully set off on the so-called spiritual path. While we would like to honor this endeavor, we may, on the other hand, not spare a mild disappointment to just those who trustingly listen to us. Because we claim that no single human being cannot NOT spiritually evolve, as unspiritual as he may seem to you.

Each of you looks back on a long history of spiritual experiences in the proper meaning. And if you evolve spiritually in this present life according to your own, time-bound ideas and criteria, training your awareness and enriching your cognitive faculties with respect to Divinity and the AllOne, this can only happen based on your numerous past experiences and findings. For that very reason it is so important that you don't hold it against anyone if they just can't get interested in Buddhism or anthroposophy, if they aren't willing to investigate their psyche but rather pray the rosary in church instead. Accept them when they aren't motivated to speak about their problems, preferring to play football or watching TV.

It is our ambition to make you understand that every single life – just the way it is – carries its own meaningfulness. When someone who played football for thirty years, after an accident quite unexpectedly and to his own surprise develops the need for a certain kind of spiritual experience or knowledge, this is no more valuable than if it doesn't happen at all and everything goes on as before.

It's about the evolvement of a previously available potential commensurate with the soul age, the level of education and the possibilities in the social fabric he or she lives in. If this potential isn't existent, it cannot be developed. Being religious or performing the specified rites and sacred acts is actually a social occurrence and shouldn't be equaled with spirituality in a narrower sense. On the other hand, there are few people in whom the exercise of specific sacred acts or the participation in religiously motivated celebrations doesn't evoke the echo of a memory of something transcendental lying beyond it. And even if it's a deep aversion that crops up during a religious ceremony: that too is a reaction contributing to the spiritual development of an individual the way we define it.

■ *I find what you said difficult to understand. So we are talking about man concerning himself with his own divinity, perhaps one can also say with his soul reality. And this active involvement doesn't have to take place within the framework of what is conventionally understood as spiritual or religious. It seems, however, to be bound specifically to moments of inner experiencing. Is this correct?*
A microbiologist investigating smallest organisms who experiences moments of astonishment and awe, touched and astounded by the conditions of such life-forms, in our mind has just as meaningful a spiritual experience as someone falling into ecstasy in a temple. It is the selective or permanent acknowledgement that life on earth is integrated into a greater whole – whether it be based on knowledge or on faith, on a discovery coined intellectually or emotionally – that is the decisive factor for the development of a spiritual potential every man carries within himself. The elaboration and variety of forms that this spiritual experiencing can take, from the rites of a tribe community up to most complex philosophical discussions, are individual and secondary. It is dependent on the historical and

social conditions, as we already said, but also on genetic factors such as certain limits of intelligence or other physical conditions, which predispose a person for one or the other. Undoubtedly, the eternal Soul Role and the rest of the variable Soul MATRIX each play a decisive, if secondary role for the specific coloring or quality of experiencing. The essential thing is humanness itself with its inherent, natural propensity for spiritual growth.

> ▪ *This sounds rather non-specific compared to the gradual development you have introduced us to, e.g. with the 35 clearly defined stages of soul development. Is the term development even adequate here? Isn't it simply a permanent questioning of and concern with the fact that soul and the AllOne exist? Is it a gradual development (growth), so that one could say: this person is spiritually far evolved, but that one isn't?*

The way a human embryo carries the information for a specific development sequence within, a soul incarnating itself also has an inherent potential which unfolds, if in a different and seemingly less mandatory way. These conditions are determined by the incarnation cycle on the one hand, and by the very own, individually designed and specific dynamics on the other. The basic condition as such consists in a succession of numerous lives, each in a new time period, new geographic space and with a new body. A newly born physical entity betakes itself into constellations never seen before, getting stamped in a way no other living being has experienced before or ever will thereafter. It provides the individual with unique development possibilities that have an evolutionary effect. Thus, each incarnating soul makes an enriching and completely novel contribution to the experiencing of the Divine. That human souls fulfill themselves in this way with an individual Soul Matrix in time and space is the principle which corresponds to the physical development. By the fixed path of incarnation as such, the human soul finds the conditions according to which it will inevitably unfold. Although there is an unpredictability factor – just as in the physical sphere due to the always new combination of genes, or in the emotional sphere by the perpetual confrontation with new conditions of life – which gives the whole its individual character and dynamic creativity. Each person evolves spiritually, physically, intellectually, emotionally and on the soul level quite independently – but within a set frame.

It's not possible to define spiritual development stages similar to the development stages of the soul's evolution. The process is much more open. The soul's development steps and stages are predetermined as a program for all souls. The other possibilities for progression are bound to worldly conditions; they require matter and contain elements of freedom. And yet, based on the necessities and wishes of an individual soul for particular incarnation objectives and correlations, certain experiences adequate to the soul age are pre-programmed in the course of an incarnation cycle.

■ *Do you have a better word for »spiritual«, then? Or shall we leave it at that?*

We think it best if you adhere to that term for the time being; otherwise we cannot make ourselves quite understood especially by those whom we speak to.

10. Fear of Death and Dying

■ *If the soul knows that, after shedding its physical body, it returns to its home in the astral world – why then do we have such a fear-laden attitude towards death?*

The soul indeed knows that it returns to its home after discarding its mortal body. But humans aren't just composed of soul. Their body doesn't know of this home. It only senses the unknown, something foreign, the void, the nothingness, the transience, its future non-existence – and is afraid of it. A body which consists of matter and is fulfilled in matter, being at home in the terrestrial world, is afraid of nothingness. It doesn't want to give up itself and the self.

In each life the soul, together with a body, a psyche and a mind, creates a new individual, an amalgamation of these four aspects of existence, and thus a unique self. Body, psyche and mind know nothing but the deep pride in the precious evolution and weaving of this individual self. Now this very life comes to an end, this unquestioned identity shall and must be given up and surrendered to the unknown. Life comes to an end, and suddenly the body shall be no more – never again! Isn't it understandable that the material vessel of an incarnated soul feels terror and fright at the thought of existing no more?

Especially in your lifetime, and particularly in the countries in which you have chosen your incarnation, is rooted a deep fear of finite demise, of tumbling into nothingness. How can one feel trust and joy at the prospect of death if one believes there is one life only? Fear of death is easily explained when you consider that your whole culture has grown on Christian soil, and Christian religion has based its center of faith on the death and resurrection of Jesus, the Savior being the only one who ever returned from the beyond? Until not long ago, your civilization was fundamentally minted by this religion of crucifixion and resurrection. It was completely focused on the memento mori, on death, on the otherworld, on torments of hell, on hope for salvation. People's whole life was headed fearfully or cheerfully towards this end.

It isn't surprising then that after such a long and intensive period of joyful expectation of death, the orientation of all worldly existence onto the end of life, a countermovement evolves in your time – in the sense of a pulsation that wants to put something else at the center of human attention at last, namely life! The beginning of that countermovement, of the pendulum swinging in the other direction, was initially marked by many misunderstandings, difficulties and conflicts with this new attitude. The turning point in this development for all those who lived at the time, but also for the following generation in their attitude towards death, were the two great wars of the 20th century. While initially most soldiers still went to war full of hope and confidence, proud to die for their people and fatherland, this changed fundamentally during WW II. The meaningfulness of dying based on religious values or bonding to a nation was hardly existent anymore. After the traumatic experiences in the face of so many millions of dead in the forties of the past century, you want none of death right now.

Europeans are currently going through a transition period. Hence the ambivalence, making death often seem desirable so as to finally leave all difficulties behind you on the one hand, while on the other, a boisterous, almost desperate zest for life is trying to push into the place of the earlier joy of death. Death is denied or euphemized, the finality of life blocked out. But that too is an extreme. There will be a gradual shift now towards a moderate and rather balanced attitude to the experience every human being has to face and must go through, just as he must go through birth.

Your collective has suffered too much, has had to look at too many corpses; it has only just begun to truly mourn. It had to cry too many tears and wasn't allowed to shed them. So it seems impossible now to encounter death serenely, either in private or in the social environment. The tremendous suffering and the general traumatization people would like to forget have led to the suppression of the eternal truth in your societies that »everybody must die«. But death cannot be suppressed. And from this fearful avoidance strategy, which was initially quite wholesome for the collective psyche, one day will arise a new, positive and free attitude towards death and life alike.

What's more – and this is something we ask you to understand and take into account as well – you are living on a planet which at present and precisely in your geographical latitudes is inhabited by a majority of Young Souls. They simply cannot understand death. Young Souls, just like teens or young adults, have got the feeling – in fact, an almost unshakeable belief – that they will live forever. They are endowed with stalwart courage to face life. Death is very far from their thoughts and feelings. They bank on immortality; and medical progress and the increasing average age seem to prove them right. When Older Souls marvel at reports about people wanting to be frozen after death or aspiring to live for several hundred years by »thinking positively«, or how some try to age agelessly by stuffing themselves with vitamins and hormones, you should understand that just this denial of degeneration and death is a major concern of the many Young Souls shaping your society. Since they outnumber Mature and Old Souls, the concerns of the latter are mostly disregarded.

However, should you incarnate in Europe again a few more times, we can hold out the prospect for you that you will see for yourselves how the attitude toward death is going to change as the percentage of Mature and Old Souls increases there. Until then, however, much water will flow under the bridge, and it's important that you, reading these lines now, show understanding for those who are frightened of what they believe they don't know. At the same time, you need to give yourselves the support and means to respect the biological fear of death as something natural, looking at it as constituted by nature, instead of scorning it. Do not, however, confound the fear of dying of the self with the apparent nothingness which, as you have learned by now, is bolstered by a beatifying light and an intimate closeness to your soul siblings. But this is something not everybody can believe in, and nobody knows for sure. But to most of you, this notion promises relief from the fear of the other side of your existence. In the certainty that you are returning to the homestead of your souls, you are going to lose the fear of this transition. Still, the fear of leaving behind that body you are so used to, the fear of letting go of your precious self, of your wonderful uniqueness and the mind you have grown so fond of, will remain. Everybody will have to cope with it – it cannot be abolished.

■ *I would like to understand the purpose of pain before and during the process of dying, or our fear of pain when we feel to be dying soon. What is the effect of opiates besides reducing the pain? Do they increase or dull the awareness process? How should we deal with that?*
Pain, emotional and physical, represents an indispensable experience for the incarnated soul. The soul needs the opportunity of exploring all conditions within the body which serve its development and evolvement. And for this very reason, we can also say that pain not serving this goal of the soul is redundant and undesirable. Sufferings which are inflicted by torture for example, no matter whether of physical or emotional kind, aren't useful to the soul's progress. Pain caused by abuse or lustfully inflicted by someone, but also such pains which could be avoided by a simple act of humanity, are an obstacle and, if we may say so, also a horror to the soul.

When the body of an incarnated soul reaches the end of life, you know that this can happen in a thousand different ways. Your question refers primarily to the process of dying as the result of disease, infirmity or old age. We would therefore like to target our response to these processes and tell you that dying as such, the transition from one state of being into another, is completely painless. Of course we know as well as you do that in the months, weeks, days and hours leading up to death, attacks of intense physical pain may occur. These are due partly to whichever sickness is prevailing, partly they arise from the tenseness caused by such pain and the fear that it might get even worse. We are of the opinion that it helps nobody, and that no soul reaps any benefit from the recommendation to suffer such pains; worse even when, based on moral or esoteric ideas or for religious reasons, the diseased is given the illusion that only fully and consciously suffered physical pain during dying ensures a good and godly transition into the otherworld.

Pain is a neuronal process affecting the brain functions. With the exception of signal pains indicating the beginning of a disease, there are only few pain conditions which promote awareness or emotional growth. We therefore recommend, within the context of medical resources, to minimize the pain or eliminate it altogether, especially around the time of the dying process. Because the anguish over taking leave from one's body, the suffering of saying farewell to the world and one's loved ones, to all the memories, belongings and experiences a human being has collected in the course of his life and which actually constitute him or her, are suffering enough. So there is no advantage in increasing the suffering with physical pain that could easily be eliminated.

Opiates, unless administered in an unreasonable overdose to sedate the individual up to total unconsciousness, have no negative influence on the awareness of dying. By this we mean the knowledge of an individual that his soul is soon to part from his body. It should be obvious to you that this parting isn't worthy only if experienced in mental clarity, but just as valuable when the individual concerned does not mentally accompany the process but rather drifts through it in a twilight state. Because not only during these final hours, but all life long, the mental aspects of consciousness cover merely small realms. They only take effect in segments, while the greater consciousness that keeps a body alive and fills every cell – if not with mentally intelligible messages – i.e., such awareness every human has of the self, remains unaffected by it.

If in future you would like to help people to better accept the time before their decease, trying to make it as comfortable as possible, you should advise them in favor of pain-killing drugs. There is little worth in bravely sticking it out. From our point of view, nothing speaks against administering strong medication. The consciousness quality is in no way dulled by it. On the contrary, opiates may even enable the diseased in his semi-conscious state to make »fleeting visits« into the astral world already days or hours before his physical death, so that he can develop an idea of the freedom and lightness and beauty of the dimensions he will soon enter.

Appendix

Table A: The Seven Cosmic Base Energies

The teachings of the soul are based on the notion of seven universal energies, which, although not further justified in their existence, can very well be perceived and felt in an earthly human context. They transcend all dimensions of the material and non-material world. In the following, we endeavour to portray these energies to you with descriptive adjectives as minted by the human world of ideas. We are perfectly aware that this can be no more than a careful approach to what the ultimate energy qualities really are.

Energy 1

Healing, nursing, soft, protecting, tender, harmonizing, uniting, accommodating, emotional, mute, comprehensive, supportive, slow, simple, heartfelt, touching, modest, restrained, composed, absorbing.

Energy 2

Joyous, childlike, funny, lively, playful, volatile, fresh, curious, fanciful, vivid, inventive, delimiting, artful, appraising, mental, thoughtful, creative, aesthetic, stimulating, original, individual, separating.

Energy 3

Forceful, invigorating, effective, defending, protective, convincing, classifying, courageous, persevering, tenacious, belligerent, creative, devoted, sensual, action-oriented, focused.

Energy 4

Instructive, thorough, attentive, instinctive, knowing, determined, clear, just, impartial, neutral, functional, observing, quiet, formative, pragmatic, preserving, regulatory, counterbalancing musing, sober.

Energy 5

Connective, expressive, friendly, communicative, content, kind, idealistic, orienting, convivial, gregarious, loquacious, collective, authoritative, powerful, wise, jovial, exuberant, generous, accepting.

Energy 6

Inspiring, elating, transcendental, motivating, trustful, still, grave, empathetic, merciful, touchy, vulnerable, charismatic, sensitive, passionate, comforting, innocent.

Energy 7

Dignified, impressive, worthy, superior, patient, perceptive, untiring, dynamic, expansive, comprehensive, orienting, structuring, integrating, responsible, agitating, radiant.

Table B: The 49 Archetypes of the Soul

The following table shows a summary of the overall structure of the Archetypes of the Soul. From this inventory on each of the seven planes, the soul selects elements to custom-assemble its individual energy structure for the respective incarnation it has planned. The basic fears represent only one plane out of seven altogether. The full dynamics of an individual Soul Matrix can only be wholly understood in the correlation of the primeval fears with the remaining six Soul Archetypes and their interaction. This greater correlation can be portrayed only very superficially at this point. For more information, we recommend interested readers to consult the volume *Archetypes of the Soul* (Septana Private Printing, by permission of Wilhelm Goldmann Verlag, a division of Verlagsgruppe Random House, GmbH.). Although we wish to emphasize and illustrate here how the archetypal seven primeval fears fit into a greater soul framework. They aren't simply individual elements conglomerated by chance, but follow the structure of a superordinate, meaningful masterplan of existence. Portraying this masterplan and step-by-step making it more comprehensible is the purpose of our work.

Archetypes of the Soul			
Soul Age VII	**Infant Soul**	**Child Soul**	**Young Soul**
Centering VI	**Emotional** – sentimental + sensitve	**Intellectual** – hair-splitting + thoughtful	**Sexual** – seductive + productive
Mentality V	**Stoicism** – resigned + tranquil	**Skepticism** – distrusting + investigative	**Cynicism** – humiliating + critical
Mode IV	**Reservation** – inhibited + restrained	**Caution** – anxious + prudent	**Perseverance** – fixated + persistent
Goal III	**Delay** – withdrawing + reviewing	**Rejection** – prejudiced + discerning	**Submission** – subjugated + devoted
Fear: Chief Characteristic II	**Self-Deprecation** *Fear of Inadequacy* – self-abasing + modest	**Self-Sabotage** *Fear of Joyfulness* – self-destructive + self-sacrificing	**Martyrdom** *Fear of Worthlessness* – victimizing + selfless
Soul Role I	**Helper/Healer** Principle: Supporting – servile + helpful	**Artist** Principle: Inventing – artificial + original	**Warrior** Principle: Fighting – overwhelmin + convincing
ENERGY	**1** sky blue	**2** butterfly yellow	**3** blood red

Quelle: *Archetypen der Seele*, Varda Hasselmann / Frank Schmolke, Goldmann Verlag, 1993

Mature Soul	Old Soul	Transpersonal Ensoulment Not Part of Incarnation Cycle	Transliminal Ensoulment Not Part of Incarnation Cycle
Instinctive thoughtless spontaneous	**Spiritual** − telepathic + inspired	**Ecstatic** − psychic + mystical	**Moving** − hectic + untiring
Pragmatism − rigid + practical	**Idealism** − vague + visionary	**Spiritualism** − gullible + verifying	**Realism** − guessing + perceptive
Observation − watchful + vigilant	**Power** − patronizing + authoritative	**Passion** − fanatic + charismatic	**Aggression** − belligerent + dynamic
Standstill immobilized + pausing	**Acceptance** − ingratiating + kindhearted	**Acceleration** − confused + comprehending	**Dominance** − dictatorial + leading
Stubbornness *Fear of Unpredictability* − obstinate + resolute	**Greed** *Fear of Privation* − insatiable + demanding	**Arrogance** *Fear of Vulnerability* − vain + proud	**Impatience** *Fear of Omission* − intolerant + audacious
Scholar Principle: Learning + Teaching − theorizing + knowing	**Sage** Principle: Communicating − talkative + expressive	**Priest** Principle: Consoling − overzealous + compassionate	**King** Principle: Leading − tyrannical + dignified
4 grass green	**5** sunny yellow	**6** ocean blue	**7** purple

SEPTANA INTERNATIONAL III

Copyright © 2014 by Varda B. Hasselmann and Frank Schmolke

All publishing rights of the present volume *The Seven Archetypes of Fear* are with Wilhelm Goldmann Verlag, a division of Verlagsgruppe Random House GmbH, Munich.

Herstellung und Verlag:
BoD – Books on Demand, Norderstedt
Printed in Germany

ISBN 978-3-7357-2430-4

CPSIA information can be obtained
at www.ICGtesting.com
Printed in the USA
FSHW010150030519
57803FS

9 783735 724304